Geschichte / History

Rajinder Singh

The Making of the Politician M. Gandhi by Muslims, Jews and Christians

Gandhi's Methods to Solve Immigration Problems

Shaker Verlag
Aachen 2015

Bibliographic information published by the Deutsche Nationalbibliothek
The Deutsche Nationalbibliothek lists this publication in the Deutsche Nationalbibliografie; detailed bibliographic data are available in the Internet at http://dnb.d-nb.de.

Sources cover picture:

Photograph:
http://www.mkgandhi.org/newannou/swmg_china.html

Map:
https://commons.wikimedia.org/wiki/
File:Map_of_the_provinces_of_South_Africa_1910-1976_with_English_labels.svg, Oct. 4, 2015.

Copyright Shaker Verlag 2015
All rights reserved. No part of this publication may be reproduced, stored in a retrieval system, or transmitted, in any form or by any means, electronic, mechanical, photocopying, recording or otherwise, without the prior permission of the publishers.

Printed in Germany.

ISBN 978-3-8440-4024-1
ISSN 0945-0815

Shaker Verlag GmbH • P.O. BOX 101818 • D-52018 Aachen
Phone: 0049/2407/9596-0 • Telefax: 0049/2407/9596-9
Internet: www.shaker.de • e-mail: info@shaker.de

Contents

Foreword xi

Preface xv

Introduction 1

Indians' Immigration to South Africa - Indentured, Free and Passenger 5

India and European Contacts 7

Indians in British and Boer Colonies 9

    Indians in Natal 9

    The Orange Free State 11

    Transvaal – South African Republic 11

    Cape Town and Indian Influence 13

Formation of Indian Organisations in South Africa 14

The Natal Indian Congress, The British Indian Association and Gandhi's Participation in Wars 21

Foundation of the Natal Indian Congress 21

Work on Political Level – Petitions and Memorials 23

Support and Propaganda on Local Level 27

N.I.C. – Participation in Wars 30

    The Second Anglo-Boer War 30

    Volunteer Stretcher-Bearer Corps and Funds Collection 30

Goodbye South Africa - Gandhi in India 31

After the Anglo-Boer War - Gandhi Returns to South Africa 33

Gandhi on Zulu Rebellion - "It is not for us to say whether the revolt of the Kaffirs is justified or not" 34

The Stretcher-Bearer Corps 35

Honours to the "War-Heroes" *38*

N.I.C. – A Party of Indian Traders with Dictatorial Methods *38*

Gandhi in Johannesburg and the Foundation of the British Indian Association *40*

The Asiatic Registration Act and a Deputation to England **49**

The Asiatic Registration Act – To Bring to Boil – H. Habib and the Gaol Going Resolution *49*

Deputation to U.K. *56*

Deputation in U.K. and Support by Local Sympathisers *57*

Deputation's Members' Meetings 59

Meeting with John Morley, Secretary, State of India *61*

Meeting with Winston Churchill, Under-Secretary of the State for the Colonies *63*

South Africa British Indian Vigilance Committee *64*

Gandhi's Opponents - W. Godfrey and C.M. Pillay *67*

Appendix C – South Africa British India Committee in London *74*

Outcome of the Deputation and Preparing for the Practical Politics **81**

Continuation of the "Asiatic Ordinance Act" War - Transvaal's Government in Action *82*

Psychological Terror - Pickets, Blacklegs, Undefined Goals and Misuse of Religion for Political Aims **111**

Gandhi's Volunteers Pickets or "Missionaries" – Controlling the 'Blacksheep' *114*

Misuse of Religion - The Making of a Hindu Hero – Priest Ram Sundar *119*

Why Struggle – Nobody Knows *123*

Arrest of Railway Workers and Others 124

Gandhi's Sword "to pierce the violent, rock-like hatred in the hearts of the whites" **131**

The Quick Compromise *131*

Causes of Quick Compromise *134*

Aftermyth of the Compromise - Finger-Prints Become a Hot Issue *135*

Useless Voluntary Registration and Asking for the Repealing of the Act *138*

The Last Blow – Gandhi's Sword "to Pierce the Violent, Rock-Like Hatred in the Hearts of the Whites" *145*

Satyagraha – A Fatalist and Fanatic Ideology – "This is a fight on behalf of religion ..." **151**

Satyagraha the Master Key *156*

A Satyagrahi as a "Super and Selfless Creator" *158*

Satyagraha - Does not Depend on the Number of Followers! *159*

The Magic of the "Soul Force" - "Your bonds will be loosened in ... less than 24 Hours" **163**

"Devil" Smuts vs. "god" Gandhi – Wanting More and More – Entry for Educated Indians *163*

Fight for 6 Educated Indians *173*

For Whom Was the Struggle – Violence of the "Non-Violents" *177*

Balance Sheet of Struggle: Years 1907 and 1908 .... *178*

Continuation of the Struggle in 1909 .... *179*

Gandhi's Critics – The Natal Indian Congress *180*

Second Unsuccessful Deputation to U.K. *182*

Indians in the Union of South Africa – Gandhi's Opportunistic Approach ... 195

Indians in the Union of South Africa	195
Smuts–Gandhi Correspondence and Gandhi's Role in the Union of South Africa	197
Extending the Field of Struggle – Gandhi's-Smuts' Problems	201
The Provisional Settlement	205
The New Immigration Bill and Protest by the Indian Community	207
A New Turn – G.K. Gokhale in South Africa	210
Aftermyth of Gokhale's Visit – Chaos Without End!	212

The Final Phase of the Struggle – "They felt that the hand of God was upon their movement" ... 219

Indian Marriages Invalid	219
The New Immigration Bill, Worse Than its Predecessor	222
Improved Immigration Regulation Act and Gandhi's Objections	224
No Settlement - New Plan of the Satyagraha	226
Three Pound Tax and the Involvement of Indentured Indians in Resistance	227
Involving the Mine Workers – "The Movement is Bound to Collapse"	231
Gandhi's Work in Past 20 Years "not only worthless but highly injurious to the Indian community"	237
Taking Christian Missionaries as Political Partners – "They felt that the hand of God was upon their movement"	238
Leaving South Africa - "Ours is a notorious family, …, we are known to belong to a band of robbers"	243
"The Relief Bill"	245

Speeches at Farewell Meetings 247

In the Den of Lions - Speech at the Hamidia Islamic Society 251

Magna Charta – Farewell Letter – "A Confidential Circular" to Serve the Empire in WWI 257

Arrival in London 259

Gandhi, Satyagraha and Money 269

Gandhi and Financial Affairs 270

The Interests of the Supporters 276

Prison as a "Palace" – Tales of Suffering 281

Living Conditions in Prisons 282

Food Problem 287

Gandhi – "They lived a most unnatural life" – "If anybody should have died it was Mrs. Gandhi" 288

Deportations 290

Ruined Families 292

Clash of Cultures – Social, Political and Religious Differences 297

Why was the White Community against Indians? 298

Indian vs. White Traders 300

Indians with the Wrong Identity 301

Indians Way of Living – "Some Don'ts" 302

Indentured and Colonial Born Indians as Scapegoats 305

"Natal-born Indian is useless as a worker" – Indentured "improve as animals" 307

Gandhi's Conflict with the Muslim Community 310

Double Standard of the British Empire - Indian Traders and the Issue of Finger Prints 312

The Origin of M.K. Gandhi's Political Ideas 323

Refusal of Tax and Protest against Carrying Passes 324

Going to Prison 324

How to Finance the Arrested Protesters? – Learn from British Women 326

Martin Luther – Burn the Documents 328

Spinning-Wheel and Weaving 328

"Passive Resistance" – vs. "Satyagraha" 329

Idea of Boycott Foreign Goods and Non-cooperation 330

The Creation of a Legend – Christian Writers and Self Propaganda by Gandhi 335

Gandhi and the Christian Biographers 336

Gandhi and the French Views 340

Gandhi in German literature 342

Gandhi and Americans 343

Propaganda by Friends 345

Self-Promotion - Autobiography – "The story of my experiments with truth" 347

Gandhi in Independent India 349

"Censorship" by the Indian State 350

Bibliography 347

Dedicated

To

Rainer Goltermann

Principal, GTS 2001 Syke, Ferdinand Salfer Str. 3, 28857 Syke

& to

My children: Simone Krah – University of Münster Michael Krah – University of Würzburg

My wife: Birgit Krah – Govt. Primary School Offen

Dr. Rajinder Singh, Research Group – Physics Education, History and Philosophy of Science, University of Oldenburg, Germany.

E-Mail: rajinder.singh@uni-oldenburg.de, *www.rajindersinghdr.npage.de*

Dr. Rajinder Singh has published more than 90 articles in national and international journals. Dr. Singh is editor of:

1. "Jugend forscht – Schüler experimentieren" – nicht nur für Hochbegabte und Überflieger, Shaker 'Verlag' Aachen 2012.

Dr. R. Singh has written the following books:

2. Nobel Laureate C.V. Raman's work on light scattering, Logos Publisher Berlin 2004.
3. Nobel Laureate C.V. Raman's science, philosophy and religion, Dharmaram Publications Bangalore 2005.
4. Characteristics of solar radiation photovoltaic pyranometers Licor 200SZ and Martix 1G, Shaker 'Verlag' Aachen 2012.
5. Upendranath Brahmachari – A pioneer of tropical diseases – A summary of his discoveries and scientific work, Shaker 'Verlag' Aachen 2013.
6. Nobel Prize Nominator Sisir Kumar Mitra F.R.S. - His scientific work in international context, Shaker 'Verlag' Aachen 2014.
7. Mahatma Gandhi – Sex scandals and the missed Nobel Peace Prize, Shaker 'Verlag' Aachen 2015.

x

Foreword

India is a country of hero-worshippers. It may be a fake Mahatma, who rapes his female disciples or gets their husbands castrated in their pursuit of "God", or an inanities-mouthing political leader - any well-publicized face can become a ruler of hearts for millions of people. It is another matter that many of such Mahatmas are presently cooling their heels in various prisons scattered over different parts of the country. While the vigilant social and visual media all over the world holds immense sway over the public opinion, these incarcerated "Gurus" can still count on the support of millions of their naive followers.

It is an inarguable truth that in a world sitting on a powder keg there can never be a better antidote to destruction than choosing the path of "Ahimsa", propounded by none other than our Father of the Nation Mahatma Gandhi. For this alone he becomes one of the greatest individuals born on this planet. Still his idea of "Ahimsa" was not completely original – Jesus Christ believed in and practiced this theory over 2000 years ago. Giving a slight twist to this belief with a blend of Hinduism, and practicing the same in the 20th century, he was able to give a new dimension to pacifism. His belief in offering penance as a remedy to violence made people - weary of two World Wars - take notice of this extraordinary man. But whenever Gandhi has been criticized, his followers have put forward Gandhi's conflicting truism that an act of violence in the defence of the defenceless is an act of bravery, and far better than cowardly submission. This contradiction came from his Hindu upbringing of doing one's Karma and observing one's Dharma. Nevertheless his maxim of offering the other cheek after having been slapped on one cheek does not hold, and never held water in a world inhabited by human race. No tyrant has ever been tamed through non-violence, neither the war of American Independence, nor the "Dharamyuddh" between Kauravas and Pandavas, as narrated in "Mahabharata", a part of the Hindu Holy Book "Bhagavad-Gita", was won through penance. In this context only one instance comes to mind – Indian King Ashoka's resolve of renouncing violence after observing the devastation his attacks on other kingdoms had brought about. But his resolve did not come from any sort of tyranny, which he or his people had to endure; it came from within. He was so devastated with the results of one Kalinga-war that he took to Buddhism, and followed the ascetic path of Buddha. The fact remains that the teachings of Gandhi have changed neither India, nor the world. Today India is world's top buyer of arms, since the country has finally come out of the idealistic illusions of Jawaharlal Nehru, the first Prime Minister of India, who, even though being aware of frequent Chinese incursions into India, and even after China had annexed Tibet, a peaceful Buddhist country, continued with the production of cosmetics in the ordnance factories of India on the assurance of his leftist Defence Minister Krishna Menon that China could never attack India.

The "Satyagraha" of Gandhi was only one of the factors, which contributed to the independence of India from British colonial rule. The fact is that Gandhi was a mitigating factor in saving British from blushes of withdrawing from India at a time when they were tired of having fought a long war against an axis led by Adolf Hitler, when the sheen of the British Empire was on the wane, who could win the war only after America joined the Allied forces in waging a war against Nazi Germany. Had the British listened to Gandhi's advice to "invite Herr Hitler and Mussolini to take" whatever they wanted of their countries they called their possessions, and to allow themselves, "man, woman and children to be slaughtered", the course of world history would have been very different.

Gandhi was awarded the title of Sergeant Major and the Kaiser-i-Hind Gold Medal by the British rulers, a fact, which hardly any Indian is aware of. The conferment of the title "Sergeant Major" was in complete contrast to the non-violent persona of Gandhi. While his propagation of "Ahimsa" won him many admirers all over the world, particularly in Europe, it suited the British to kowtow with Gandhi, since a fading British Empire was finding it difficult to handle the rising, most of the time violent, tide of resistance to British rule by different revolutionary groups, mainly from Bengal and Punjab. While Gandhi and his party Indian National Congress dithered in saving the life of revolutionary Bhagat Singh and his associates Rajguru, and Sukhdev, even when the whole country stood behind the incarcerated revolutionaries and urged Gandhi to persuade Lord Irwin to save the real freedom fighters from going to gallows, Gandhi never mentioned anything about this in his writings, nor did he pursue the matter seriously with Lord Irwin in an important meeting with him, which brought about the famous Gandhi-Irwin Pact. His abhorrence of violence did not allow him to favour the commutation of the death-sentence awarded to the true freedom fighters of the country.

The world is aware of Gandhi's fight against racism in South Africa and against untouchability in India, whereas in his earlier years in South Africa the struggle pertained mainly to win parity with the whites at the cost of blacks. Gandhi detested being bracketed with the kaffirs, a term used for black South Africans, whom he considered inferior in the scale of civilization, and, "whose occupation is hunting, and whose sole occupation is to collect a certain number of cattle to buy a wife with and then, pass his life in indolence and nakedness," as he stated in a speech delivered in Bombay in 1896. In his eyes Kaffirs were the quite opposite of "clean Indians". It was a vicious tirade against the Kaffirs, which Gandhi led in his politically formative years in South Africa. His rise to greatness is attributed to an incident, in which he was thrown out of a train compartment meant only for whites, but it is a little known fact, at least in India, that he despised being "huddled together in the same compartment with the natives of South Africa."

Rajinder Singh has, in his quest for truth, spent many years looking for documents in different archives in London, Oslo etc. This tome is a commendable effort to unravel the mysteries of the history of a crucial period, when the destiny of a free India was being structured.

Dr. Amrit Mehta

Editor-in-Chief Saar Sansaar, New Delhi

Preface

There are a number of books on the Indian politician Mohandas Gandhi alias Mohandas Karamchand Gandhi alias Mahatma Gandhi. Only a few deal with his life and political work in South Africa. While writing "Mahatma Gandhi – ... the missed Nobel Peace Prize – ...", Shaker 'Verlag', Aachen 2015, my attention was drawn to Gandhi's peculiar behaviour towards the natives of South Africa (abbreviated as S.A.). In order to know more about his political activities in South Africa; I started reading "Collected Works of Mahatma Gandhi" and other books. Consequently the present book has been written. It gives a short review on: (a) Indians' immigration to South Africa between 1860 and 1914 (b) Foundation of the Natal Indian Congress and the British Indian Association by M. Gandhi and his associates; (b) The role played by them during the Second Anglo-Boer- and Anglo-Zulu Wars. (c) The creation of a "new" political ideology "satyagraha" (insistence on truth) by Gandhi. (d) The financial support to Gandhi's political activities by traders, Indian politicians and Europeans. (e) Gandhi's opportunist approach to involve workers and indentured Indians, in the final phase of the political struggle (f) The heavy price paid by the Indian community to get a few rights, which he proudly called "the Magna Charta." (g) The cause of conflict between Gandhi, colonial born Indians and traders.

In general, historians blame the white community for suppressing Indians in South Africa. It is shown that it is wrong to reduce the whole issue to one point, that is, racism. To understand the reaction of the Europeans, in particular the Boers', one needs to consider social, financial and political aspects. So far as I am aware; the "origin of Gandhi's political ideas" had not been discussed in the literature. It has been attempted to find out: From whom he borrowed the ideas? History books as well as the "Collected Works of Mahatma Gandhi" show that his achievements in S.A. were more than modest. However, propaganda by Christian missionaries (Joseph J. Doke and C.F. Andrews) and European writers (Romain Rolland, France; and E.F. Rimensberger, Germany) created Gandhi's legacy. More importantly Gandhi himself propagated his own image by writing autobiography.

The letters (from Gandhi and his associates) and articles from different newspapers and journals referred to in this book are taken from the "Collected Works of Mahatma Gandhi." To make the text readable, information is given in parenthesis. The text quoted from the "Collected Work", if in parenthesis, is given so in the original. The emphasized text, if not mentioned explicitly, is from me.

One of the weak points of the present work is that it is heavily based on the "Collected Works of Mahatma Gandhi." They are not intended to give critical image of M. Gandhi. However, I have tried my best to "read between and lines" and occasionally compared the information with published literature. Books on Gandhi's life in South Africa are rare. I had a limited approach to them. What I could obtain and read; has been referred to.

I am not an expert on Gandhi. Without question any critical remarks or comments are most welcome by the readers of this book.

Acknowledgements

I am thankful to Prof. Dr. Michael Komorek, Head of the Research Group - Physics Didactics and History of Science, for supporting my research work by providing research facilities. Without his support, as well as that of the members of the group (Prof. Dr. Falk Riess, Sebastian Peters, Friederike Kirschner, Marko Mansholt, Chris Richter, Tanja Ruberg, Steffen Smoor, Ghassan Azkoun and Wolfgang Engels) this work would have never been completed. Also, I would like to thank my family members (Birgit Krah, Simone Krah, Michael Krah, my brothers Ajit Singh, Pritam Singh, Mohinder Singh and their families) for their moral support. Thanks are due to: Rev. Christiane Cuno; Retired Judge Mr. Bernd Drünner; German Teacher Mrs. Renate Henkenberg-Schröder; Greek friends Rizos Evangelos and Papanastasiou Nikos (Santorini Rastaurant); Colleague from GTS 2001 School Syke - Director Rainer Goltermann, Deputy Director Mazen Hamade, Werner Wordtmann, Dr. Melanie Buss and Annegret Göken; for helping me by one way or another in my life. Furthermore, I thank Mr. Gunnar Shaffer, B.Sc., Engineering, University of Oldenburg, Germany, for correction of this manuscript. Last but not least, thanks are due to Mrs. Leany Maaßen (Shaker 'Verlag') and the Shaker 'Verlag' Aachen, for printing this work.

Introduction

There are a number of books on the Indian politician Mohandas Gandhi alias Mohandas Karamchand Gandhi alias Mahatma Gandhi.[1] However, less has been written on his two decades stay and political activities in South Africa; or to formulate correctly in Natal and Transvaal, as South Africa Union came into existence in 1910.

Mohandas Gandhi, son of a "Prime Minister", went to England and qualified himself as a barrister. In India, he was an unsuccessful lawyer. Due to his elder brother's contacts he got a contract for one year; however, his employee was in South Africa. The one year stay turned into nearly two decades. Being one of the few educated Indians, he became a successful lawyer. He had an aptitude of a journalist. With the help of Muslim Indian traders, Gandhi founded the Natal Indian Congress and the British Indian Associations. To safe-guard their interests, the members of the N.I.C., between 1897 and 1902, wrote about 20000 letters, pamphlets and telegrams. This process continued until Gandhi left S.A. in 1914.

In general, political history concentrates on an individual's achievements. The main question ignored is – who were the helping hands? Most of the literature on M. Gandhi; and in particular his autobiography are based on the same lines. In the present work, it has been attempted to give due place to the "helping hands." How far the present author (R. Singh) had been successful will be judged by the readers. This book will present, Why Indian traders supported; and later opposed him?; How Gandhi and his associates supported the British Empire during the Second Anglo-Boer-, and Anglo-Zulu Wars?; How Gandhi created a "new" political ideology "satyagraha" (insistence to truth)?; What was the origin of Gandhi's political ideas? Why Gandhi initially ignored workers and indentured Indians, but finally involved them in political struggle?; Which heavy price was paid by the Indian community to get a few rights?; and finally, Why he left South Africa? History books as well as the "Collected Works of Mahatma Gandhi" show that his achievements in S.A. were more than modest. How he himself and his Christian followers like the Literature Nobel Laureate Romain Rolland, missionaries Joseph J. Doke (Gandhi's first biographer) created Gandhi's legend? What were their intentions? This has been explored in detail.

Practically, Africa and in particular South Africa does not play any role in Indian schools or University text books. South Africa was one of the few countries which had no political contact with India. In connection with Gandhi's struggle in South Africa, the role of Europeans, in particular the Boers' is presented as that of the "suppressers" and "unjust." Surprisingly, Gandhi, neither in "Indian Opinion" nor in his autobiography mentioned that during the Second Anglo-Boer War, the latter lost one fourth of their population and 50% of their children died. During the war period, Indian traders flourished. It has been attempted to better understand the behaviour of the Boers' towards the Indian community; from a social and financial point to view.

Notes and Refences

[1] A few of the books on Gandhi, which fascinated me are: Mehta V., Mahatma Gandhi and his apostles, Yale University Press, New Haven 1993; Rau H., Mahatma Gandhi, Rowohlt Taschenbuch Verlag GmbH, Hamburg 1996; Grabner S., Schwert der Gewaltlosigkeit – Mahatma Gandhi, Leben und Werk, Pahl-Rugenstein Verlag Köln 1984; Fischer L., Gandhi – Prophet der Gewaltlosigkeit, Wilhelm Heyne Verlag, München 1983; Gandhi M., Mein Leben, Suhrkamp Taschenbuch Verlag, Frankfurt 1983; Erikson E.H., Gandhi's truth - On the origins of nonviolence, W. W. Norton & Company, New York 1971; Kumar G., Brahmacharya Gandhi and his women associates, Vitasta Publishing Pvt. Ltd., New Delhi 2008; Singh R., Mahatma Gandhi – Sex scandals and the missed Peace Nobel Prize, Shaker 'Verlag', Aachen 2015.

Indians' Immigration to South Africa - Indentured, Free and Passenger

Indians' immigration to South Africa started in the 1860s. Almost four centuries before that, in the 1480s the Portuguese navigator Bartholomeu Dias, was the first European who travelled round the southern tip of Africa. His countryman Vasco da Gama, "the discoverer of India", in 1497, landed on Natal coast (see Figure 1). The Dutch, Jan van Riebeeck, a representative of the Dutch East India Company, in 1662, founded the Cape Colony at Table Bay. More than a century later, the British forces seized Cape Colony from the Netherlands.

Figure 1: South Africa – Below: the old Provinces.[2]

The natives of the South Africa were not passive spectators in world politics. Between 1816 and 1826, Shaka Zulu founded then expanded the Empire and named it after himself. In the time period of 1835 and 1849, the Boers left the Cape Colony and founded the Orange Free State and the Transvaal (see Figure 1). The latter was declared a Republic by the Dutch in the late 1850s. A few years later, it was annexed by Britain. Transvaal restored its status as Republic after the First Anglo-Boer War in 1880-81.

In 1899, the British went to war against the Boer, which later came to known as the Second Anglo-Boer War (Oct. 1899 – May 1902). A British woman, Emily Hobhouse, protested against the policies of the British Government. By August 1901, 93940 Boers and 24457 natives were in concentration camps. By the end of the war, 50 percent of the Boer's children under the age of 16 had died of starvation and diseases in the camps. All in all, about one fourth of the Boer's inmates died. The war ended with the Treaty of Vereeniging signed on 31 May 1902. As a sign of goodwill and for future politics, in 1906-1907, the British gave Boers 3000000 pounds for reconstruction and limited self-government.[3] Shortly after that the idea of the foundation of the South Africa Union was born, with General Jan Christiaan Smuts being the driving force behind it.

In 1908, at the occasion of the Inter-Colonial Conference; the Asiatic question was one of the points to be discussed. Gandhi reported that General J.C. Smuts proposed the formation of a Union of different Colonies. The Dutch are interesting in such a Union as they are dominant in the Orange River Colony, the Transvaal and the

Cape. They want to weaken the influence of British settlers.[4] In 1910, the Union of South Africa was founded by former colonies: Cape, Natal, South African Republic (that is, Transvaal) and Orange Free State (Figure 1).[5]

India and European Contacts

Trade between India and Europe by sea route began due to the Portuguese, Vasco da Gama, who sailed into the South West Coast of India on May 27, 1498.[6] Nearly a hundred years later, the British traders formed the East India Company (E.I.C.) to do business in India. On Aug. 24, 1608, its first ship "Hector" dropped anchor off Surat – Mughal Empire's principal port.[7] Due to trade between Indians and Europeans, a new class of Indian traders came into existence that later supported the foreigners to win political and economic influence. The direct intervention in political policies by the E.I.C. began after the battles of Plassey and Buxar on June 23, 1757, and Oct. 23, 1764, respectively.[8] In the former case, the out-numbered British were supported by the Indian traders and the upper caste Hindus against a Muslim ruler.[9]

The British, being minute in number, were also handicapped due to language, and had to seek the help of the educated Indian elite – Brahmins or Muslim priests, in order to communicate with the public and to study the social, judicial and economic laws that were based on religion and were implemented by the rulers in India. Particularly, for Brahmins it was advantageous to co-operate with the British as they had lost their privileged position in the society with the breakdown of old feudal structures. Apart from Brahmins, the other upper castes like Baidyas and Kayasths made contact with the British and eagerly sought after modern scientific knowledge, setting out to seek positions in judiciary, schools and offices which were opened up by the colonial administration.[10] Another type of people to embrace the Western system were progressives. Their opinion was that scientific and technical knowledge was the right way to combat against superstitions and religious prejudices. Two of these pioneers were Raja Ram Mohan Roy and Mahendra Lal Sircar. Roy belonged to a well-educated Brahmin family and had worked as a British official. He was one of the persons who supported the establishment of the Hindu College in Calcutta. In 1830, he went to England with the objective of presenting evidence regarding the introduction of Western education before the Parliamentary Committee, which was going to consider the renewal of the Charter of the E.I.C.[11] In 1857, officially India became a colony of the British Empire.

M.L. Sircar, with some other educationists like Rev. Father Lafont,[12] appealed for the introduction of natural science courses in the syllabus of the Calcutta University[13] which was founded (along with Bombay and Madras Universities) by an act of incorporation passed by the Government of India on January 24, 1857.[14] At the inception, these universities adopted the rules and regulations of the London University. The functions of the Universities were to examine and reward the academic degrees. M. Gandhi and other educated Indians who came to South Africa or other colonies, were a product of the British education system. Without obtaining B.A. degree Gandhi proceeded to the U.K. to study law. After finishing the studies he came back to India. In 1893, the young, M. Gandhi came to South Africa. His contract was limited for a year. However, the circumstances "forced" him to stay in his new home land for about two decades.

Indians in British and Boer Colonies

There were three types of Indians who migrated to S.A. (a) Those who came under work contract for some years, were the so-called "indentured" or "Coolies."[15] (b) After the contract term was over, the immigrant could either stay in Africa or go back. Those who stayed or returned after a short stay in India were called the "free Indians." To earn their livings the "free Indians" worked as either hawkers or began petty trades. (c) In order to trade with Indians some businessmen (mainly Muslims and Parsees from Bombay) followed. The Asian traders and educated persons, who paid their boat passage, were called as the "Passengers."[16] However, after a few years, the primarily White Europeans started calling all Indians as "coolies."

Indians in Natal

In 1856 Natal become a Crown Colony. A law was passed to import workers for sugar plantations and mines. It was a welcomed opportunity for farmers in Calcutta and Madras, as during the war of 1857 and famines they had lost their existence. The first batch of so-called Indian "coolies" reached Natal in Nov. 1860.[17] In 1866 their number was 6448. In 1874 the Government of India sent 6025 workers. According to some historians until 1884 the Natal

Government treated them well and took care of their welfare and rights. They were allowed to buy land.[18] In 1896 Natal's population comprised 400000 blacks, 50000 whites and 51000 Indians.[19] Outside Natal Indians' population was rather low.[20] Indian traders tried to maintain formal contacts with higher political authorities. For instance, Dada Abdulla, Dawod Mahomed, M.C. Camroodeen, Amod Jeewa, Amod Tilly, Parsee Rustomji and A.C. Pillay sent a welcome message to the representative of Her Majesty the Queen, Empress of India.[21] As we shall see later, all of them played important role in Gandhi's political activities.

In 1900, within Natal over 300 Indians had store or shops and about 500 were hawkers.[22] A new law was passed, which forced Indians to pay a poll tax of three pounds. About which the author C.F. Andrews wrote that out of 11175 indentured in Natal, 7585 men and 5334 women had become free Indians by Dec. 31, 1904. After the introduction of the 3 pound poll-tax; the Government had collected 28290 pounds from them. It is a huge some, if we see that, on average an Indian earns 30 rupees (about two pounds) per year.[23] In Natal at the initial stage the Indian traders were entitled to vote or stand as candidates for the Legislative Council of Natal. Some of them made use of the right and got their names entered on the electoral roll.[24]

In 1909, in Natal Indians held properties, valued at nearly a million pounds.[25] In the year of foundation of the South Africa Union in 1910, Natal Indians numbered over 100000, of whom about 10000 were traders. The rest were either indentured or free Indians.[26]

According to a report, referred to by "Indian Opinion" the number of Natal born Indians was more than 27000.[27]

The Orange Free State

The Orange Free State was strict with Asians. For trading, farming and long stay they needed special permission from the State President.[28] "All Indian businesses are forced to close by 11 Sept. 1891, and the owners are deported from the State without compensation."[29] In 1914 Gandhi signed a settlement, which gave some rights to Indians (details later). However, Indians were not allowed to live in the Free State.[30] Until 1961, Indians were officially not considered as a permanent part of the South African population.[31]

Transvaal – South African Republic

The first Indian recorded in Transvaal is from the year 1881.[32] In Transvaal, in 1885, a law was passed which forced the Indian traders and merchants to pay three pound registration fee. There was no limit to immigration. According to law the Indians were allowed to make trade only in settlements. However, the law was never followed strictly.[33] Later, in order to control the influx of Asians (Indian and Chinese workers, who mainly worked in mines), as far as back 1885, in Transvaal a law was passed, according to which the coolies, Arabs and other Asiatic were not allowed to live in particular areas and own property. Apart from that they were devoid of political and civil rights.[34] In 1898, the Transvaal Government wanted to strictly apply the 3rd Law of 1885, as amended in 1886; which denied the indentured, Arabs, Malays and Mahomedan subjects of the Turkish Empire citizenship rights, including the right of owning immovable property. However, the Imperial Government differed in opinion on the application of the law to Indians.

In Oct. 1895, the Transvaal Volksraad passed a resolution, which exempted British subjects from compulsory military service. They were not included as "British subjects." The Natal Indian Congress sent a cablegram and a memorial to the Imperial Government, with the request, not to give Royal ascent to the obnoxious resolution.[35]

In 1896 the Transvaal Government passed a new law, which forced Indian traders to leave particular areas. At that time Gandhi was in India. After he was informed by Indian traders, he sent a telegram to the Viceroy of India and wrote a letter to a local newspaper. In part it was as follows: "…, I venture to think, constitutes a breach of international courtesy, if nothing more. I venture to remind you that the assets of the Indians in the Transvaal amount to over £100000, and that removal to locations would practically mean ruin to the Indian traders."[36]

In 1897, in Transvaal, it was a criminal offence for an Indian to marry a white woman. A year later Indians were prohibited from operating in gold mining areas. In 1899, according to new regulations the trading and residential areas were supposed to be separated. After the Anglo-Boer War Indians' could enter the state with a special permit. Further restrictions followed: Such as the introduction of three pound poll-tax, carrying a passport and compulsory registration by the giving of finger prints. As we shall see in the following chapters, this led to a mass movement by the Indians.

In 1905, a survey made by the Agricultural Council of Barberton showed that some parts of the Colony are suitable for tobacco crop. It was suggested that Indians should be allowed to enter as in Natal. However, from India, Lord Curzon wrote that as long as Indians do not receive proper rights in the colony, the laborers will not be sent. "Indian Opinion" wrote: "... If, therefore, the Transvaal Government does really need Indians, Lord Curzon will have a golden opportunity to exert pressure in order to secure the rights of Indians. The Transvaal is not likely to achieve prosperity so long as agriculture is not introduced there. And there is little likelihood of agriculture being developed without Indians."[37]

According to the 1904 census for the Transvaal there were 11321 Indians (mainly merchants), 299000 whites and 945000 Africans.[38] In 1909, Gandhi wrote: "Indians actually resident in the Colony since the war have probably never been more than 10000 at any time. At the present moment, owing to the Asiatic struggle, there are probably not more than 5000 in the Colony."[39]

Cape Town and Indian Influence

The Cape Colony was established by Dutch East India Company in 1652. After the battle of Blaasuwberg, under the Anglo-Dutch treaty, in 1814, it came under British occupation. In 1872 it became self-governing. According to the author, Uma Dhupelia-Mesthrie: "It was a colony where irrespective of race, people could secure the franchise provided they met the educational and property qualifications."⁴⁰ After the Anglo-Boer War, due to an economic boom, there was an increase in immigration.

> "The city of Cape Town grew from a population of 79000 in 1891 to 170000 in 1904, among the newcomers were Europeans (mainly British), Australians and Indians. From its early numeration in 1891 at 1453, the Indian population of the colony grew to 8489 in over a decade. While a distinct minority - for the total population of the colony was 2409804, their growing presence was cause for concern. ... In 1904 the Indian population was overwhelmingly male, 7648 to just 841 females."⁴¹

By 1904 there were 10192 Indians in Cape Province.⁴² They worked as traders, hawkers, gardeners, interpreters etc. According to another author, "The Cape of Good Hope Colony had 900000 Negroes, 10000 Indians, and 400000 Europeans; ....." ⁴³ "In 1911 the Indian population at the Cape was significantly smaller since the last census, reflecting the tyranny of permits that lasted just a year. Numbering 6606, it was still predominantly male with just 1016 females."⁴⁴

Formation of Indian Organisations in South Africa

It will be wrong to believe that before Gandhi came to S.A. in 1893, the Indians were politically inactive. For instance, when the Asians were placed under the same category as the indigenous Africans, British Indians sent a petition to the South African Republic.⁴⁵ In order to protect the rights of Indians, in 1893, the British Indian

Political Association was established by Indian residents of Kimberley.[46] With the increasing number of Indians, due to religious, social and political deeds various institutions were founded by them. For instance: Hindu Thirukatam Association (Ladysmith), Sanatahn Dharm Soodhur Sabha (Ladysmith), Young Men's Vedic Society (Durban), Aryan Youth Progressive Association (Pietermaritzburg), Newcastle Tamil Association. They were all associated with Hindu culture. The Muslims had their own, such as, Anjuman Fejeh (Johannesburg), Anjuman Islam (Somerset Strand), Hamidia Islamic Society (Johannesburg), Mehafil Eslam Mota-Varachha (Pietermaritzburg), Ladysmith Islamic Society, Natal Memon Community, Point Mahomedan Society, Durban. Somewhat of secular nature were: British India League (Cape Town), British Indian Association (Johannesburg), British Indian Union (Cape Town), Cape British Indian Association, Colonial Born Indian Association (Natal), Colonial Born Hindu Benefit Society (Port Elizabeth), Durban Indian Women's Association, Durban Fruiterers Association, Indian Young Men's National Union (Kimberley), Indian Political Association (Kimberley), Indian Chamber of Commerce (Durban), Ladysmith Farmers Association, Natal Indian Congress, Natal Indian Association.[47]

Out of them the Natal Indian Congress, the British Indian Association, Transvaal, and Hamidia Islamic Society, Johannesburg, were closely connected with Gandhi's political activities. The N.I.C. was founded in 1894. Gandhi remained its General Secretary until 1901. The Hamidia Islamic Society was founded in 1906. The reason for its foundation was that some of the members of the

Muslim community were of the opinion that N.I.C. did not safeguard their interests. The British Indian Association, Johannesburg (Transvaal) or Transvaal British Association was founded in 1903. The President of the B.I.A. was, Abdul Gani; Gandhi was the Honorary Secretary. The political activities of the N.I.C. and B.I.A. are given in the following Chapters.

Notes and References

[2] https://www.lib.utexas.edu/maps/africa/safrica_provinces_95.jpg, Feb. 2, 2015.

[3] http://en.wikipedia.org/wiki/Second_Boer_War, Feb. 2, 2015.

[4] Indian Opinion, 9-5-1908.

[5] http://www.bbc.com/news/world-africa-14094918, Feb. 2, 2015.

[6] Wolpert S., A new history of India, Oxford University Press, New York 1997, p. 135.

[7] Wolpert S., A new history of India, 1997, p. 142.

[8] James L., Raj – The making and unmaking of British India, Little, Brown and Co., London 1999, p. 35; p. 41.

[9] Raj K., Knowledge, power and modern science - The Brahmins strike back (in: Science and empire – Essays in Indian context: 1700-1947, Kumar D. (Ed.)), Anamika Prakashan, Delhi 1991, pp. 115-125.

[10] Raj K., Knowledge, power and modern science - ..., 1991, pp. 115-125.

[11] Chatterjee A., Burn R., British contribution to Indian studies, Longmans, Green & Co., London 1943, pp. 33-34.

[12] Biswas A.K., Science in India, Firma KL Mukhopadhyay, Calcutta 1969, pp. 67-84.

[13] For details on the history of the University see: Banerjee P., Ray N., Gupta P., et al., Hundred years of the University of Calcutta – A history of the university issued in commemoration of the centenary celebrations, University of Calcutta, Calcutta 1957.

[14] Bose D.M., Scientific education and research in the Calcutta University during the last hundred years, Science and Culture 22, 405-412, 1957.

[15] http://scnc.ukzn.ac.za/doc/HIST/LAWS.htm, Jan. 2, 2015.

[16] Copley A., Gandhi against the tide, Basil Blackwell Inc., Cambridge 1989, p. 17.

[17] Andrews C.F., Mahatma Gandhi's ideas – Including selections from his writings – Mahatma Gandhi: His own story – Mahatma Gandhi at work – His own story continued, The Macmillan Company, New York 1931, pp. 40-41.

[18] Jaffer I.A., The early Muslims in Pretoria 1881-1899, M.A. thesis, Rand Afrikaans University 1991, pp. 18-19.

[19] Wolpert S., Gandhi's passion - The life and legacy of Mahatma Gandhi, 2001, pp. 34-35.

[20] Copley A., Gandhi against the tide, 1989, p. 19.

[21] The Natal Mercury, 30-9-1893.

[22] The Times of India, 6-1-1900.

[23] Andrews C.F., Mahatma Gandhi's ideas - ..., 1931, p. 49.

[24] Indian Opinion, 22-4-1905.

[25] The Englishman, Calcutta, 3-8-1909.

[26] C.W.M.G. 10, 1909-1910, p. 47.

[27] Indian Opinion, 27-8-1910.

[28] C.W.M.G. 2, 1897-1902, pp. 396-399.

[29] http://www.sahistory.org.za/topic/history-indians-south-africa-timeline1654-2008, Jan. 14, 2015.

[30] http://www.sahistory.org.za/politics-and-society/anti-indian-legislation-1800s-1959, May 13, 2015.

[31] http://en.wikipedia.org/wiki/Indian_South_Africans#Orange_Free_State, May 13, 2015.

[32] Jaffer I.A., The early Muslims in Pretoria 1881-1899, 1991, p. 21.

[33] Doke J.J., Gandhi in Südafrika – Mohandas Karamchand Gandhi – Ein indischer Patriot in Südafrika, Rotapfel Verlag, Erlenbach-Zürich 1925, p. 209.

[34] http://scnc.ukzn.ac.za/doc/HIST/LAWS.htm, Jan. 2, 2015.

[35] C.W.M.G. 2, 1897-1902, pp. 295-313.

[36] The Englishman, 8-12-1896.

[37] Indian Opinion, 29-4-1905.

[38] Copley A., Gandhi against the tide, 1989, p. 19.

[39] Indian Opinion, 10-4-1909.

[40] https://worldhistoriesfrombelow.files.wordpress.com/2011/08/engaging-with-immigration-laws1.pdf#page=1&zoom=auto,-107,842, Feb. 2, 2014.

[41] https://worldhistoriesfrombelow.files.wordpress.com/2011/08/engaging-with-immigration-laws1.pdf#page=1&zoom=auto,-107,842, Feb. 2, 2014.

[42] Copley A., Gandhi against the tide, 1989, p. 19.

[43] Fischer L., Gandhi – His life and message for the world, New American Library, New York 1954, pp. 23-24.

[44] https://worldhistoriesfrombelow.files.wordpress.com/2011/08/engaging-with-immigration-laws1.pdf#page=1&zoom=auto,-107,842, Feb. 2, 2014.

[45] http://www.sahistory.org.za/topic/history-indians-south-africa-timeline1654-2008, Jan. 14, 2015.

[46] http://www.sahistory.org.za/topic/history-indians-south-africa-timeline1654-2008, Jan. 14, 2015.

[47] http://www.mkgandhi-sarvodaya.org/social_reform/appendix.htm, Feb. 4, 2015. Bhana S., Vadeh G.H., The making of a social reformer - Gandhi in South Africa, 1893 – 1914 (online).

The Natal Indian Congress, The British Indian Association and Gandhi's Participation in Wars

Gandhi in his autobiography devoted just about eight pages (out of 420) on the work of Natal Indian Congress. The main part belongs to "his work and achievements."[48] According to Gandhi, he saw in a newspaper that voting rights for Indians were going to be abolished. They were not aware of it. When he told them, they said that we have no idea about law. They requested him to extend his stay. "I ascertained the names of those who were on the list of voters, and made up my mind to stay on for a month."[49] For political work, Gandhi founded different institutions in S.A. In the following we shall see the activities of the Natal Indian Congress and the British Indian Association, Transvaal until 1907. In particular their participation in wars.

Foundation of the Natal Indian Congress

In Natal from the initial stages the Indians (possessing education and a definite amount of money) were entitled to vote or stand as candidate for the Legislative Council of Natal. Some of the Indians had got their names entered on the electoral roll.[50] In 1893 Natal was a British colony with self-governing status. In June 1894, the Natal Government introduced the Franchise Law Amendment Bill in the Legislative Assembly. It limited the rights of Indians. In spite of protests, the bill was passed by both the Houses.

To take action meetings were held on the premises of Messrs. Dada Abdulla & Co.: ""The effect of the agitation was that all the Indians recognized the absolute necessity of establishing a permanent institution that would cope with the legislative activity, of a retrograde character, of the first responsible Government of the Colony with regard to the Indians, and protect Indian interests."[51]

The constitution of the N.I.C. was drafted by Gandhi.[52] Though the political work began about three months earlier, officially, the Natal Indian Congress was founded on August 22, 1894; with Abdoola Hajee Adam as President, M.K. Gandhi as Honorary Secretary and twenty-two Vice Presidents (see Appendix A). The Objectives of the N.I.C. were:

> "1. To promote concord and harmony among the Indians and the Europeans residing in the Colony.
>
> 2. To inform the people in India by writing to the newspapers, publishing pamphlets, and delivering lectures.
>
> 3. To induce Hindustanis-particularly Colonial-born Indians - to study Indian history and literature relating to India.
>
> 4. To inquire into the conditions of the Indians and to take proper steps to remove their hardships.
>
> 5. To inquire into the conditions of the indentured Indians and to take proper steps to alleviate their sufferings.
>
> 6. To help the poor and helpless in every reasonable way.
>
> 7. To do such work as would tend to improve the moral, social and political conditions of the Indians."[53]

The minimum membership fee was fixed to 5 Shilling (0.25 pounds) per month. It was too much for workers, who had an average income of 14 Shilling (0.70 pounds).[54] On June 4, 1896, that is, the time Gandhi left for India, the Congress had 300 members.[55] A written credential, which was signed by 38 persons, allowed him to represent the Indian community in Natal.[56] He was given a draft for 75 pounds to cover the travelling, printing and other expenses in connection with his work on South Africa.[57]

According to the first report of the N.I.C., Europeans did not show interest in the meetings. In general the attendance was poor and the members were unpunctual. In particular the Tamil community had not shown much zeal in the political work.[58] Gandhi was accused of taking money for his services. He refuted.[59]

Activities of the N.I.C.

Work on Political Level – Petitions and Memorials

In 1894, the Natal Legislative Assembly was passing a bill, which could devoid Indians of their voting rights. As a reaction to the bill on July 14, 1894, a petition was sent to Lord Ripon, Principal Secretary of the State for Colonies by H.M.H. Dada, Vice-President N.I.C., and sixteen others.[60] One of the 36 points in the petition was that according to the Natal Government Gazette of March 27, 1894, in 26 schools 2589 scholars are studying. Out of them many are born in the Colony. Their way of living is more like Europeans than Indians. They are able to compete with Europeans. They deserve the Franchise privilege.[61]

On May 5, 1895, a petition was sent to the Viceroy and Governor-General of India. In which it was stated that:

"If an intelligent stranger were to visit the South African Republic, and were told that there was a class of people in South Africa who could not hold fixed property, who could not move about the State without passes, who alone had to pay a special registration fee of £3 10s as soon as they entered the country for purposes of trade, who could not get licenses to trade, and who would shortly be ordered to remove to places far away from towns, where only they could reside and trade, and who could not stir out of their houses after 9 o'clock, and that stranger were asked to guess the reasons for such special disabilities, would he not conclude that these people must be veritable ruffians, anarchists, a political danger to the State and society?"[62]

Indian traders were forced to live in particular settlements. One of the arguments of the South African State was that the hygienic conditions in Indian's houses and working places were not satisfactory. However, some of the Europeans had different opinions. For Instance, according to a document, dated March 14, 1895, signed by 51 individuals and firms of Europeans:

"1st. That the aforementioned Indian merchants, the majority of whom come from Bombay, keep their business places, as well as their residences, in a clean and proper sanitary state - in fact, just as good as the Europeans. 2nd. That it is a distinct error in calling them "Coolies" or inhabitants of British India of a "lower caste", as they decidedly belong to the better and higher castes of India."[63]

Another local group signed a petition, which was sent to the President of the South African Republic Pretoria. It reads:

"In view of the gross misrepresentation by certain interested Europeans residing in the Republic, to the effect that the burghers of this State are opposed to the Indians residing or trading in the State, and their agitation against these people, we, the undersigned burghers, beg respectfully to state that so far from the burghers being opposed to these people fully stopping and trading in the State, they recognize in them a peaceful and law-abiding, and therefore desirable, class of people. To the poor they are a veritable blessing inasmuch as by their keen competition they keep down the prices of necessaries of life which they can do owing to their thrifty and temperate habits."[64]

According to another document:

"We, the undersigned Europeans residing in this Republic, beg to protest against the agitation set up against the Indians, residing or trading freely in the country, by certain interested persons. So far as our experience is concerned, we believe their sanitary habits to be in no way inferior to those of the Europeans, and the statements about prevalence of infectious diseases among them are certainly without ground, especially as regards the Indian traders. We firmly believe that the agitation owes its origin not to their habits as regards sanitation, but to trade jealousy, because, owing to their frugal and temperate habits, ...".[65]

And further:

> "We do not believe any good cause exists for compelling them to reside or trade in separate quarters. We would therefore humbly request Your Honour not to adopt or countenance any measure that would tend to restrict their freedom and ultimately result in their withdrawal from the Republic, a result that cannot but strike at the very means of their livelihood and cannot, therefore, we humbly submit, be contemplated with complacency in a Christian country."[66]

A few other examples about the work of the N.I.C. to be quoted are:

- Regarding the Franchise Law Amendment Bill, on July 10, 1894, Gandhi and seven others sent a petition to the Natal Governor.[67]

- A.H.H. Adam and several others on May 5, 1895, opposed the extension of term for indentured from five years to an indefinite period; and the introduction of 25 pound tax for those, who want to live in Natal after the termination of the term.[68]

- A memorial was sent by the representatives of the British Indian community to Joseph Chamberlain, Principal Secretary of State for the Colonies, London. In it Her Majesty's Government was requested not to accept the bill, which support the purchase of freedom by paying an annual tax of three pounds.[69]

- Chamberlain was told that "out of the 9000 signatories, not a hundred, besides those who were already on the Voters' Roll, possessed the legal property qualifications."[70]

- Other active members like M.C. Kamroodeen, A. Gani, M. Ismail *et al.* sent memorial to J. Chamberlain to inform that the Government of the South African Republic consider only the white persons as the "British subjects."[71]

- In Natal, A.K. Hajee and 39 others sent a memorial to the Natal Governor and complained against the fact that they are not allowed to acquire property in the Nondweni Township.[72]

- From time to time petition and memorials were sent to Indian politicians like Dadabhai Naoroji[73] or to the influential members of the Indian National Congress as Pherozeshah Mehta.[74]

- The help was also sought from the authorities of the British-India Empire as indicated by a letter from A.K.H. Adam to Elgin, Viceroy and Governor-General of India, Calcutta.[75]

Support and Propaganda on Local Level

Why Indians should not get the right of franchise? The opponents had the following arguments:

"(1) The Indians do not enjoy the franchise in India.

(2) The Indian in South Africa represents the lowest-class Indian; in fact, he is the scum of India.

(3) The Indian does not understand what the franchise is.

(4) The Indian should not get the franchise because the native, who is as much a British subject as the Indian, has none.

(5) The Indian should be disfranchised in the interests of the native population.

(6) This Colony shall be and remain a white man's country, and not a black man's and the Indian franchise will simply swamp the European vote, and give the Indian political supremacy."[76]

In 1895, in a long pamphlet "An appeal to Briton in South Africa", young Gandhi masterly refuted one point after the other, with numbers and quotations from literature. He showed that though the number of Indians is little bit higher than the whites, only a few had the right of voting. Only those inhabitants, who are above 21 and possess "an immovable property to the value of £50 or who rents any such property of the yearly value of £10 within any electoral district and who is duly registered in the manner hereinafter mentioned, shall be entitled to vote at the election of a member for such district."[77]

Then he reproduced the data of voters to show that under these condition Indians cannot over swamp Europeans (see Appendix B).[78] Gandhi wrote:

"List further shows that most of the Indian voters are those Indians who have settled in the Colony for a very long time; that out of 251 (out of them 40 are either dead or left the colony; 9 Africa born Indians) whom I have been able to get identified, only 35 have been at one time indentured Indians, and that they have all been in the Colony for over 15 years."[79]

According to the first report of the N.I.C. about 1000 letters, in connection with the Franchise petition, Transvaal petition and the Immigration petition were sent to the Home Government and U.K.[80] The British Government does not sanction the Franchise Act, but the Act was reintroduced in 1896.

Gandhi left for India on June 4, 1896.[81] A few months later, that is, in Jan., 1897, he returned back with his family. He continued political work. On Jan. 29, 1897, he wrote a letter to the British Agent in Pretoria and asked why Indians are not allowed to enter even if they possess 25 pounds security.[82] On March 27, 1897, a circular was issued by A.K.H. Adam (Dada Abdoolla & Co.) and forty others on some of the legal disabilities the Indians had in Colonies. For instance, unlike Europeans, they cannot go out without pass after 9 p.m.; free Indians were liable to be arrested if they did not possess passes; in Durban the registration of native and Indian servants was needed; those who became free Indians, either must return to homeland and pay travelling, or annual poll-tax of three pounds; and High Schools were closed from Indians. However, the most important point in the circular was that: "Indians, unlike Europeans, in order to be entitled to the Franchise must prove that they belong to a country "possessing elective representative institutions founded on the Parliamentary Franchise," or, must receive an order of exemption from the Governor-in-Council."

Natal Indian Congress was a bureaucratic body, which sent one petition/memorial/letter after the other on different issues; with the hope that the British- or the British-Indian Empire will support its causes.[83] Between 1897 and 1902, "about 20000 pamphlets, copies of memorials and letters" were written and distributed by the N.I.C.[84]

N.I.C. – Participation in Wars

The Second Anglo-Boer War

The roots of the Anglo-Boer War was the discovery of Gold in Transvaal. In order to have control over Gold mines the British sought cause for the war. One of their arguments was the mistreatment of British-subjects. Gandhi saw rightly that injustice was being done to the Boers. Still he was of the opinion that "... every single subject of a state must not hope to enforce his private opinion in all cases. The authorities may not always be right, but so long as the subjects own allegiance ... *it is their clear duty* ... to accord their *support to acts of the state.*"[85]

In the following we shall see, how Gandhi and his followers helped the brutal British Empire.

Volunteer Stretcher-Bearer Corps and Funds Collection

By the end of 1899 due to war many started leaving Transvaal. Some of them obtained refuse in Natal. For that the N.I.C. thanked the government. A resolution was passed to support the government. On Oct. 19, 1899, Gandhi wrote a letter to the Colonial Secretary, Maritzburg, stating that 32 (...) educated and English speaking Indians would like to support the Empire. However, they are untrained in using weapons, but they can help in taking care of the wounded soldiers. He assured that the interested participants had been medically checked up by a European doctor.[86] On Dec. 2, 1899, Gandhi sent a telegram to the Colonial Secretary, Pietermaritzburg, and offered services of his countrymen. A few weeks later, Colonel Gallwey, P.M.O. Headquarters, Natal, was told that 500 free Indians are ready to do ambulance work until the end of the war. In March 1900, the number of members of the Stretcher Bar Corps was reported to be 1000. Most of them were indentured laborers.[87] For their work they were paid one pound per week; whereas their thirty leaders had served without any remuneration. The Corps was disbanded after six weeks.[88] Four years later, only eight leaders were honoured with medals.[89]

Goodbye South Africa - Gandhi in India

While the war was going on, Gandhi decided to leave the country forever. On Oct. 15, 1901, a farewell party was given to Gandhi. Abdul Cadir, President N.I.C. and others thanked him for his work. Before leaving Gandhi resigned from the organisation as its Honorary Secretary.[90] He donated all valuables like Gold medals to the N.I.C. He reached India in the middle of Dec. 1901; and met G.K. Gokhale and other politicians. To inform the Indians about the situation in South Africa he delived a lecture. He wrote to Gokhale: "I think I have told you that if I receive the funds expected from Natal, I would settle in Bombay. Having received over Rs. 3000, I have opened an office here and propose giving a year's trial to this place."[91]

In May 1902, the war was over. The British were "victorious." The war cost around 75000 lives; 22000 British, 20000 natives and the rest were Boers.[92] On the political level, the cards were to be mixed new. During the war the Indian community was loyal to the British Empire. Now, the question was: What will they get under the British rule in S.A.? They needed to deal with the British authorities. In the beginning of Nov. 1902, Gandhi wrote to a friend, saying that, he had been asked to return to Natal. During the last eight years stay he had done extensive political work but he confessed that he had no more energy. Thus before making a final decision, he wrote a letter to the N.I.C. and imposed some conditions.[93] Gandhi told to Gokhale:

> "When I was just feeling that I had settled down in Bombay, I received a message from Natal asking me immediately to go there. From the cablegrams exchanged between our people in Natal and myself, I think it is in connection with Mr. Chamberlain's approaching visit to South Africa that I am required there. I propose to leave by the first steamer available. That would be probably the 20th instant."[94]

The above communication indicates that he was asked to attend a short meeting with J. Chamberlin. Also Gandhi was feeling well in Bombay. Under these conditions – Why he decided to leave Bombay and take his whole family with him? It remains unclear.

After the Anglo-Boer War - Gandhi Returns to South Africa

On Dec. 27, 1902, Gandhi and 27 other "humble servants" wrote a petition to J. Chamberlain. They wanted to talk about trade licenses and the immigration act. The deputation was to be led by Gandhi.[95] In the beginning, Transvaal's authorities refused to include Gandhi in the deputation list, as he was not living in the state. T.H.K. Mahomed requested the Colonial Secretary, Pretoria, to include Gandhi as he was well-informed about laws.[96]

Gandhi and Co., who believed that they would recieve better rights after the war were mistaken. Shortly after the war, refugees in Pretoria were not given trading licenses; steamship companies were instructed not to take Asian passengers from Cape Town to Durban.[97] A circular by M.C. Camrooden and nineteen others show that in the South African Republic (Transvaal): Indians had to pay a three pound registration fee; they were also not allowed to travel on trains in the first or second class apartments; they had no right to do business with gold; in Pretoria they could not use footpaths and public vehicles.[98] So far as the political achievements of Indians were concerned, in 1905, Gandhi wrote: *"Whether we look at Natal, the Transvaal, the Cape, or the Orange River Colony, it is not possible to recall anything that may be considered in the light of an achievement."*[99]

Apart from supporting the Anglo-Boer War, Gandhi and the N.I.C. supported the British Empire against "Kaffir rebellion" (detail below).

Gandhi on Zulu Rebellion - "It is not for us to say whether the revolt of the Kaffirs is justified or not"

In the April 7, 1907, issue of the "Indian Opinion", it was reported: "The British Empire received (a) set-back as Kaffirs in Natal revolted against the poll-tax. Sergeants Hunt and Armstrong were killed by Zulus. As a reaction to it, the martial law was declared and twelve natives were blown up at the mouth of a cannon. Neighbouring natives and their chief were forced to see the scene."[100]

Lord Elgin, Secretary of State for the Colonies, criticized Natal's Governor.[101] W. Churchill threatened to send an expeditionary force, if the local Government is unable to keep the Kaffirs under control.[102] Meanwhile, the Zulus had kidnapped the Chief, who was placed by the British at the place of Bambata. In an encounter the British soldiers were defeated by Bambata's army.[103] A journalist of the "Indian Opinion" wrote: "At the time of writing, Bambata is at large. Meanwhile, his followers go on increasing. There is no knowing how all this will end."[104] Then Gandhi posed a question and answered as follows:

> "What is our duty during these calamitous times in the Colony? *It is not for us to say whether the revolt of the Kaffirs is justified or not. We are in Natal by virtue of British power. Our very existence depends upon it.* It is therefore our duty to render whatever help we can. There was a discussion in the Press as to what part the Indian community would play in the event of an actual war. We have already declared in the English columns of this journal *that the Indian community is ready to play its part;*

and we believe *what we did during the Boer War should also be done now.*"¹⁰⁵

Under the auspicious of the N.I.C., a meeting was held in Durban and D. Mahomed was the Chairperson. Gandhi was critical of the government, which was not taking Indians in the army. Some Indians were not ready to support British. To convince them, Gandhi argued:

> "Opinions, too, may differ as to the cause of the native revolt. But it was their duty not to be prejudiced by any such thoughts. If they claimed rights of citizenship, they were bound to take their natural share in the responsibilities that such rights carried with them. It was, therefore, their duty to assist in averting the danger that threatened the Colony. *The Indians had done good work during the Boer war.*"¹⁰⁶

In a meeting a resolution was moved, in which the Chairman of the N.I.C. was asked to make an offer to the Government to support the war against the Natives.¹⁰⁷

The Stretcher-Bearer Corps

In general, the white community was least interested in taking help from Indians. In contrast they were suspicious that if they are armed, they would sell their weapons to the natives.¹⁰⁸ One of the newspapers "satirically suggested that Indians, so that they may not run away, should be placed in the front-line, and that then the fight between them and the natives will be a sight for the gods."¹⁰⁹ Others thought it under their dignity to be defended by Indians. Gandhi, the future pacifist, pleaded the Government to train Indians for military purpose and at the same time he attacked a politician as follows: "... Watt will like to apply Indians for digging trenches; but his will not like to be defended by them."[110] "Will Mr. Watt and his fellow-ministers wake up to a sense of their duty in the matter?" wrote Gandhi.[111] In the "Indian Opinion" he stated:

> *"We have to learn much from what the whites are doing in Natal. There is hardly any family from which someone has not gone to fight the Kaffir rebels. Following their example, we should steel our hearts and take courage. Now is the time when the leading whites want us to take this step; if we let go this opportunity, we shall repent later."*[112]

On April 24, 1906, the N.I.C. passed a resolution to support the war with an Ambulance Corps.[113] They informed the Government about their decision and received a positive reply.[114] The secretaries of the N.I.C. thanked the Government for accepting the offer. The arrangements for uniform, equipment and transportion were to be made by the Government. "At the same time, we beg to submit that it is not possible to raise the Corps on a salary of less than one pound per week, which sum, we are instructed to say, the Indian community is willing to pay as long as the services of the Corps are required", wrote the secretaries of the N.I.C.[115]

The stretcher bearers took the following pledge:

> "We, the undersigned, solemnly and sincerely declare that we will be faithful and bear true allegiance to His Majesty King Edward the Seventh, His Heirs and Successors, and

that we will faithfully serve in the supernumerary list of the Active Militia Force of the Colony of Natal as Stretcher-Bearers, until we shall lawfully cease to be members thereof, and the terms of the service are that we should each receive Rations, Uniform, Equipment and 1s. 6d. per day. M.K. Gandhi, U.M. Sehlat, H.I. Joshi, S.B. Medh, K. Mahomed, Mahomedshaikh, Dada Mian, Pooti Naiken, Appa Samy, Kunjee, Shaikh Madar, Mahomed, Alwar, Muthusamy, Coopoosamy, Ajodhyasing, Kistama, Ali, Bhailal, Jamaludin."[116]

The Red Cross badges for the members of the Corps were made. Albeit, the readers were told: "These badges cannot be very important in the Kaffir rebellion; but among European nations there is a convention that arms cannot be used against persons wearing such badges."[117] However, the list with names and ranks published in the "Indian Opinion" differs from the forgoing. It reads as follows:

"..., in connection with the operations against the natives, consists of twenty Indians whose names are as follows: M.K. Gandhi (Sgt.-Major), U.M. Shelat (Sgt.), H.I. Joshi (Sgt.), S.B. Medh (Sgt.), Parbhu Hari (Corporal), Khan Mahomed, Jamaludin, Mahomed, Sheikh Madar, Sheik Dada Mia, Mahomed Essop, Puti Naiken, Appasamy, Kitama, Kupusamy, Bomaya, Kunji, Ajodhyasing."[118]

Honours to the "War-Heroes"

After six weeks at the front, the Stretcher Bearers were disbanded on July 19, 1906. Gandhi in his speech stated: "If, for any reason, the traders could not enlist, other educated Indians as well as the servants and clerks of traders could easily do so. From experience gained during the fighting, he could say that *the whites treated the Indians very cordially*, and *distinctions based on colour had ceased to exist.*"[119] The N.I.C. paid tributes to them. In a meeting it was decided to present silver medals to members of the Stretcher-Bearer Corps."[120]

N.I.C. – A Party of Indian Traders with Dictatorial Methods

In 1906 there was a change in the N.I.C. as Dowd Mahomed was elected President.[121] Mahomed Cassim Anglia, who was educated and had experience in political work became secretary.[122] Though the N.I.C. was founded to safe-guard the interests of all Indians in S.A., it remained a party of traders and businessmen. The indentured played a negligible role. "The Natal Advertiser" and "The Star" published articles indicating that the "Colonial Hindus and Christianized Indians" are planning to found a new party as they are unhappy with the N.I.C. politics. Immediately the "Indian Opinion" reacted to it as follows: "There is no doubt that this is the work of some disgruntled Indians. It is obvious enough that they will receive help from the Europeans. We have with us a circular notice of that meeting, signed by Messrs. Bryan Gabriel, V. Lawrence and A.D. Pillay; and the meeting was held at Mr. A.D. Pillay's house...."[123]

Gandhi and Co. were arrogant to see fault in the programme of the N.I.C. They were of the opinion that the meeting was simply a threat. Most probably, V. Lawrence (who later, 1908, with A.D. Pillay *et al.* founded "The Natal Indian Patriotic Union") under pressure from Gandhi and others, wrote a letter to the media and stated: "The object of that meeting was to form a very influential and representative committee to approach the Natal Indian Congress, which is recognized by the Imperial and Colonial Governments as the representative institution of the Indian community in Natal, to make it a more representative body than it is at present."[124]

Why one should support the traders? V. Laurence's wording, which fits only to Gandhi's way of thinking, was:

> "If the Indian traders today loom large at the Congress meetings, it is because they are the most in danger; and if they were neglected or allowed themselves to be neglected, who will suffer? Certainly the whole Indian community; for *throughout the world it is the commercial class that supplies the sinews of war and even common sense to the community or nation to which it belongs.*"[125]

Though Gandhi tried to "hide" the conflict at this stage, later the reality came into light. The fact is that African born Indians saw rightly that the N.I.C. did not safeguard their rights. V. Lawrence, A.D. Pillay and P.S. Aiyer *et al.* founded the "The Natal Indian Patriotic Union" (1908) and the Colonial Born Indian Association (1911), South African Indian Committee (1911). In 1908, P.S. Aiyer started publishing the "African Chronicle" in the Tamil language.[126] The N.I.P.U. protested against the three pound tax on the indentured workers. In 1911, "The African Chronicle" started a mass campaign. So far as Gandhi was concerned, it was not until 1913, that he took the issue seriously, though, in 1909, he had urged the business community to agitate against the tax. In July 1911, per law the import of Indian indentured labour was stopped. Gandhi and Co. welcomed it. But the members of the N.I.P.U. were against it, as their policy and demand was that the position of labour should be improved.[127]

Gandhi in Johannesburg and the Foundation of the British Indian Association

In Feb. 1903, Gandhi settled down in Johannesburg.[128] Shortly after that, on March 23, 1903, the British Indian Association was founded; with A. Gani as President. The political work was started soon. A. Gani wrote a number of letters to defend the interests of the Indian traders and shopkeepers.[129-130] A deputation of the British Indian Association (consisting of M.K. Gandhi, Abdul Gani, Haji Habib, H.O. Ally, S.V. Thomas, and Imam Shekh Ahmed) met Lord Milner, Governor of Transvaal. He refused to remove the three pound tax. His argument was that other communities give 18s annually, whereas the Asians had to pay only once.[131] The B.I.A. worked on the same pattern as the N.I.C., namely, writing petitions and informing its supporters in the U.K. and India. For instance:

- The Chairman wrote to the local authorities that the British Indians are not allowed to pass through the former Orange River Colony on their way to Cape Colony; they are not allowed to enter Delagoa Bay in spite of the possession of permits.[132]

- After the plague break out in Johannesburg, B.I.A. sent a petition of letters with support from whites. For example, H. Prior Veale, B.A., M.D., B.C. (Cantab.) wrote "Generally, in my opinion, it is impossible to object to the Indian on sanitary grounds, provided always the inspection of sanitary authorities is made as strictly and regularly for the Indian as for the white."[133]

- On Dec. 3, 1904, A. Gani wrote to the Acting Lieutenant-Governor, Pretoria regarding the financial help to be given to persons, whose property was destroyed at the instruction off the health officer at the outbreak of plague.[134]

- Also, the B.I.A. protested against the contemplated transfer of the control of the Bazaars to the municipalities;[135] or putting Indians on the same level as the natives.[136]

- In Sept., 1905, A. Gani stated that it is insulting and lack of faith in Indian testimony as the refugee Indians require to furnish two Europeans as reference to get permit. Also it is impractical as most of the Indian storekeepers, salesman and domestic servants have no contact with the white community. Most importantly, "it would put a premium on perjury, as it is quite conceivable that a few unscrupulous Indians will not find it difficult to find a few unscrupulous Europeans who would be prepared to perjure themselves for a consideration."[137]

We have seen above that the organisations founded by Gandhi were more or less passive. Passive in the sense that they wrote petitions and letters to official authorities, with the hope to get better rights. As we shall see in the next chapter, it was going to change in future.

Appendix A – N.I.C. - Vice Presidents

Most probably to appease the businessmen, the number of Vice Presidents was limited to twenty-two. Their names are: Hajee Mahomed Hajee Dada, Abdool Kadir, Hajee Dada Hajee Habib, Moosa Hajee Adam, P. Dawjee Mahomed, Peeran Mahomed, Murugesa Pillay, Ramaswami Naidoo, Hoosen Miran, Adamjee Miankhan, K.R. Nayanah, Amod Bayat (P. M. Burg), Moosa Hajee Cassim, Mahomed Cassim Jeeva, Parsee Rustomjee, Dawad Mahomed, Hoosen Cassim Amod Tili, Doraiswamy Pillay, Omar Hajee Aba, Osmankhan Rahamatkhan, Rangaswami Padayachi, Hajee Mahomed (P.M. Burg), Camroodeen (P.M. Burg).[138] Out of them, some, such as A. Kadir, H. Habib, A. Miankhan, P. Rustomjee and D. Mohomed played important roles in Gandhi's struggle.

Appendix B

No.	Electoral divisions	Europeans	Indians
1	Pietermaritzburg	1521	82
2	Umgeni	0306	Nil
3	Lion's	0511	Nil
4	Ixopo	0573	3
5	Durban	2100	143
6	County of Durban	0779	20
7	Victoria	0566	1
8	Umvoti	0438	1
9	Weenen	0528	Nil
10	Klip River	0591	1
11	Newcastle	0917	Nil
12	Alexandra	0201	"
13	Alfred	0278	"
	Total	9309	251

Notes and References

[48] Gandhi M.K., An autobiography – The story of my experiments with truth (translated from Gujarati by Mahadev Desai), Jonathan Cape Ltd., London 1972, pp. 123-131.

[49] Gandhi M.K., An autobiography or the story of my experiments with truth, Navajivan Publishing House, Ahmedabad 1940, p. 73.

[50] Andrews C.F., Mahatma Gandhi's ideas – Including selections from his writings – Mahatma Gandhi: His own story – Mahatma Gandhi at work – His own story continued, The Macmillan Company, New York 1931, p. 49.

[51] C.W.M.G. 1, 1888-1896, pp. 262-268.

[52] The Natal Mercury, 27-9-1895.

[53] C.W.M.G. 1, 1888-1896, pp. 178-182.

[54] Gandhi M.K., An autobiography – The story of my experiments with truth, 1972, pp. 123-131.

[55] The Natal Advertiser, 5-6-1896.

[56] C.W.M.G. 1, 1888-1896, p. 358.

[57] C.W.M.G. 1, 1888-1896, p. 461.

[58] C.W.M.G. 1, 1888-1896, pp. 262-268.

[59] The Natal Mercury, 4-10-1895.

[60] C.W.M.G. 1, 1888-1896, pp. 163-173.

[61] C.W.M.G. 1, 1888-1896, pp. 163-173.

[62] C.W.M.G. 1, 1888-1896, pp. 236-237.

[63] C.W.M.G. 1, 1888-1896, pp. 232-233.

[64] C.W.M.G. 1, 1888-1896, p. 233.

[65] C.W.M.G. 1, 1888-1896, p. 234.

[66] C.W.M.G. 1, 1888-1896, p. 234.

[67] C.W.M.G. 1, 1888-1896, p. 162.

[68] C.W.M.G. 1, 1888-1896, pp. 246-248.

[69] C.W.M.G. 1, 1888-1896, pp. 249-260.

[70] Adam A.K.H. *et al.* to Chamberlain J., May 22, 1896.

[71] C.W.M.G. 1, 1888-1896, pp. 281-283.

[72] Hajee A.K. *et al.* to Governor, Natal, Feb. 26, 1896.

[73] C.W.M.G. 1, 1888-1896, p. 238.

[74] Gandhi M.K. to Mehta F., Aug. 9, 1895.

[75] C.W.M.G. 1, 1888-1896, pp. 260-262.

[76] C.W.M.G. 1, 1888-1896, pp. 283-307.

[77] C.W.M.G. 1, 1888-1896, pp. 283-307.

[78] C.W.M.G. 1, 1888-1896, pp. 283-307.

[79] C.W.M.G. 1, 1888-1896, pp. 283-307.

[80] C.W.M.G. 1, 1888-1896, pp. 262-268.

[81] The Natal Advertiser, 5-6-1896.

[82] Gandhi M.K. to British Agent, Pretoria, Jan. 29, 1897.

[83] Adam A.C.H. to Governor Natal, April 6, 1897, Adam A.C.H. to Chamberlain J., July 2, 1897. Adam A.C.H. to Natal Governor, July

2, 1897; Jeewa C.M. *et al.* to Naoroji D. *et al.*, Sept. 18, 1897. Gandhi M.K. to Naoroji D., Sept. 18, 1897.

[84] C.W.M.G. 2, 1897-1902, pp. 295-313.

[85] Wolpert S., Gandhi's passion - The life and legacy of Mahatma Gandhi, Oxford University Press, Oxford 2001, p. 46.

[86] Gandhi M.K. to Colonial Secretary, Maritzburg, Oct. 19, 1899.

[87] C.W.M.G. 2, 1897-1902, p. 371.

[88] C.W.M.G. 2, 1897-1902, p. 371.

[89] Indian Opinion, 12-11-1904.

[90] C.W.M.G. 2, 1897-1902, pp. 421-423.

[91] Gandhi M.K. to Gokhale G.K., Aug. 1, 1902.

[92] http://en.wikipedia.org/wiki/Second_Boer_War, Feb. 2, 2015.

[93] Gandhi M.K. to Shukla D.B., Nov. 8, 1902.

[94] Gandhi M.K. to Gokhale G.K., Nov.14, 1902.

[95] C.W.M.G. 3, 1902-1904, pp. 6-11.

[96] Mahomed T.K.H. to Colonial Sec., Pretoria, Jan. 2, 1903.

[97] C.W.M.G. 2, 1897-1902, pp. 392-393.

[98] C.W.M.G. 2, 1897-1902, pp. 396-399.

[99] Indian Opinion, 30-12-1905.

[100] Indian Opinion, 7-4-1906.

[101] Indian Opinion, 7-4-1906.

[102] Indian Opinion, 14-4-1906.

[103] Indian Opinion, 14-4-1906.

[104] Indian Opinion, 14-4-1906.

[105] Indian Opinion, 14-4-1906.

[106] Indian Opinion, 28-4-1906.

[107] Indian Opinion, 28-4-1906.

[108] Indian Opinion, 12-5-1906.

[109] Indian Opinion, 12-5-1906.

[110] Indian Opinion, 28-4-1906.

[111] Indian Opinion, 28-4-1906.

[112] Indian Opinion, 30-6-1906.

[113] Mohamed D. to Colonial Sec. Pietermaritzburg, April 25, 1906.

[114] Johari O.H.A., Anglia M.C. to Colonial Secretary, Pietermaritzburg, June 2, 1906.

[115] Johari H.A., Anglia M.C. to Principal Medical Officer, June 2, 1906.

[116] Indian Opinion, 16-6-1906.

[117] Indian Opinion, 23-6-1906.

[118] Indian Opinion, 21-7-1906.

[119] Indian Opinion, 28-7-1906.

[120] C.W.M.G. 5, 1905-1906, p. 282.

[121] Indian Opinion, 10-3-1906.

[122] Indian Opinion, 10-3-1906.

[123] Indian Opinion, 26-1-1907.

[124] Indian Opinion, 26-1-1907.

[125] Indian Opinion, 26-1-1907.

[126] Switzer S. (Ed.), South Africa's alternative press - Voices of protest and resistance, 1880s-1960s, Cambridge University Press, Cambridge 1997, p. 113.

[127] Switzer S. (Ed.), South Africa's alternative press ..., 1997, p. 114.

[128] http://www.gandhi-manibhavan.org/aboutgandhi/chrono_detailed_gandhiinsafrica.htm, March 22, 2014.

[129] C.W.M.G. 3, 1902-1904, pp. 35-36.

[130] For more detail see, C.W.M.G. 3, 1902-1904, pp. 29-62; 90-117.

[131] Indian Opinion, 11-6-1903.

[132] Gani A. to Rand Plague Committee, June 24, 1904.

[133] Gani A., Gandhi M.K. to Colonial Sec., Pretoria, Sept. 3, 1904.

[134] Indian Opinion, 10-12-1904.

[135] Indian Opinion, 22-7-1905.

[136] Gani A. to Private Secretary of Governor, Orange River Colony, Aug. 30, 1905.

[137] Gani A. to Chief Sec. for Permit, Sept. 1, 1905.

[138] C.W.M.G. 1, 1888-1896, pp. 178-182.

The Asiatic Registration Act and a Deputation to England

After the Anglo-Boer- and Anglo-Zulu Wars, "theoretically", the British were the masters of the colonies in South Africa. However, still the individual colonies had political power on issues of law and order. In order to unite the white community and to have peace with Boers, the British were forced to find solution. After the war was lost, Generals Smuts and Botha were received in London as friends. Gandhi and Co. had supported the wars as they identified themselves as "British subjects." Their expectation was to get the same rights as other British. In the following sections we shall see:

- How far the British Empire supported British Indians after the wars?
- Which steps were taken by Indian community to get rights?
- The extent of Gandhi's success.

The Asiatic Registration Act – To Bring to Boil – H. Habib and the Gaol Going Resolution

From the very beginning the Transvaal Colony was not Indian friendly. After the British came to power, the situation even became worse, as shown by Gandhi *et al.* (Appendix A).[139] In order to discuss the situation, an Indian deputation met the Constitutional Committee with the following members: Abdul Gani (Chairman), Haji Ojer Ali (also written as Ally), Ebrahim Saleji Coovadia (Johannesburg), Ismail Patel (Klerksdorp), Ibrahim Khota (Heidelberg), Ibrahim Jasaat (Standerton), E. M. Patel

(Potchefstroom) and M.K. Gandhi. Due to the pressure of work, Haji Habib did not join the party.

> "Gandhi gave a full account of the difficulties relating to the use of trams and added that there was another difficulty which caused greater harassment to the Indians: they were not only denied the right to purchase land, but they could not hold it in their own names even for religious purposes. Constant difficulties were experienced in the matter of transferring such lands in Pretoria, Johannesburg, Heidelberg and other places. *It was a gross injustice to seek to place Indians in the same class as the Kaffirs.*"[140]

In the first half of the 1906, in order to control the "Asian flux" and its influence in the society, the Asiatic Registration Act was drafted in Transvaal. From the Transvaal's Governmental point of view, it was meant to improve the management in the case of immigration. However, for Indians it was an insult, because in the registration applications, one needed to give his "mother's name" and "finger prints" (Appendix B), which was generally taken in the case of criminals. The "Indian Opinion" under "Effect of rules" commented as follows: "The rules include the following additional points not anticipated earlier:

> "1. *In India, Hindus and Muslims respect the mother so deeply that if anyone compels them to make a reference to her name, that may lead to murder. The name of the mother will have now to be entered in an application.*
>
> 2. It was never dreamt that impressions of all fingers would be required from children. Now they will take eighteen such

prints. It is the usual experience that delicate children of nine years will start crying if touched by a stranger. These delicate Indian children will now have contact with rough hands. *Fathers will look on while impressions of their fingers are being taken.*

3. Not only that impressions of all fingers will have to be given, but it will be done twice - together and separately.

4. The police have orders to take impressions of children as well as of adults.

5. If a merchant goes out, and the application for licence is made by his partner, he will need to have with him the power of attorney from the merchant, bearing the thumb-impression of his right-hand. This is insulting in the extreme. From now on, a signature will not be sufficient on the power of attorney by an Indian, but a thumb impression will be required.

6. All applications will be prepared by officers. No one can have them prepared by a lawyer or agent."[141]

In order to react against the act, a meeting was held. It was presided over by Abdul Gani, Chairman, B.I.A.[142] On Sept. 11, 1906, Gandhi gave a speech and called for action.[143] At the meeting, one of the members, Haji Habib proposed that all who want to oppose the ordinance should take a solemn oath. Gandhi was rather surprised at the idea. He said: "The manner of making the resolution suggested by our friend is as much of a novelty as of a solemnity. I did not come to the meeting with a view to getting the resolution passed in that manner, which redounds to the credit of Sheth Haji Habib as well as it (sic) lays a burden of responsibility upon him. I tender my congratulations to him."[144]

In the meetings of the B.I.A., on Sept. 11, 1906, resolutions were passed and copies were sent to the President of the Legislative Council, Pretoria; and Lieutenant-Governor, Transvaal and Johannesburg.[145] "The Rand Daily Mail" reported that hall was full up to the capacity. In order to take part, the shopkeepers and hawkers had closed business. According to the Newspaper:

> "..., it must be admitted that much of the credit for holding such a meeting goes to the Hamidia Islamic Society. The Society's Hall was thrown open to all, Hindus and Muslims alike. ... The meeting was attended by representatives from a number of places. Telegrams or letters expressing sympathy and agreement with the aims of the meeting were received from Middelburg, Standerton, Klerksdorp and other places. Both the Colonial Secretary and Mr. (Montford) Chamney were invited. .... In addition, white gentlemen like Mr. Lichtenstein, a lawyer from Pretoria, Mr. Israelstram, Mr. Littmann Landsberg and Mr. Stuart Campbell's manager were present. ... The President, Mr. Abdul Gani, began his speech exactly at three o'clock. ... His speech in excellent Hindustani was brief and eloquent. His narration of the facts was quite moderate, yet forceful. His voice was loud and so audible everywhere. His speech was received with acclamation. When he spoke of gaol-

going, the audience shouted in one voice we shall go to gaol, but will not register ourselves again."[146]

One of the speakers, Nanalal Valji Shah stated that according to officials we need new registrations as the old one could be fake or sold. He argued that:

> "Suppose a bank finds that some forged notes bearing its name have passed into currency, will it cancel all the notes? …. Producing his own register Mr. Shah declared, "This register contains my name, my wife's name, my caste, my profession, my height, my age," and slamming the paper on the table, he added: It bears even my thumb-impression. Is all this not enough? How can anyone else use this register? Does the Government want now to brand us on our foreheads? I will never return my register. Neither will I be registered again. I prefer going to gaol, and I will go there."[147]

One of the resolutions was entitled as "The gaol resolution." Hajee Habib told the public that we are not going to get justice at the hand of the British Government, which "kills us with sweet words; we should not be deceived." He said that if a bill is passed he will never register again and he will be the first who will prefer to go to gaol. He suggested the others to do the same. H. Habib seems to be the person, who knew, when and how to hit the nail. He stood up and asked the audience: "Are you all prepared to take the oath? (The Assembly stood up to a man and said, 'Yes, we will go to gaol!')."[148] He told the pubic that:

> "We tried this method in the days of the Boer Government also. Some 40 of our men were once arrested for trading without licences. I advised them to go to gaol and not to seek release on bail. Accordingly, they all remained there without offering bail. I immediately approached the British Agent, who approved of our action and ultimately secured justice for us. ..., the meeting greeted his resolve with applause."[149]

Hajee Ojer Ally, the Secretary of the B.I.A., who supported H. Habib's resolution, told that he is a father of eleven children, but he is ready to take up the responsibility; and will prefer to go to jail than registering. He stated that due to the efforts of the Hamidia Society, the registration of women was dropped. [150] While telling about his past he said that:

> "In the Cape I exercised the right to vote and other rights as well. Nowhere except here in the Transvaal have I seen such oppression of our people. And the Transvaal is still a Crown Colony. When it was under the Boers, the British whites came to me for my signature to their petition. Now they are against us. We will not take up rifles as they did but like them we shall go to gaol" [151-152]

About two weeks later, probably to motivate the public, "Indian Opinion" published an article to show the importance of resistance as follows:

> "When there were difficulties about licences, the Indians carried on their business in the towns fearlessly without licences, did not bow to the Boer Government, and

succeeded. That Government tried hard to send us to the Locations, but failed. .... When Lord Milner brandished the sword of the Bazaar Notice against the Indians, the people for once were scared, but later they thought over the matter and finally decided not to go to the Location. The summons that had already been issued at Potchefstroom had to be withdrawn. The Indian people refused to accept the passes bearing their photographs that Mr. Moore had issued, and the Regulation had to be withdrawn."[153]

It seems that some of the persons were not clear about the movement. They did not know, what would happen with their property and family, if they were to go to jail? A reader sent eight questions to the "Indian Opinion." They were answered on Oct. 20, 1906. For instance, "How will it affect the traders?" The reply was that it is not that all traders will have to go to goal. But, if it comes so, the shops should be closed or may be entrusted to a reliable white. Three other questions according to the list were: "8. What shall we do if nothing is gained even by going to goal? 9. And if some take out new Registers? 10. What is the harm in taking out a Register?" As the whole discussion was based on theoretical bases, the answers were far from reality. For example, the person was told that *going to goal is in itself a gain.* "What could be worse than giving one's finger-prints and disgracing oneself? How can we do that which we consider disgraceful? Further, "If some persons take out the new Register, they will lose their good name and earn the contempt of the Indian community." And further, "The disadvantage in taking out the new Register is that *our condition will thereby become worse than that of the Kaffirs.*"[154] After that followed the moral pressure, namely, "For those who cannot stand a gaol sentence, the better course will be to leave the Transvaal. It is, of course, cowardly to leave the land, but it is even more cowardly to take out a new Register."[155] Strange as it may sound, those who suggested the community not to give finger prints, were the first to do so (detail later). At a meeting of the Hamidia Islamic Society, Gandhi asked to refuse registration and protest, as: *"Even the half-castes and Kaffirs, who are less advanced than we,* have resisted the Government."[156]

Deputation to U.K.

After discussions with the local authorities, in particular an unsuccessful delegation to the Earl of Selborne, High Commissioner in South Africa, it became clear that the Indian community could not expect justice. Thus it was decided upon to send a delegation to U.K., before the Asiatic Registration Bill gets Royal assent.

In the beginning Haji Ojer Ally alone (see Appendix D) was suggested to represent the Indian community. Gandhi's supporters advocate Reinhold Gregorowski and attorney Lichtenstein were of the view that the presence of Gandhi is essential.[157] So far the finances were concerned, the Committee of the B.I.A. sanctioned up to 900 pound, of which 300 pounds for special purposes were reserved for H.O. Ally.[158] On Sept. 30, 1906, a meeting of the B.I.A. was held to bid farewell to the members of the deputation.[159]

The deputation arrived in England on Oct. 20, 1906. H.O. Ally being severely sick during the passage, after arrival in the U.K., he had to be admitted to a hospital. In Southampton a representative of "The Tribune" talked to Gandhi. He was told by Gandhi that some of the problems, which Indians face in South Africa, are: 1. Every Indian now settled in the Transvaal must carry a pass, just as the Kaffirs. However, the Indian passes, must bear ten finger impressions of the holder. 2. They can hold land-property only in specific locations. 3. They cannot ride in tram-cars and trains in Johannesburg or Pretoria. What further planned is that Asiatics should not use foot-paths in Johannesburg and Pretoria.[160] A similar interview was given to "The Morning Leader."[161]

Deputation in U.K. and Support by Local Sympathisers

Two Indians, namely, Dadabahi Naoroji (A Parsi cotton trader and educator; the first Asian to be elected as a British M.P. Apart from that he was in the House of Commons for three years) and Sir Mancherjee Merwanjee Bhownagree (Also a Parsi and M.P. in U.K.) were well informed about the affairs as they were regularly getting copies of various petitions and memorials from Gandhi. Same information was being sent to G.K. Gokhale in Indian. All of them were members of the Indian National Congress. Gandhi sent a telegram to Amir (also written as Ameer) Ali[162] (A former Judge of the Calcutta High Court, he was at this time a Member of the Privy Council; and author of "The Spirit of Islam" and "A Short History of the Saraeens") and asked him whether he would like to support the deputation for the introduction to Lord Elgin. Further, he was told that Sir G. Birdwood will be the spokesman.[163] G. Birdwood agreed under the condition that he will do if Sir M. Bhownaggree approves.[164] Gandhi's aim was to get support from various quarters in politics and religions.

Due to local support, on Nov. 7, 1906, at the House of Commons, Gandhi, Ally and other members of the deputation addressed a meeting in Parliament to represent their point of view. "The Times" reported about it as follows:

> "Sir Henry Cotton, the Chairman of the meeting, said that, under this Ordinance, British Indians were placed under the surveillance of the police in a manner which could not be differentiated from the treatment given in England to prisoners who were released from jail. Mr. Ally appealed in the name of Christianity and humanity for the support of British Members of Parliament in freeing Indians from a degrading law. ....."[165]

And further:

> "Lord Derby tried to mitigate their grievances, and Mr. Chamberlain afterwards wrote a strong dispatch to the Boer Government about British Indians, whom he described as honourable men and an asset of great importance to the Transvaal. The result of this was that British Indians went about the country as free citizens, and there was absolutely no restriction upon their movements."[166]

Deputation's Members' Meetings

On Oct. 29, 1906, Gandhi wrote a letter to the Secretary to Lord Elgin, Principal Secretary of State for Colonies, London, stating that Sir Muncherji M. Bhownaggree, Sir George Birdwood, Sir Henry Cotton, the Hon'ble Mr. Dadabhai Naoroji, and Mr. Ameer Ali, among others will be the members of the deputation team.[167] L. Griffin led the deputation. He introduced Ally and Gandhi to Lord Elgin and gave a short speech. Same was done by other members. However, before starting with conference, Elgin told that it is to be seen as a private talk, thus no press is allowed. But he made arrangement that minutes of the meeting were recorded. He started with a formal talk, telling that he is happy to see some of the colleagues with whom he worked in India.[168] Then he came to the reality of the political life. He told that according to his communication with colleagues in S.A., the intention of the new laws is to improve the conditions of British Indians. So far as the three pound poll-tax was concerned, he agreed that it is not quite fare. Then he came to the question of permits or registration. He told that the permits given under the Boer administration were some sort of receipts for the money. According to the new rules the idea is to improve the administrative work. It is not meant to discriminate Indians.[169] So far as the finger prints were concerned, Gandhi and Co. had argued that they are taken in the case of criminals. To support Gandhi, H. Cotton had criticized it in his talk in the House of Commons. Eglin rebutted that Cotton was the first to introduce "thumb marks" in India as it has advantage over the hieroglyphics. Then he turned to Gandhi by saying: "on the permit which he has handed to me, issued under the present Ordinance, there is a thumb mark already imposed under the present Ordinance in just the same way as it will be imposed under the new Ordinance."[170] Gandhi said that it "is a purely voluntary act done by us on the advice and the instigation of Lord Milner. He asked us to do it."[171] Elgin was of the opinion: "Quite so; but still here is a certificate which is an official certificate, and it bears a thumb mark." H. Cotton insisted again that it is done in the case of criminals. Elgin refused to discuss on the matter. He stated that he assented to the Government of Transvaal regarding the carrying of a pass and permits, because they will not be inspected all the times, perhaps once a year. He proceeded further to tell that he had many telegrams from municipalities urging him to pass the Ordinance. Gandhi told Elgin that information regarding permits given to him were not correct. He promised to send documents to prove his (Gandhi's) point of view. The final point in the petition was to form a commission to examine the subject. Elgin suggested postponing the idea.

In the meeting Elgin let a bomb-shell explode (detail below), namely, "I have got telegrams from the Transvaal advising me of the forwarding of a petition from British Indians which they say had been largely signed, in opposition to the views which have been placed before me today; ...."[172]

Though the meeting with Elgin was private and without the presence of media, information leaked out, and an article was published by "The Times." Gandhi wrote to Sir Henry Cotton: "Sir Lepel is of opinion that the information must have been given by someone in the Colonial Office. Lord Elgin's speech has been given practically word for word."[173]

Gandhi was quite realistic about the results of the meeting: He wrote to Abdul Qadir, Editor of "Lahore Observer and Urdu": "I am satisfied with the result of the interview with Lord Elgin, not because I am assured of success, but because of the necessary work done. However, Lord Elgin, instead of giving a blank, negative reply, has promised to consider the proposal about the commission. There is therefore some hope yet left."[174]

The outcome of the meeting was published in the "Indian Opinion." In part it reads: "It was true in a sense that the remission of the £3 tax afforded, as Mr. Gandhi had pointed out, no relief in fact. .... There did not seem to be much objection to the giving of thumb-impressions. It was unlikely that the police would look into the passes every day and harass the people."[175]

Meeting with John Morley, Secretary, State of India

Apart from the meeting with Elgin, Gandhi organised a conference with J. Morley, Secretary of State for India. The idea seems to be born in London. Again the meeting had private character.[176] Gandhi requested an interview and sent different documents regarding the African issue. The request was granted. Including Gandhi and Ally, the following other 19 members of the deputation met Morley on Nov. 22, 1906: Lord Stanley of Alderley; Sir Chas. Dilke; Sir Lepel Griffin; Sir Henry Cotton; Sir M.M. Bhownaggree; Sir Charles Schwann; Sir William Wedderburn; Dadabhai Naoroji; Harold Cox;

Ameer Ali; J.D. Rees; Theodore Morison; T.J. Bennett; W. Arathoon; Dr. T.H. Thornton; Dr. Rutherford; Lorain Petre; L.W. Ritch and A.H. Scott.[177] After hearing the views of the members, Morley expressed the helplessness of the U.K. Government in the following words:

> "No doubt *the position of the Imperial Government towards a Colony such as the Transvaal is going to be, and such as Natal is, is a great paradox.* There is no other word for it. But there it is. You have to accept our present system, miscalled an Imperial system. You have to accept that, and you have to recognize this plain fact - and you ought to recognize it - that *we cannot dictate to these Colonies.* What can we do, and what ought we to do? What I hope is that such gatherings as this Deputation to Lord Elgin and to myself, and perhaps to other Ministers and other persons, will promote this operation."[178]

About the work done by the British-Indian Government in S.A. he read from a document by Lord Curzon, the previous Viceroy of India:

> "In context of dealing with the Natal Government in 1903, regarding the budget as follows: 'We stipulated for the eventual abolition of a tax of £3 a head which had been imposed on such persons for leave to reside; we stipulated for the amendment of an Act placing traders, of however old a standing, under the power of local corporations, who had absolute authority to refuse licenses to trade; we stipulated for the removal of Indians from another Act, under which they were classed with barbarous races; and for the provision of a summary remedy for free Indians, that

is to say, Indians who had served their indenture, and had become free Indians, who might be wrongfully arrested on the ground that they were coolies under indenture or prohibited immigrants'. That was Lord Curzon's position dealing with the Government of Natal in 1903. What did the Government of Natal say? 'In reply,' says Lord Curzon, 'we were given to understand that there was no prospect of obtaining the consent of the local legislature to these conditions, and the negotiations were dropped.'"[179]

The above paragraph clearly shows that the U.K. Government had nothing to say in S.A. Still it is surprising that British Indians (including Gandhi) sought support from it.

Meeting with Winston Churchill, Under-Secretary of the State for the Colonies

W. Churchill was not only a politician, but also military man. He had taken part in Anglo-Boer War, and fought against General Botha, the Boers' representative. Though the Boers lost the war, in 1907, within Transvaal they won the election. To deal with the future of the colony, Churchill and Botha met again. Irony of the dignity, Gandhi requested for a meeting with the man, Churchill, who after some decades would be the Prime Minister of England and call Gandhi "a naked Fakir", a "fraud" and "scoundrel."'[180] On Nov. 15, 1906, Gandhi wrote to W. Churchill that Ally and he as a deputation from Transvaal on behalf of the British Indians. They requested for a short meeting. It was granted. After that they were optimistic as reported in the "Indian Opinion":

> "Mr. Ally then reminded him that he was the same person who had been present at the Point to receive Mr. Churchill on his return from the war (Boers war). And it was with the same Mr. Churchill that he now pleaded for redress on behalf of the Indian community. Mr. Churchill smiled, patted Mr. Ally on the back and said that he would do all he could. This answer added to our hopes."[181]

Apart from different meetings with political leaders and friends, Gandhi and Ally achieved something more, that is, the foundation of a committee in London to safeguard the interests of the British Indians in S.A. (detail below).

South Africa British Indian Vigilance Committee

Idea of forming a Committee by Ally: As H.O. Ally was admitted to a hospital, most of the work fell on Gandhi's shoulders. He communicated with Ally either by letters or telephone calls. On Oct. 29, 1906, Gandhi wrote to Ally:

> "I have been discussing with Sir Muncherji and Sir William Wedderburn the advisability of establishing a permanent committee for British Indians in South Africa. *Perhaps you recollect that you made the suggestion long ago*. I think that our work could be usefully continued if such a permanent committee composed of people representing all shades of opinion is established, say, for one or two years. I am, therefore, most anxious that such a committee be

formed. We could then perhaps afford a second deputation."[182]

It did not last long that Gandhi give credit to others (that is, Muncherji) for the idea. For instance: "Sir Muncherji has been working hard on our behalf. *He and some others are of the opinion that, for a few years at least, it is necessary to have a standing committee here.*"[183]

Neglecting the question of priority, the fact remains that within a short time, Gandhi found the persons for the Committee, which was supposed to be called "South Africa British Indian Vigilance Committee." Gandhi in a letter asked H.O. Bennett from "The Times of India", whether he will like to join. He was told that the following persons have agreed to do so: Sir William Wedderburn, Sir Lepel Griffin, Sir Henry Cotton, Mr. J. D. Rees, Mr. Dadabhai Naoroji, Sir Muncherji Bhownaggree, and other sympathizers have kindly consented to join the committee. L.W. Ritch was supposed to be secretary.[184] Gandhi, a man of action, wrote to his friend Henry S.L. Polak: "A room has been engaged for the permanent committee at £40 per year. Furniture has been bought for £25. Sir Muncherjee will probably be the chairman."[185] On Nov. 16, 1906, in a letter George Birdwood suggested Gandhi to strike off the word "Vigilance." Gandhi successfully found the South Africa British India Committee and wrote its Constitution, Rules and Regulations (see Appendix C).

Gandhi was quite satisfied with his mission. Before leaving for S.A. he wrote to Gokhale:

> "The importance of the question was fully realized by everyone in London. I am aware that Sir Pherozeshaw

does not see eye to eye with us in this matter but I venture to think that he is mistaken. Anyhow if a committee were formed, even if it did not do much good, it could not do harm. In order to have a committee you certainly need some local man with an accurate knowledge of the position in South Africa. As to that I can make no suggestion."[186]

Gandhi had written a number of documents during his stay. In particular, the official documents had to be typed and copied. The person, who did this work, was Miss E. Lawson. Before leaving, on Nov. 27, 1906, Gandhi and Ally gave her the following experience certificate:

"We have much pleasure in certifying that Miss Edith Lawson has done secretarial work for the British Indian Deputation from the Transvaal to the Imperial authorities. During the time, we found her a highly intelligent young lady, very obliging, punctual and energetic. What struck us most, however, was her capacity to identify herself with her work and we believe that she is capable of occupying a position of trust."[187]

Now, we come to the last part of the story, namely, Gandhi's opponents, who were of the opinion that he did not represent the Indian community. Why they reacted so? What was Gandhi's reaction? The details are given below for the preceeding questions.

Gandhi's Opponents - W. Godfrey and C.M. Pillay

During the interview, Lord Elgin told Gandhi and Ally that he had got document from S.A. which shows that the present deputation did not represent the opinion of the Indian community. The document was signed by 437 persons.[188] Elgin did not disclose the names of the persons who sent petition. In a letter to H.S.L. Polak, Gandhi rightly speculated that it must be W. Godfrey.[189]

Gandhi and Ally requested Lord Elgin for a copy of the petition and they were provided with. After receiving it; in their defence, on Nov. 20, 1906, they sent the following letter to Elgin's Secretary:

> "1. The "petition" is signed by Dr. William Godfrey and C.M. Pillay both of whom are personally known to the Delegates.
>
> 2. Petitioner William Godfrey is a doctor of Edinburgh University and is practising in Johannesburg.
>
> 3. The petitioner C.M. Pillay is an interpreter of no standing. He has been found to be the worse for liquor and may be described as a loafer.
>
> 4. So far as the recollection of the Delegates serves rightly, the points made in the "petition" are as follows:
>
> (a) Delegates have no mandate from the general body of Indians.
>
> (b) Mr. Gandhi is a professional agitator who has made money out of his work.

(c) Mr. Gandhi has caused an estrangement between Europeans and Indians and his advocacy has resulted in harm to the community.

(d) He was mobbed at Durban by the European community.

(e) He is proprietor of "Indian Opinion."

(f) Mr. Ally is Chairman and founder of a politico-religious body which has as its object recognition of the Sultan as both the spiritual and political head of the Moslems.

(g) Mr. A. Abdul Ganie (Gani) is President of the British Indian Association.

(h) The petitioners have not been able to receive support for their contentions because of the intimidation on the part of the British Indian Association.

5. As to (a), the Delegates enclose herewith letter signed by the Chairman of the British Indian Association. Their election was unanimous. It took place at a meeting of the Association that was largely attended. There was no protest sent to the Association although the election was before the public for a long time.

6. As to (b), Mr. Gandhi has received no remuneration for his public work throughout his thirteen years' career. He has from time to time contributed to the funds of the Association. The work has been purely a labour of love. His Lordship is further referred to correspondence that took place in "The Star" of Johannesburg on the 25th October in

refutation of a somewhat similar statement made by "The Star" on the 23rd October."[190]

Gandhi and Ally reacted immediately and asked for information from B.I.A. On Nov. 12, 1906, Gandhi wrote to H. Cotton that he received the following cablegram: "Have affidavits Godfrey obtained signatures blank paper false pretences using name bias (code word for British Indian Association). Signatures now withdrawn. Cabling (Lord) Elgin. ...." Further:

> "Mr. Ally and I know the gentleman well. Personally I can only say that he is a little insane. He is a medical man and has taken his degree at Edinburgh and in measures to be taken against the Ordinance he would go much further than we should. Indeed he even advocated violent measures, that is simply because there is no problem placed before him for solution but he loses his mental balance. There are other matters connected with Dr. Godfrey proving the statement made by me which I need not touch upon at any rate for the present."[191]

Due to W. Godfrey's petition, the issue became a point of discussion in the House of Commons, London. Gandhi was presented as a "professional agitator", who does so to earn money, and does not represent the Indian community.[192] In his defence, on Nov. 16, 1906, Gandhi sent a letter to "The Times", London, which was not published. Later, it was done by the "Indian Opinion."[193] On Nov. 16, 1906, Gandhi was interviewed by the newspaper "South Africa." He stated that W. Godfrey had obtained 437 signatures on blank paper, using the name of the B.I.A.[194] In "Indian Opinion", Gandhi told that

Godfrey's two brothers in the U.K. have actively supported the deputation by writing against their brother. Gandhi "preached" his readers *not to be angry at Godfrey, as he is like a child who lacks understanding.*[195]

Practically, the deputation came back empty handed as the British Empire did not give support to the "British subjects" in S.A. Gandhi, who had supported the Empire by all means must had been disappointed. What does a disappointed man/woman does? He/she seeks consolation either from religion or alcohol. Gandhi, with his primitive views of religion, sought console in it. However, he was intelligent enough to combine his religious views with Christianity, the religion of the Colonial powers (details later). With that he attracted the attention of the Christian world, as we shall see later.

Appendix A

The Asiatic Registration Act – Contrast[196]

	Now	Under the new law
1	"Malays are subject to Law 3 of 1885."	"They are exempted from the new law. Many Indians have Malay wives and relatives. The position of such Indians when they meet their Malay relatives can be better imagined than described."
2	"Every Asiatic in possession of a permit *bona fide* obtained is a full-fledged and lawful resident of the Transvaal."	"He becomes dispossessed of this title and the burden of showing that the permit lawfully held by him was not fraudulently obtained is thrown on him to entitle him to receive the new registration certificate."
3	"An Asiatic child born since the 31st day of May, 1902 in the Orange River Colony, is entitled to enter and remain in the Transvaal."	"Such child is debarred."
4	"Present permits held by Asiatics entitle them to enter and reside in the Transvaal and Orange River Colony. Whether these are of any use for going into the Orange River Colony is not the question."	"This right, so far as the permit can give it, is taken away."
5	"Asiatics holding permits to reside in the Orange River Colony are in a position to enter the Transvaal on the strength thereof."	"These are not allowed."
6	"Present permits cannot be changed without the consent of the holders."	"They are subject to alteration at the will of the Government."
7	"Asiatic children are not required to take out permits."	"The guardian of such child is bound, under heavy penalty, to have particulars of identification of: such child, no matter how young, endorsed on his

		registration. When the child reaches the age of 8 years, the guardian is bound to again approach the Registrar and take out registration for such child, furnishing further particulars as to identification, etc."
8	"Minors who are at present in the Transvaal are entitled to remain without a permit, and are not liable to leave the country on attaining majority."	"All such boys on reaching the age of 16 are liable to be deported unless they obtain from the Registrar registration certificates, the granting of which is at his discretion."
9	"No Asiatic is bound to furnish particulars of identification."	"Even a Kaffir policeman may demand production of certificate and particulars of identification, which may be fixed by regulation from time to time. Such policeman may, notwithstanding, take the Asiatic to the nearest police station, where the same inquiry may be repeated, and, if the Officer at the station is not satisfied, he may detain the Asiatic in the cell overnight."
10	"An Asiatic can demand a trade licence as a right against payment without production of permit."	"No Asiatic may receive such licence unless he produces his registration certificate and furnishes means of identification, as may be prescribed by regulation. If, there- fore, there are partners in any Asiatic firm, the Licensing Officer may insist upon the presence of all the parties and submit them to a humiliating examination before giving them their licence."
11	"Any Asiatic is free to employ any other Asiatic."	"Any Asiatic who brings into the Colony an Asiatic under the age of 16 (even his son!) without a permit for him, or who employs such child, is liable to be heavily fined or sent to gaol, and to have his own right to reside in the Transvaal cancelled."
12	"The Registrar, at present, has fairly strong authority."	"The Registrar practically becomes the master of Asiatics with almost unlimited power over their personal liberty."
13	"Asiatics who come in possession of certificates belonging to others commit no crime."	"Asiatics having such certificates (evidently a father having his son's register) are bound to deliver same by post under pain of being fined £50 or, in default, sent to gaol."

"Additional points to be noted -

1. The new law does not apply to Kaffirs, to Cape Boys, and Christian subjects of the Turkish Empire, whereas it applies to the Mahomedan subjects of that Empire, and it thus insults Indians and their religion in a cold-blooded manner. It reduces them to a state of serfdom although belonging to civilized countries. It reduces them to a position lower than that of the Kaffirs, Cape Boys[197] and Malays.

2. It puts a premium on fraud. It might have occurred to the framers of the law that there is nothing to prevent an Asiatic impersonating a Malay or Cape Boy.

3. It opens up a fertile field for permit agents to prey upon harmless Asiatics. It must be well known to the Permit authorities that Asiatics are not, as a rule, capable of filling in complicated

Application forms, being ignorant of the ways of Government departments and easily terrorized. At the very least, therefore, assuming that Indians and Chinese combined would make 12000 applicants, they would be robbed of £36000, counting the fee at £3 per head on an average.

Who, then, can wonder if Asiatics prefer gaol to submission to such an extraordinary law and to such extortion? Verily, the whole of the Transvaal would to them become, during their residence therein, a wretched gaol. It does, indeed, need the intoxication of power to blind one to the wretched state of misery to which the new law reduces Asiatics."[198]

Appendix B – Obnoxious Law

"... 3. Persons above the age of sixteen should apply in Form B. ...

4. Every adult shall appear before such person as the Colonial Secretary may appoint, and furnish such person with the required particulars in Form B. and shall produce and surrender to such person his permit, the registration certificate obtained on payment of a fee of £3, and any other documents which he may desire to produce in support of his application. ... "[199]

"Form B
Form of application by an adult

Name in full ....   Race ...

Caste or sect ....   Age ...   Height .....
Residence...   Occupation....
Physical description...
Place of birth ...
Date of first arrival in the Transvaal ....,
Where resident on May 31, 1902 ....
Father's name....   **Mother's name** ...
Wife's name ....   Residing at ....
Names and ages of children under eight years of age, their residence, and relationship to the guardian ...
Signature of applicant ....
                Signature of the person taking application...
Date ....   Office ...
                Right-hand impressions
    Thumb   Index   Middle   Ring   Little
            Separate impressions of the left-hand as above.
                Simultaneous impressions
Left-hand - The four fingers   **Right-hand—The four fingers**
Impressions of adult taken by ....
Date ...."

Appendix C – South Africa British India Committee in London

Provsional Draft

"President

Vice-President

Sir Lepel Griffin, K.C.S.I.

Members of the Committee: Ameer Ali, Esq., C.I.E.; T.J. Bennett, Esq., C.I.E.; Sir Muncherji Bhownaggree, K.C.I.E.; Sir George Birdwood, K.C.I.E., C.S.I.; Harold Cox, Esq., M.P.; Sir William Markby, K.C.S.I.; Theodore Morison, Esq.; Dadabhai Naoroji, Esq.; J.H.L. Polak, Esq., J. P.; J.D. Rees, Esq., M.P.; L. W. Ritch, Esq.; J.M. Robertson, Esq., M.P.; Dr. Rutherford, M.P.; Sir Charles

Schwann, Bart., M.P.; A. H. Scott, Esq., M.P.; Sir William Wedderburn, Bart.; Sir Raymond West, K.C.S.I.

Sub-Committee: Chairman - Sir Muncherji Bhownaggree, K.C.I.E.; Members - Ameer Ali, Esq., C.I.E.; Harold Cox, Esq., M.P.; J.H.L. Polak, Esq., J.P.; J.D. Rees, Esq., M.P.; J.M. Robertson, Esq., M.P.; A.H. Scott, Esq., M.P.

Secretary: L. W. Ritch, Esq.

Honorary Solicitors

Bankers: The Natal Bank Limited.

Offices: 28, Queen Anne's Chambers, The Broadway, Westminster, W.

The Constitution

Name: The Committee shall be called South Africa British Indian Committee.

Object

The Committee is established for the purpose of

(a) Concentrating and giving continuity to the efforts to secure fair and just treatment to British Indian settlers in South Africa of those friends who have heretofore exerted themselves to that end in Parliament and in other ways; (b) and of helping the Imperial Government to arrive at a proper solution of this difficult problem.

Rules

1. There shall be no subscription for membership of the Committee and members shall not be personally liable for any expenses incurred in the name of the Committee.

2. The Committee shall consist of a President, Vice-Presidents and members.

3. There shall be a sub-Committee of not more than six members besides Chairman and Secretary, who shall be ex-officio members of such Committee.

4. The sub-Committee shall meet every week on...at...

5. ....members shall form a quorum.

6. As to any matters touching which no provision is made in the foregoing rules, the ordinary rules of meetings shall apply.

7. The above rules are subject to change at the discretion of the sub-Committee."[200]

Appendix D

Haji Ojer Ally

1853: Born in Mauritius, where he received an early education.

1868: Took up a job as a printer in the office of the "Commercial Gazette."

1873: Employed as a clerk in a wharf.

1876: Joined a shipping clerk in the firm of Messrs, Charles Jacob and Son.

1884: Came to Cape Town and set up business as a manufacturer of aerated water.

1885: Began doing public work. In Cape Town, he was a voter both for Parliament and the Municipality.

1892: He went to Kimberley and other places. He was elected Chairman of the Coloured Peoples' Organization. He took a leading part in the movement against the Franchise Law Amendment Act of the Cape, when a petition signed by 22000 Coloured people was sent to London.

1893: He settled in Johannesburg.

Allay was the founder of the Hamidia Islamic Society and was its President.[201] He held liberal views regarding female education.[202] He communicated with important local politicians like Sir Richard Solomon, Lord Loch, Lord Rosemead, Sir Gordon Sprigg and Sir James Sievright[203]

Notes and References

[139] Indian Opinion, 2-6-1906.

[140] Indian Opinion, 26-5-1906.

[141] Indian Opinion, 6-7-1907.

[142] C.W.M.G. 5, 1905-1906, p. 332.

[143] Indian Opinion, 22-9-1906.

[144] Indian Opinion, 22-9-1906.

[145] C.W.M.G. 5, 1905-1906, p. 343.

[146] C.W.M.G. 5, 1905-1906, p. 343.

[147] Indian Opinion, 22-9-1906.

[148] Indian Opinion, 22-9-1906.

[149] Indian Opinion, 22-9-1906.

[150] Indian Opinion, 22-9-1906.

[151] Indian Opinion, 22-9-1906.

[152] Indian Opinion, 22-9-1906.

[153] Indian Opinion, 6-10-1906.

[154] Indian Opinion, 20-10-1906.

[155] Indian Opinion, 20-10-1906.

[156] Indian Opinion, 22-9-1906.

[157] Indian Opinion, 6-10-1906.

[158] Indian Opinion, 6-10-1906.

[159] Indian Opinion, 6-10-1906.

[160] The Tribune, 22-10-1906.

[161] The Morning Leader, 22-10-1906.

[162] Ameer Ali belonged to those Muslims, who were sceptical that Hindu political leaders in National Indian Congress (I.N.C.). For instance, on January 13, 1888, Badruddin Tyabji, President I.N.C. (1887), wrote to Ameer Ali: "I understand your objection to be that the Hindu, being more advanced than ourselves, would profit more by any concessions made by government to educated natives, ..."

(in: Pandey B.N. (Ed.), The Indian nationalist movement, 1885-1947, St. Martin's Press, New York 1979, p. 15).

[163] Gandhi M.K. to Ali A., Oct. 25, 1906.

[164] Gandhi M.K. to Bhownaggree M., Oct. 25, 1906.

[165] The Time, 8-11-1906.

[166] The Time, 8-11-1906.

[167] Gandhi M.K. to Sec. Lord Elgin, Oct. 29, 1906.

[168] C.W.M.G. 6, 1906-1907, p. 31.

[169] C.W.M.G. 6, 1906-1907, pp. 44-45.

[170] C.W.M.G. 6, 1906-1907, pp. 44-45.

[171] C.W.M.G. 6, 1906-1907, pp. 44-45.

[172] C.W.M.G. 6, 1906-1907, pp. 46-47.

[173] Gandhi M.K. to Cotton H., Nov. 10, 1906.

[174] Gandhi M.K. to Qadir A., Nov. 10, 1906.

[175] Indian Opinion, 8-12-1906.

[176] Gandhi M.K. to Smith A.H., Nov. 22, 1906.

[177] Gandhi M.K., Ally H.O. to Sec. of Morley J., Nov. 20, 1907.

[178] Journal of the East India Association, April 1907 (in: C.W.M.G. 6, 1906-1907, pp. 140-151). Detail of J. Morley speech and Gandhi's expectations from the deputation were published in Indian Opinion, 22-12-1906.

[179] Journal of the East India Association, April 1907 (in: C.W.M.G. 6, pp. 140-151).

[180] Wolpert S., Gandhi's passion - The life and legacy of Mahatma Gandhi, Oxford University Press, Oxford 2001, p. 62.

[181] Indian Opinion, 29-12-1906.

[182] Gandhi M.K. to Ally H.O., Oct. 26, 1906.

[183] Indian Opinion, 1-12-1906.

[184] Gandhi M.K., Ally H.O. to Bennett T.J., Nov. 15, 1906. It was a circular letter sent to Sir Henry Cotton, Sir George Birdwood, Sir Lepel Griffin, Sir Charles Dilke, Lord Stanley Of Alderley, Sir Charles Schwann, Sir William Wedderburn, A. H. Scott, J. M. Robertson, Harold Cox, T. H. Thornton and J. D. Rees. C.W.M.G. 6, 1906-1907, p. 90.

[185] Gandhi M.K. to Polak H.S.L., Nov. 16, 1906.

[186] Gandhi M.K. to Gokhale G.K., Dec. 3, 1906.

[187] C.W.M.G. 6, 1906-1907, p. 175.

[188] C.W.M.G. 8, 1907-1908, p. 48.

[189] Gandhi M.K. to Polak H.S.L., Nov. 9, 1906.

[190] Gandhi M.K., Ally H.O. to Sec. of Lord Elgin, Nov. 20, 1906.

[191] Gandhi M.K. to Cotton H., Nov. 12, 1906.

[192] Indian Opinion, 15-12-1906.

[193] Indian Opinion, 15-12-1906.

[194] Interview to South Africa by Gandhi M.K. on Nov. 16, 1906. Republished in "India", 23-11-1906.

[195] Indian Opinion, 15-12-1906.

[196] Indian Opinion, 8-6-1907.

[197] There are different views about the term "Cape boys" – They were defined as either non-African immigrants or children of "mixed races." They were stigmatized as the part of the S.A. society, which was responsible for evils like, prostitution, drinking and stealing. For more detail see, Muzondidya J., Walking a tight rope - Towards a social history of the coloured community of Zimbabwe, Africa World Press Inc., Trenton 2005.

[198] Indian Opinion, 8-6-1907.

[199] Indian Opinion, 6-7-1907.

[200] C.W.M.G. 6, 1906-1907, pp. 164-165.

[201] Indian Opinion, 6-10-1906.

[202] Indian Opinion, 6-10-1906.

[203] C.W.M.G. 6, 1906-1907, p. 129.

Outcome of the Deputation and Preparing for the Practical Politics

Now, during his stay in the U.K., Gandhi had worked day and night. The delegations main success was to make the problem known in U.K. It led to debate in the House of Commons. Most importantly, Gandhi was able to form a permanent body in London, the South African British Indian Committee (SABIC), which supported the Indians' cause in the following years.

As we have seen in the previous chapter, Gandhi and Ally did not obtain definite promises from the Imperial Government. In March 1907, Gandhi wrote:

> "The Blue book containing the correspondence that passed between Lord Selborne and Lord Elgin regarding the Ordinance has now been received. It shows that Lord Elgin, who had heard only one side of the case, had at first approved the Ordinance, but his eyes were opened after he had heard the Deputation that visited England, and then he refused it (Royal) assent."[204]

It was re-enacted in 1908.[205]

As we shall see later, from Elgin's side, it was a political tactic to win time, as shortly after the visit of the deputation, a meeting with General Botha, the representative of the Transvaal Colony, was called for. In the following, we shall see:

- What happened after the Deputation returned back to S.A.?

- What role was played by the SABIC in the future politics of S.A., U.K. and India?

- Which action was taken by Gandhi to motivate for protest the Indian community after the Registration Act was passed?

Continuation of the "Asiatic Ordinance Act" War - Transvaal's Government in Action

South African politicians were not passive spectators on the Asiatic Ordinance. For Quinn, a Member of Parliament, it was a question of self-defence, irrespective of skin colour. He confessed that there are many white British subjects, with whom he would have nothing to do. Like most of the white traders he was jealous that the Asians can manage to live with one tenth of the money that whites require. Quinn and his colleagues had no desire to live with people of low standard. According to his own statement, in Johannesburg, out of 5000 licences, ten percent belong to Asiatics. His proposed solution was that their business and shops should be closed down; and they should be compensated.[206] So far the interference by the Imperial Government was concerned, he opinioned:

> "The British Government withheld assent to the Asiatic Ordinance because they were not aware either of our real condition or of our feelings in the matter. I do not believe that the British Government intend to do us harm. They have not taken the side of the sufferers, and if they have withheld assent to the Ordinance for that reason, they will not hesitate to accord sanction to the Ordinance when the (new) parliament of the Transvaal meets and reenacts it unanimously."[207]

The anti-Indian newspaper, "The Star", reproduced (from "The Morning Post") an article from Ritch, Secretary SABIC, in which Indians were highly praised for being hard working, and having influential friends in U.K. "The Star" wrote: "The whites are sitting back without being interested in the Ordinance. "The Star", therefore, suggests that the whites should hold big meetings and take steps to see that the Ordinance was passed. Otherwise Indian infiltration would increase to the detriment of the whites."[208] Richard Solomon, a local politician, who had been to England; and met authorities of the Colonial Office in London, as well as other politicians, was optimistic. In an election speech he said that the Imperial Government will not reject an act passed by local parliament.[209] As a reaction to it, Gandhi stated:

> "When that happens, there should be only one thought in the mind of every Indian: *never to accept such a law*. And, if it is enforced, *he will rather go to gaol than carry a pass like a Kaffir*. True victory will be won only when the entire Indian community courageously *marches to the gaol - when the time comes—and stays there as if it were a palace*. .... And the *whites must be made to realize* that their policy of repression is not at all called for."[210]

In the end of Feb. 1907, Selborne and Richard Solomon made it clear that the Asiatic Ordinance should be (re-)enacted. Elgin was clever enough to appease the British Indian community as well as Natal authorities as Gandhi's article shows. In part it reads: "He (Elgin) says that the *term "uncivilized" should not be defined so as to include sons of indentured laborers.* Moreover he says that it is not legitimate to include Indians among "Coloured persons", ... Lord Elgin therefore hopes that the Natal Government will consider the point."[211]

Elgin's tactic was to wait for the elections in Transvaal. Surprisingly, not British, but Dutch politicians won the election. The British candidate, Richard Solomon was defeated at Pretoria. His dreams to become Prime Minister were shattered. Gandhi predicted: "But it is being said that some elected member will resign his seat and Sir Richard will thus be given an opportunity to enter parliament. If this comes about, it seems probable that Sir Richard will become Minister for Justice. General Botha is likely to be the Prime Minister. That is to say, he will be as good as President."[212]

Gandhi, who had fought against the Boers stated: "For us there is not much in this either to rejoice or to regret. However, one may hope that the Dutch will do the Indian community some measure of justice. Some of them know the Indian community well. It does not seem likely that they will be wholly unjust."[213]

As to be expected, just in two days the "Asiatic Ordinance" was passed on 22nd March, 1907, by the Transvaal parliament without changes, that is, as it stood in September 1906.[214]

In protest B.I.A. sent a telegram, which was read out before the Council; but it was ineffective.[215] From the official side, General J.C. Smuts, Colonial- and Education Secretary, stated that:

> "The whole white population of the Transvaal was of one mind in the matter. Indians should be stopped from coming in. They come in large numbers. The Dutch Government

attempted to prevent them, and this led to the (Boer) war. The Bill that had been presented that day had come up before the former Council. Its aim was just to have every Indian registered. Law 3 of 1885 was defective, and its drawbacks would be removed in the new Bill. The Imperial Government had vetoed the Bill because it was passed by the former Council. They were now in a position to show that they were unanimous in passing it. Further legislation would be necessary after that Bill had become law; but they would have to look into the matter later. For the time being it was necessary for them to know who had the right to live in the Colony. For these reasons the Bill must be passed the very same day."[216]

Even before the law was enforced, at some places, such as in Rustenburg, the police authorities took finger prints and examined permits. A. Gani, President B.I.A., sent a telegram to the Registrar of the Asiatics, and told:

"Association informed by Rustenburg Indians. Their finger impressions taken by police authorities and permits examinded. While Association has no object to examination of permits Association respectfully protests against fingerimpression being taken. If information Rustenburg true, Association requests reasons for taking finger-impressions and assurance of discontinuance practice."[217]

"Indian Opinion" supported the action taken by A. Gani as follows:

"We congratulate the British Indian Association on having moved so promptly in the matter. Our correspondent informs us also that the British Indian Association has circularized all the sub-committees warning them against giving finger-impressions, and informing them that there is absolutely no law justifying such a degrading procedure."[218]

At the same time, Indians were scolded for giving finger prints as follows:

"It is shameful of the Rustenburg Indians to have surrendered their freedom by giving their full hand-prints. As the Gujarati proverb says, so long as the axe does not have a wooden handle to it, it cannot cut wood. Rustenburg has served as the handle by starting the giving of finger-prints. If, as a result, the Indian community comes to harm, the blame will be with the Rustenburg Indians. We are glad to find that prompt action has been taken by the British Indian Association."[219]

The Countdown Starts

One of the main objections from the Indian community was the giving of finger prints for registration. In Feb. 1907, Gandhi wrote:

"Now when people are wrongfully *treated as criminals and asked to give their finger-prints*, will they quietly give them or will they go to gaol? *If they give their finger-prints and suffer dishonour, we shall regard them as doubly unmanly.* Hence we ask: will Indian men be effeminate? Or will they emulate the manliness shown by English women (here he meant the women in U.K. who were fighting for voting right) and wake up? Will they choose to find happiness in prison taking it to be a palace, or will they submit to oppression when the Transvaal Government starts it? In a few days our mettle will be tested."[220]

Here the pin point is that Gandhi gave too much stress to "fingerprints." It did not last long that he took 180 degree turn and said that it is not a major issue (detail later).

In order to discuss the planning of a politcal movement, in March 1907, a mass meeting was organized. The "Indian Opinion" suggested to collected funds.[221] Gandhi was ready to use any means to motivate his countrymen. The man, who later will preach love and truth; and appreciated the British Empire in his autobiography and speeches, wrote:

> "*Why do the Dutch and the British both hate us?* We believe the root *cause is not the colour of our skin, but our general cowardice, our unmanliness and our pusillanimity.* They will begin to respect us the moment we impress upon them that we can stand up to them. There is no need actually to fight, but courage is necessary. If a man kicks us, we take it lying down. He therefore thinks that we deserve nothing better. This is the cowardice in us. There is a kind of courage in receiving a blow without returning it; but we are not speaking of that courage here. We receive kicks passively out of fear."[222]

The moral pressure was increased by reminding the British Indians that:

> "If the Transvaal Indians do not rigidly adhere to the resolution on going to gaol, they will lose everything. Not only they, but other South African Indians also will lose their rights. If the Indian community in the Transvaal does not carry out the resolution in regard to going to gaol, it will be eating its own words. The Europeans will laugh at the Indians. They will think us timid and cowardly and take it that we shall endure any burden imposed on us."[223]

On the political side he informed the Indians in Transvaal that:

> "This Ordinance is about to be enacted again in the Transvaal parliament. Almost word for word it is identical with the Ordinance which was cancelled. We here have an instance of the tenacity of the Europeans. Whatever they undertake they see through. .... If the Transvaal Indians are prepared to go to gaol, they have nothing to fear. .... We would suggest that every Indian male should call to mind, on this occasion, the great deeds of British women."[224]

The B.I.A. and the Hamidia Islamic Society held their meetings. "At both the meetings, it was solemnly resolved after due consideration to adhere to the Resolution about going to gaol" and the issue of collecting funds for the movement of anti-Indian law were discussed.[225] To protest against the Asiatic Act and pass resolution, on March 29, 1907, B.I.A. held its meeting under the Chairmanship of A. Gani. About the consequences of the Asiatic Ordinance

Gandhi produced a long list (see Appendix A). Gandhi stated: "We request the Indian community to bear all this in mind and to adhere firmly to the resolution on courting imprisonment. And we pray to God to give us the courage to renew that pledge."[226]

On April 8, 1907, Natal Indian Congress passed a resolution of sympathy for Transvaal Indians. The Chairman of the meeting was Dawad Mahomed.[227] A. Gani sent a petition to the official quarters, stating:

> "We should be very much surprised if it were not a fact that the Transvaal Ministry is not pining for a tussle with the Imperial Government. It should be thankful to take up the Indian suggestions, nor need Indians be at all frightened over the resolution whilst it undoubtedly exposes them once more to irksome procedure, in view of the prejudice existing in the Colony, it is necessary for them to undergo it."[228]

A deputation (with its members: Abdul Gani, Coovadia, Essop Mian[229], Haji Ojer Ally, Moonlight, Gandhi, Mahomed Haji Joosab and Gaurishankar Vyas) met Smuts and Montford Chamney, Registration Officer. Smuts heard their arguments and promised to send a reply in written.[230] After the meeting with Smuts, Gandhi reminded the Indians in Transvaal about the "going to gaol resolution." He wrote:

> "On that basis too, the Deputation went to England, and on that basis several whites have been helping us. .... It was because the resolution about gaol-going was passed that the Kimberley people as also the Natal Congress have sent

telegrams. .... The Transvaal Indians have to adhere steadfastly to the gaol-going Resolution for the *sake of their own honour and that of the entire Indian community.* .... Our demand will not be accepted until we force them to do so."[231]

To convince them he referred to an example from the history of colonial Africa, namely:

"... It is because the *Cape Coloured opposed the Pass Act, refused to take out passes and went to gaol* that the Cape Government does not any longer compel them to take out passes. Though the Pass Act applies to them, the Government is unable to enforce it. *We should under no circumstances prove ourselves more timid than the Coloured persons.*"[232]

Smuts' reply to the deputation was straight forward. He regretted that for the identity sake:

"Compulsory registration is necessary. Moreover, I cannot see how you could say with certainty that your word would be binding on other Asiatic communities, and particularly on those residing without a permit. ... There is no doubt that many whites hold that a number of Asiatics is infiltrating into this territory without permits. And they also find that people have been doing so because there is no adequate law in force to identify the (lawfully resident). .... It is not possible for the Government to ignore this feeling. Moreover, the Government has strong evidence of such unlawful infiltration."[233]

The Acting Chairman of the B.I.A., Essop Mian, thanked Smuts for the reply. Like in the previous years, once again a long proposal followed from Indians. In part it reads: "My Association would humbly state that there is no need to make a promise, as the proposal is such that it could be immediately implemented. Moreover, it can be ascertained, without loss of time, how many Asiatics are agreeable to taking out the new registers in place of their present permits."[234] After offering the solution for registration, E. Mian proposed the following idea regarding the control of permit-less persons: "When fresh registration is completed, it will remain only to detect those without permits, and to serve them with 'quit' notices for unlawful residence in the Colony."[235]

Seeing the "war" inevitable, Gandhi suggested traders that only those should stay in Transvaal, who possess genuine permits. "The pre-war residents and others, who have come after the war but hold genuine permits, have to put up a fight."[236] Further:

> "As shopkeepers and hawkers will have taken out their licences for the whole year, they will have no difficulty in carrying on their business. A *shopkeeper can entrust his shop to any other person* and himself *enjoy life in gaol.* For *hawkers* there will be no difficulty at all. I know from experience that *many of them have been living such a miserable life that they will be much better off in gaol.*"[237]

On April 30, 1907, Gandhi took an oath (for detail see, Appendix B). In part it reads: "I hereby declare my Pledge that, *should the new law come into force, I will never take out a permit or register under the law but will go to goal; and even if I am the only one left who has not taken a permit, ...*"[238]

Shortly after the above stated pledge, probably to motivate Indians, Gandhi published an article to report about revolts in Punjab, India.

> "The people in the Punjab appear to be preparing for a revolt. This is the first upheaval of the kind seen in India after 1857. The native Press has been inciting the people both openly and secretly. It was not right that (the editor of) the "Punjabi" should have been prosecuted. What only a few men knew is now known to the whole of India. The journal has become more powerful. People have ceased to be afraid of the repressive measures of the Government. ... *In the Punjab, judges have enlisted themselves as volunteers and taken up arms.* .... The present is a critical time for India as indeed it is for us here in South Africa. We have to do our duty here. If ever manliness and courage were needed in the country's cause, it is now."[239]

Smuts had doubt that the B.I.A. represents all Indians. Such views were made public by "The Times", to which Gandhi gave the following reply:

> "Under the Registration Act, all Indians have to be compulsorily registered. Under the Indian offer they can be voluntarily registered, and that now. But, supposing that the lowest class of Indians, as you have been pleased to classify some Indians, who enter the Colony, do not accept the proposal of the British Indian Association, the key to the situation is in the hands of the Government. A bill can then

be passed cancelling all permits save those issued under the compromise, unless they are exchanged within a certain time. The law will then reach the culprits and leave the innocent free. The Act at present punishes the vast majority of the innocent, self-respecting people, for the sake of the guilty few."[240]

The support neither from India, nor from the U.K. availed. "Indian Opinion" informed its readers that the Transvaal Act has received (Royal) assent by the Imperial Government.[241] Gandhi stated that Lord Elgin "Out of fear of the whites, ... has done injustice to the Indians."[242] So far as W. Churchill was concerned, at the Colonial Conference he "declared that the people of South Africa have the freedom to make whatever laws they wish relating to Kaffirs and Asiatic immigration."[243]

Gandhi asked his Transvaal's traders to *learn from indentured Indians in Durban*:

"As a result of the Durban Corporation's decision to reduce the rice ration, the indentured Indians employed by them have struck work, and have got ready to go to gaol. They did this earlier also. On that occasion, the Magistrate was kind. He observed that, even though it was legal to give them maize instead of rice, it would be cruel to insist on the (letter of the) law. He therefore let the men off and advised the Corporation to give them rice as usual, even if it was dearer. .... *If indentured laborers can do so much in self-interest*, who will deny that the Indian community in the Transvaal ought to do no less?"[244]

Fidget in Dark

People took an oath to support the struggle and go to gaol if the bill would be passed. No one explained to them: What the exact plans are? What will happen with their shops, children and wives during this time? From what will they live? Gandhi replied such questions in "Indian Opinion". For instance:

> "... At the time Mr. Gandhi himself will say that he had advised the entire community not to take out permits as required by the new law but instead to go to gaol in all humility, and that was why his client had not taken out a fresh permit. ... When the counsel himself says this, it is possible that the defaulter may be set free and the counsel arrested. That is, Mr. Gandhi will be arrested and his client let off. At that time, a similar deposition will! If possible, be made on behalf of the Association also. ..... If many persons are thus prosecuted and all of them go to gaol, the chances are that they will be soon released and the law amended suitably. ... The wife and children of a person so going to gaol will, if necessary, be maintained on subscriptions from the public."[245]

A reader of the "Indian Opinion" who was running a shop with his son, asked, what he can do, if both of them are in prison? He got four alternative replies: First:

> "*Going to gaol is a great adventure*, which will benefit not only the person concerned, but all the Transvaal Indians and, in fact, the Indian community as a whole. To win such great benefits, one must put up with whatever loss may

occur. I believe that *going to gaol will please Khuda (Muslim's God) or Ishwar (Hindu's God).* The Creator always helps us in anything we do in fear of Him. We reap the fruit of our labour in proportion to our faith in Him...."[246]

Further, Gandhi wrote:

"Before it becomes necessary for an Indian to go to gaol, he will receive a notice to quit the Transvaal. He will be arrested after the expiry of the notice period, then sentenced to pay a fine and to imprisonment in case of default. One must then go to gaol instead of paying the fine. It will thus be possible for the trader, during the notice-period, to make over his goods to his creditors. For the small trader this will be the best remedy. He is unlikely to find any difficulty in earning his daily bread after release from gaol."[247]

It seems that Gandhi had some fascination to suicide. He suggested the British Indians: "It will be better for every worthy son of India to *leave the Colony or commit suicide than to submit to a law* with such dire consequences."[248] In 1946, Gandhi told his biographer Louis Fischer that it would have been a great victory for Jews if they "...*should have offered themselves to the butcher's knife. They should have thrown themselves into the sea from cliffs* ...."[249]

It will be of interest to note that in 1907 there was no deportation law in Transvaal. For, Gandhi wrote in a letter to "The Star":

"You say in your leatherette that those who oppose the Indians would not be sorry if their leaders were deported. But *I ought to point out to such opponents that there is no law authorizing the Government forcibly to deport anyone.* If that is to be done, another law will have to be passed. Then the Transvaal Government will be able to deport those Indians who are ready to serve their country and even the government."[250]

As we shall later, it did not last long till this law was introduced and many Indians were deported.

On May 11, 1907, a meeting of the Executive Committee of the B.I.A. was held. It was presided over by Essop Mian. Gandhi told the audiences that *for the sake of India's honour* it is our duty to go to gaol. A resolution was passed, which stated:

"The Honorary Secretary should write to people everywhere, asking them to stop having any dealings with the Permit Office. Telegrams should be sent to Bombay and other places to say that those intending to go to the Transvaal should give up their plans for the time being. No one should give all the ten finger-impressions. Meetings should be held at all the places and people should be asked to refuse to submit to the new Ordinance."[251]

As we have seen above, Gandhi is supposed to be the lawyer, who will defend Indians in court. One of the readers asked rightly: "What if Gandhi is arrested first?" The answer was a mixture of stupidity and irrationality, namely: *"Even while in gaol, Mr. Gandhi can put up* a defence, that is, he can pray to God to give courage to all Indians."[252]

In June 1907, Gandhi once again reminded his people to collect more money for the political work. Referring to the report of the Women Association, U.K., he stated that they are spending 100 pounds per week. Some of them have suffered imprisonment for about six years.[253] Then he told to his countrymen that if they want to have their rights, they have much to do, that is, "Such a mighty task if they had to spend £13000 and 13000 Indians had to go to gaol. Till now Indians have not spent even £2000 all told, and no Indian has so far suffered imprisonment. And yet to believe that we could get our rights is, it would seem, a patent mistake."[254]

To instigate British Indians, in particular the Muslim community, "Indian Opinion" wrote:

> "The new law does not apply to Kaffirs, to Cape Boys, and Christian subjects of the Turkish Empire, whereas it applies to the Mahomedan subjects of that Empire, and it thus insults Indians and their religion in a cold-blooded manner. It reduces them to a state of serfdom although belonging to civilized countries. It reduces them to a position lower than that of the Kaffirs, Cape Boys and Malays."[255]

Government had given special concession to religious preachers for railway travelling. Later it was confined only to Christian (Indian Christian priests excluded) and Jewish preachers.[256]

At the initial stage, Chinese were also considered as Asians. They had supported N.I.C. petitions. Probably, to apply the policy of divide and rule, in the new law, the term "Asiatic" was reserved only for Indians, coolies, and Muslim subjects of Turkey.[257] Before proceeding further, it will be worthwhile to mention that in the Transvaal Parliament, some had sympathy for Indians. Without mentioning the name of Hoskin, Gandhi wrote: "I had a meeting with a prominent member of the Transvaal Parliament. ....., he promised to give us as much help as he could. Moreover, he added, the entire Liberal Party in England would come to our rescue and the new law would be repealed."[258] During the second reading of the Immigration Bill, while Smuts clarified the aims of the Bill; Hoskin, "speaking on the Indian side, said that the new Bill would be appropriate only in Russia. The Bill contained some provisions which ought to have no place under British rule."[259]

Meanwhile Gandhi was seen as the leading figure. "The Daily Rand Mail" asked him about the number of persons, who will take part in passive resistance. Gandhi, based on the letters received by him and the editor of "Indian Opinion", speculated that *50 per cent of British Indians*[260] in the Transvaal will remain firm in the policy of non-submission."[261]

To find a way out of the deal-lock, B.I.A. proposed the voluntary registration by the Indian community. It was flatly refused by Smuts, as there was no warranty that all will follow the call of Gandhi and B.I.A.[262] Shortly after that a mass meeting was held in the mosque of the Hamidia Islamic Society. Haffejee Abdul Samad was the Chair person. Gandhi explained the consequences of the new laws. In order to challenge the "manhood" of the audience, Gandhi said: "If the women of England were strong enough to go to gaol, would the men among the Indian people be scared by having to go to gaol or by having to suffer other losses?"[263] Soon after that "Indian Opinion" published the demands which were placed before Smuts:

"(1) They should not be required to give ten digit-impressions,

(2) The mother's name should not be required,

3) Registration should be required only in the case of grown-up children, the younger ones being spared the harassment.

(4) *The Kaffir police should not have the power to examine (the permits).*

(5) The distinction made between the Christians and the Muslims of Turkey should be dropped.

(6) The name of the Orange River Colony should continue to be mentioned in the permit.

(7) The determination of the age of a minor should not be left to the arbitrary decision of the Registrar, but should be left to the court.

(8) Temporary permits should be freely available for the entry of merchants' employees.

(9) An assurance should be given that this legislation is now final."[264]

Smuts remained polite and made some compromises. "Indian Opinion" wrote: *"He says that the obligation to give one's mother's name will be withdrawn if all Indians get themselves registered. The*

Kaffir police will not ask for finger-prints (which means that they may ask for the permit. Whether this law will be the last of its kind or not depends on the Indian community itself. If the community carries out the provisions of the law faithfully, there will perhaps be, says Mr. Smuts, no further legislation."[265]

So far the issue of "mother's name" was concerned; even a lawyer like Gandhi was out of control. He wrote:

> "As I summarize this reply, my blood boils. ... It should be noted that on no single point has Mr. Smuts given up his obstinacy. *For he does not say categorically that the mention of the mother's name will not be required.* If all Indians agree to registration, it will be left to our discretion whether *that sacred name should be mentioned or not. The native police* will not ask for the finger-prints, that is, they may certainly ask for permits. If we submitted to the new law, we would never be able to escape the music of "Your pass, please.""[266]

Before proceeding further, in order to understand the "foreign support" for Indians' political struggle, it will be necessary to say a few words on the South African British Indian Committee (abbreviated as SABIC), which was founded by Gandhi in U.K.

Activities of the South African British Indian Committee

The main activities of the SABIC members were either write articles in British newspapers[267-270] or publish pamphlets[271] or impose questions in the House of Commons about the issue of Indians in

S.A. "The Morning Post" called it a very powerful institution.[272] Gandhi and Co. continued communicating with SABIC. In Jan. 1907, the N.I.C. sent a cable to the SABIC to take necessary measures regarding the licences issue for Indian Traders in Vrededrop.[273] Gandhi praised Ritch, Secretary of SABIC, as follows: "There is at present no one in London who can replace Mr. Ritch for vigilance and ability. Sir Muncherji and our other well-wishers do all they can to help us but not much can be done unless there is an able Secretary to bring them all together and to work under their guidance. Almost weekly we see from Reuter's cables that the Committee is active."[274]

The newly elected Prime Minister of Transvaal, Louis Botha came to England to attend the Conference of Colonial Premiers. During the visit, a deputation of the SABIC, led by Lord Ampthill met him. L. Botha promised that "there was no intention whatever of humiliating Indians, and that he would use his influence as practicable to preserve their honour."[275]

Confrontation: Gandhi thanked the Deputation and its communication with L. Botha; but was very critical due to the "mistakes", namely, during the talk the Committee gave the impression that giving of finger-print is the main objectionable issue in the new law.[276] Gandhi had suggested Indians to disobey the laws. This was against the way of thinking of many members of the SABIC. They threatened to leave it. Gandhi was annoyed. He stated: "It is likely that such members will advise us to submit to disgrace. Even so, we need not be afraid, for the Indian community holds it to be a virtue not to submit to the new law, and in doing a good deed we need not be afraid of anyone."²⁷⁷ All of sudden, not human beings, but God became his supporter. He stated: "*Knowing that God always protects the righteous*, the Transvaal Indians should keep to the straight path they have chosen for themselves."²⁷⁸

In the next communication, the Committee disapproved the resolution on gaol-going, because it stated that Gandhi's method means to disobey the government's laws. Gandhi's interpretation was that the members of the SABIC oppose his ideas because "Its chief members are well-known retired officials from India. It is possible that they may again hold such offices. It would be surprising if they advised us to oppose the law. It is not at all surprising that they should have asked us to submit to the law."²⁷⁹

Gandhi had dictatorial power in the B.I.A. Not surprisingly, he stated:

> "Leaving aside all other considerations, Indian community, if it were to submit to law, would be dishonouring its oath taken in name of God, and Committee ought not to advise such a course. It is hoped, therefore, that the Committee's sympathy for Indians will be continued. .... But the task undertaken by the Indian community should not be abandoned even if the Committee should break up. *The true support of the Indian community is Khuda - Ishwar. The Resolution was made with Him as witness and, with trust in Him, we shall swim across to the other shore.*"²⁸⁰

In spite of differences in opinion, SABIC continued constitutional fighting.²⁸¹ For instance, "When Churchill was asked by Robertson and Cox, members of the SABIC that before the monetary assistance, that is, a loan of £5,000,000 to the self-governing Transvaal is given, the interests of the British Indians must be considered. He promised to do so.[282] This was a tactic from Churchill as in the end the results were different than promised. Also, Sir Henry Campbell-Bannerman refused to meet SABIC as he was of the opinion that though he personally finds the law bad, but he would not interfere as Transvaal is self-governing. To it Gandhi said that "For, if the Imperial Government does not protect innocent people when they are being oppressed, commonsense tells us that *God will deprive it of its power.*"[283]

So far the financial support for the SABIC was concerned, from the very beginning the Indian community in S.A., mainly N.I.C. and B.I.A. were responsible for it.[284] Ritch stated that to maintain the work of the Committee 250 pound annually is not sufficient. Later the amount was increased to 300 pounds.[285] Gandhi made hope to the traders that if the political war is won, they will be repaid a hundred times over. After one year, instead of 300 pound, as previously planned; 500 pounds were found to be insufficient. Ritch estimated that at least 1000 pounds are required annually.[286]

Appendix A – Other Reasons for Opposing Ordinance

"1. Under the Ordinance all (existing) permits will be withdrawn and new ones issued after fresh inquiry.

2. *These permits will have to be produced before a Kaffir or any other constable.*

3. Licences will not be issued to those who do not produce the permits.

4. Even when the permit is produced, the police have the right to lock up a man for the night.

5. Even a child of eight years will have to be registered by its parents, and its identification marks noted.

6. It is not the people with forged permits or without permits who will have to face this harassment, since they will have left the Transvaal. It is the others with valid permits who will have to go through it all.

7. All the officers have said that the new permits will carry the impressions of all the ten digits.

8. There is a great difference between giving our thumb-impressions in the past and the same provision under the new law. So far, the thumb-impression was given voluntarily, now it is made compulsory under the law.

9. Hitherto the giving of thumb-impressions was not a statutory requirement, so that it had no consequences elsewhere, but now under the new law, it will have consequences everywhere.

10. If a stranger reads this Ordinance, he will only get the impression that those to whom it applies must be thieves, bandits or traitors.

11. The clauses of the Ordinance are such that these can only apply to criminals.

12. The reason advanced for the Ordinance is also of the same nature: the leaders of the Indian community secure entry for Indians into the Transvaal under false pretexts—which means that the leaders are criminals.

13. The Ordinance raises the question whether the Indian community has any status at all.

14. If the Indian community submits to this Ordinance, the result will be that Indians like Sir Muncherji Bhownaggree who may enter the Transvaal will also be required to take out permits with finger-prints. The responsibility for this will rest on the Transvaal Indians.

15. The Ordinance applies only to Asiatics, and not to Cape Boys, Kaffirs, or Malays. That means that all these three communities will laugh at the Indians. Supposing an Indian marries a Malay. No one will be able to ask the Malay to produce a pass, but everywhere the Kaffir police will accost the Indian and demand, "Your pass, please!" This means that the status of the Indian will be lower than that of his Malay wife."[287]

Appendix B – Gandhi's Pledge

"I do not think that they will come forward to take out the compulsory registers. However, lest I should be guilty of this sin of omission, I hereby declare my Pledge that, should the new law come into force, I will never take out a permit or register under the law but will go to goal; and even if I am the only one left who has not taken a permit, my pledge shall stand for the following reasons:

1. I consider it a humiliation to submit to this law, and I prefer to go to gaol rather than submit to such humiliation;
2. I believe that my country is dearer to me than my person;
3. If, after having announced the September Resolution to the world, the Indian community submits to the law, it will lose everything;
4. I believe that prominent men who have been helping our cause in England rely upon the Fourth Resolution; if we shrink back, we shall not only bring dishonour on them but forfeit their help for ever;
5. the remedy of gaol-going cannot be applied against other laws, but for this Act, it is an infallible remedy and it can be adopted by everyone, whether small or great;
6. if I now retract, I shall be deemed unfit to serve the Indian community;
7. I believe that Indians will rise in public esteem if all of them remain staunch in not submitting to the law, and that, moreover, it will evoke sympathy in India also for the cause of the Transvaal Indians.

…. I appeal to every Transvaal Indian not to miss this occasion and not to turn back. I beg the Indians of Natal, the Cape and Delagoa Bay to encourage us, the Transvaal people, and render help when the need arises."[288]

Notes and References

[204] Indian Opinion, 16-3-1907.

[205] https://www.nelsonmandela.org/omalley/index.php/site/q/03lv01538/04lv01646/05lv01727.htm, Sept. 20, 2015,

[206] Indian Opinion, 12-1-1907.

[207] Indian Opinion, 12-1-1907.

[208] Indian Opinion, 4-5-1907.

[209] Indian Opinion, 2-2-1907.

[210] Indian Opinion, 2-2-1907.

[211] Indian Opinion, 23-2-1907.

[212] Indian Opinion, 2-3-1907.

[213] Indian Opinion, 2-3-1907.

[214] Indian Opinion, 30-3-1907.

[215] Indian Opinion, 30-3-1907.

[216] Indian Opinion, 30-3-1907.

[217] Gani A. to the Registrar of Asiatics, Pretoria, March 4, 1907.

[218] Indian Opinion, 9-3-1907.

[219] Indian Opinion, 9-3-1907.

[220] Indian Opinion, 23-2-1907.

[221] Indian Opinion, 23-3-1907.

[222] Indian Opinion, 9-3-1907.

[223] Indian Opinion, 30-3-1907.

[224] Indian Opinion, 23-3-1907.

[225] Indian Opinion, 30-3-1907.

[226] Indian Opinion, 30-3-1907.

[227] Indian Opinion, 13-4-1907

[228] Indian Opinion, 6-4-1907

[229] In 1908, "Mr. Essop Mia has announced his intention to resign (from the chairmanship of the British Indian Association) as he wishes to go on a pilgrimage to Mecca. …. The meeting has resolved to entrust the chairmanship to Mr. Adam Mahomed Cachalia in succession to Mr. Essop Mia." Indian Opinion, 12-9-1908.

[230] Indian Opinion, 13-4-1907.

[231] Indian Opinion, 20-4-1907.

[232] Indian Opinion, 20-4-1907.

[233] Indian Opinion, 20-4-1907.

[234] Indian Opinion, 20-4-1907.

[235] Indian Opinion, 20-4-1907.

[236] Indian Opinion, 27-4-1907.

[237] Indian Opinion, 27-4-1907.

[238] Indian Opinion, 4-5-1907.

[239] Indian Opinion, 4-5-1907.

[240] Indian Opinion, 11-5-1907.

[241] Indian Opinion, 11-5-1907.

[242] Indian Opinion, 11-5-1907.

[243] Indian Opinion, 25-5-1907.

[244] Indian Opinion, 11-5-1907.

[245] Indian Opinion, 27-4-1907.

[246] Indian Opinion, 18-5-1907.

[247] Indian Opinion, 18-5-1907.

[248] Indian Opinion, 18-5-1907.

[249] The Hindustan Times, 22-1-2011.

[250] The Star, 11-5-1907.

[251] Indian Opinion, 18-5-1907.

[252] Indian Opinion, 1-6-1907.

[253] Indian Opinion, 29-6-1907.

[254] Indian Opinion, 29-6-1907.

[255] Indian Opinion, 8-6-1907.

[256] The Rand Daily Mail, 2-7-1907.

[257] Indian Opinion, 8-6-1907.

[258] Indian Opinion, 8-6-1907.

[259] Indian Opinion, 20-7-1907.

[260] At that time 13000 Indians were living in Transvaal. Indian Opinion, 24-8-1907.

[261] The Rand Daily Mail, 29-6-1907.

[262] Indian Opinion, 29-6-1907.

[263] Indian Opinion, 20-7-1907.

[264] Indian Opinion, 20-7-1907.

[265] Indian Opinion, 20-7-1907.

[266] Indian Opinion, 20-7-1907.

[267] Indian Opinion, 4-5-1907.

[268] Indian Opinion, 4-5-1907.

[269] Indian Opinion, 4-5-1907.

[270] Indian Opinion, 4-5-1907.

[271] Indian Opinion, 7-12-1907.

[272] Indian Opinion, 4-5-1907.

[273] Indian Opinion, 26-1-1907.

[274] Indian Opinion, 23-3-1907.

[275] Indian Opinion, 4-5-1907.

[276] Indian Opinion, 8-6-1907.

[277] Indian Opinion, 8-6-1907.

[278] Indian Opinion, 8-6-1907.

[279] Indian Opinion, 29-6-1907.

[280] Indian Opinion, 29-6-1907.

[281] Indian Opinion, 17-8-1907.

[282] Indian Opinion, 10-8-1907.

[283] Indian Opinion, 7-9-1907.

[284] Indian Opinion, 9-3-1907.

[285] Indian Opinion, 23-3-1907.

[286] Indian Opinion, 12-10-1907.

[287] C.W.M.G. 6, 1906-1907, pp. 340-342.

[288] Indian Opinion, 4-5-1907.

Psychological Terror - Pickets, Blacklegs, Undefined Goals and Misuse of Religion for Political Aims

In the previous chapter we have seen that the South Africa British Indian Committee was safeguarding Indians' interests. It wrote a letter to General Botha. His reply was straight forward, namely: "He will not permit a single Indian to remain here. Rights in regard to ownership of land are not to be conceded, finger-prints will remain necessary, and tram regulations are in the interests of Indians! .... , since Indian leaders do not wish to submit to the law, he does not intend to consult them."[289]

"The Leader" and "The Star", the local newspapers suggested Indians to cooperate with Smuts. To that Gandhi reacted violently, stating that *Indian community in Transvaal is neither under the protection of whites nor Smuts, but God.*[290] At this stage Gandhi was confident that Smuts can neither imprison nor deport 13000 Indians.[291]

We have seen above that for more than a year, he was inciting the Indian community that "finger prints" is the main issue in the law. They are for the criminals only. That is what Gandhi's supporter SABIC, and opponents "The Star" understood. Gandhi sent a rejoinder to the newspaper to say that his proposal has not been read carefully, as: "..., *though finger-prints are not the chief point, they certainly are one of the objectionable points. .... Even voluntarily, Indians will not give ten-finger prints.*"[292]

In a meeting of the Hamidia Islamic Society, Gandhi suggested that a resolution should be passed to know that those who agree with that B.I.A. should carry on in the struggle on behalf of Indians and should sign a petition. Some members, like M.S. Coovadia were not ready to give sole responsibility as they feared that others Indian organisations like N.I.C. will lose their importance. It was not possible to reach a compromise. The discussion was postponed.[293] On Nov. 11, 1907, a petition signed by 4522 persons was sent to the Colonial Secretary.[294] In the petition, there was not only a question of finger prints, but to force the British Empire to give them rights as other British in Transvaal. Gandhi wrote:

> "... *The fundamental issue, therefore, is - are Indians or are they not to be recognised as self-respecting citizens of the Empire?.* Our contemporary, "The Star", the other day twitted Indians on having misled their friends in England as to the real cause of the struggle, and it credited British Indians with fighting against ten digit imprints only. .... But to rightly understand the full measure of the burden of disability borne by our Indian fellow-subjects in the Transvaal, it is necessary to recognise that this humiliation is but an incident, and unimportant compared with the larger particular principle involved in the question of the right of the Transvaal British Indian community to treatment as civilised subjects of the Empire, and as such to protection by their overlord from their invasion and dispossession of that most elementary right. The case for Indians could not be put more clearly."[295]

In a letter dated Sept. 21, 1907, from the B.I.A. to the Sec. of Prime Minister, Johannesburg, it was stated that:

"*Finger impressions themselves have never been a primary cause of the opposition to the Registration Act. .... I take the liberty to quote from the grounds of objections* framed (emphasis in original):

1. It is manifestly in conflict with the past declarations of His Majesty's representatives;

2. It recognises no distinction between British and alien Asiatics;

3. It reduces British Indians to a status lower than that of the aboriginal races of South Africa and coloured people;

4. It renders the position of British Indians in the Transvaal much worse than under Law 3 of 1885, and therefore, than under the Boer regime;

5. It sets up a system of passes and espionage unknown in any other British territory;

6. It brands the communities to which it is applied as criminals or suspects;

7. The alleged influx of unauthorised British Indians is denied;

8. If such a denial is not accepted, a judicial, open, and British inquiry should be instituted before such drastic and uncalled for legislation is enforced;

9. The measure is otherwise un-British, and unduly restricts the liberty of inoffensive British subjects, and constitutes a compulsory invitation to British Indians in the Transvaal to

leave the country. Thus, it will be seen that, when the Law was first introduced last year, the main objections did not contain even so much as a reference to finger prints. The whole flavour about the Act is, in my humble opinion, that of criminality, and submission to it would make the lives of British Indians in the Transvaal intolerable."[296]

The law had become reality. Gandhi and Co. advised the Indian community to avoid the Permit Office. In July 1907, the following poster was to be found on the walls of the Permit Office in Transvaal: "BOYCOTT, BOYCOTT PERMIT OFFICE! BY GOING TO GAOL WE DO NOT RESIST, BUT SUFFER FOR OUR COMMON GOOD AND SELF-RESPECT. LOYALTY TO THE KING DEMANDS LOYALITY TO THE KING OF KINGS. INDIANS BE FREE!"[297]

Gandhi's Volunteers Pickets or "Missionaries" – Controlling the 'Blacksheep'

To prevent "weak-kneed" Indians (in Gandhi's words) from going to registration office, pickets were posted at different stations and around the Permit Office.[298] In Transvaal "some Indians beat up an Imam for having escorted an Indian to the Permit Office and also poisoned the dog of the Indian who had taken out the permit; and at Germiston, a Hindu priest started a brawl."[299] A picket, P.K. Naidoo, who had beaten a Madrasi for registering, was sentenced by court.[300] In Pretoria, Hajee Ebrahim, for having taken out a register and broken the oath; was dealt with a blow with a stick by

Banutkhan, a Pathan.[301] Gandhi took time to suggest his people not to use violence.[302]

In some cases people got registered, but later apologized for the act. For instance, "Indian Opinion" reported: "Mr. Gani Ismail and Mr. Hasan Mahomed Kala write from Pietersburg that both of them feel extremely sorry for having made the application for new registers in Johannesburg, that their remorse knows no bounds, and that the thought of their plight when the law comes into force gives them a stab in the heart."[303]

Those who were afraid of their countrymen, they tried to get registered at night. One such case was reported by the "Indian Opinion" under the title: "New law – Ghastly betrayal". It will be of interest to note that in Pretoria, at 10:00 PM, Gandhi and his friends knocked at Ali Khamisa's house. Gandhi stated: "...I have regretfully to say that Mr. Khamisa sent word to each of his Indian customers that, if they did not apply for the new title-deed of slavery by Monday morning, they should pay up all his dues, failing which he would have summons taken out against them. This created a great stir."[304]

What created greater stir was the letter of H.O. Ally, who was of the opinion that the idea of going to gaol is poisonous for Muslims and will destroy them, as most of them are traders, whereas Hindus hawkers. As usual, Gandhi took the role of a preacher and wrote:

> "We do not wish to hurt Mr. Ally in any way by discussing the matter in public. Those who disagree with him need not be angry with him; rather, they should pity him for his mistake. The main point to be learnt from this is that every person engaged in public work should take a vow that he

would not, under any circumstances, act in a way that might harm public interests. We would advise Mr. Ally to correct his mistake."[305]

Probably to avoid confrontation and save his business, he decided to settle in Cape. "Indian Opinion" wrote about his farewell party and stated: "He has left the Transvaal rather than submit to the law; this is a step on which, condoning his mistake, we should congratulate him. We shall succeed in the end if many Indians stand up to do even as much."[306]

It did not last long that Gandhi had to write:

"It is with a sense of extreme shame and regret that we publish in this issue the petition that has been made by "leading Indians" from cities like Pretoria. We consider this to be a base step, and lay the blame for it chiefly on Mr. Hajee Cassim. His name is mentioned in every meeting of Indians; hence we feel no hesitation in making it public. We consider it our duty to do so. .... Therefore, we regard his disgrace as the disgrace of us all. The language of the petition is abject and worthy of a slave. In using the words "we are wax in the hands of law", they have sinned against God, who alone holds sway over us. Why then should we use towards oppressive rulers language which is appropriate in regard to Him alone?"[307]

Shortly after that: "The four gentlemen of Pietersburg having, as it were, stormed a castle in taking out their title-deed of slavery, Mr. Cassim Hajee Tar of Mafeking thought that he was left behind. Accordingly, he too has melted. What then to talk of Lazarus (Tamil) and Joseph (Tamil) of Durban? These two Tamil gentlemen have also received the brand of registration."[308]

In order to degrade them socially, they were told that they *"ought to dress themselves like women."*[309] Not only in Germiston, also in Johannesburg, there were some "who have no sense of shame", as they got registered.[310-311]

In Aug. 1907, the individual as well as a particular community became point of attack as they were not "loyal" to the B.I.A. For instance, from Pretoria, some persons from the Memons (an ethnic group from Kathiwar) and Konkanis (a minority group from Maharashtra and Kerla) groups get themselves registered. Their names were published by "Indian Opinion."[312-314] Gandhi's "favourite group" to be attacked was Memons in the Transvaal.[315] He published a list of blacklegs or black-faces or 'piano players'". Understandably majority of them were Memons.[316] Almost in every issue of the "Indian Opinion", there were such lists.[317-322] In the beginning of January 1908, he told "I appeal to them all, and especially to the Memons, not to allow the ship to go down just when we are about to sight land. If all the Memons become deserters, that will be a blot on Porbandar, Bhanvad and Ranavav."[323]

Once Gandhi's man, a Hindu Priest Sundar Ram, who refused to renewed his permit (detail below) was arrested. Consequently he was sent to gaol. In protest most of the British Indians closed their shops. Those, who did not follow the said strike, were defamed as follows: "There was a businessman in Offerton, Mr. Kamalkhan by name; who kept his shop open. Likewise in Heidelberg, Messrs. Khota, Abou Mian Camroodeen and Adam Mamuji kept their shops open. This has caused resentment in the whole of the Indian community."³²⁴ However, the most shocking for Gandhi and Co. was that out of 511 registrations; some were close associates. Gandhi wrote:

> "..., there is the more painful information that gentlemen like Mr. Hasan Mia Camroodeen Zatam, of the firm of Sheth M. C. Camroodeen, Mr. Gulam Mahomed Hurzug, the Treasurer of the Anti-Indian-Law Fund, Mr. Hajee Cassim, Mr. Haji Jusab of Pretoria and Mr. Ally Habib have had their faces blackened. I shall not say anything about Mr. Hasan Mia. I think he has lost his balance of mind in connection with this law. Mr. Gulam Mahomed's case is very much to be regretted. It appears that they performed the black deed in great secrecy. There have been rumours about them for quite some time, but I did not (so far) attach any weight to them. I feel ashamed to find that the rumours have proved true. Mr. Hajee Cassim and Mr. Ally also appear to have registered themselves quite secretly. Their words come back to me even as I write this. There is no point in reproducing them. But I think it is at any rate my duty to say that, if persons like Mr. Hajee Cassim and Mr. Ally wanted to get themselves registered, they should have come out boldly in the open to do so."³²⁵

After a compromise between Smuts and Gandhi, the latter changed his tone. Under the title: "To those who submitted to the obnoxious law" he wrote: *"We have been describing blacklegs as black-faced people. That was done deliberately and without anger. It was our* duty to do so. We did not, however, use that description with any ill-will, only we felt grieved because of our love for them."[326]

Interpretation of the above statement in the present political situation means that the U.S.A. and Europeans Governments sent their armies to kill the so-called terrorists because of their love for them; or Muslim terrorists kill Christians in the west, because they love "Christianity?" This seems to be the logic of Gandhi's world view.

Misuse of Religion - The Making of a Hindu Hero – Priest Ram Sundar

A Hindu priest Ram Sundar said in the courts that he refuse to obey the law, because:

> "Mr. Gandhi informed me that *it was against the religion of Indians -* …- because it took away the personal liberty of every Asiatic coming within the meaning of the Act, the result being that, instead of his *being the creature of God only*, he became the creature of any official appointed under the Act, and *a man believing in God would never even dream of submitting to an Act* which really enslaved him. … Consequently, the priest has actively interested himself in seeing that the people do not register, and that rather than look to the things on earth, they look to those from above. This accounts for his (Ram Sundar Pundit) having acted as chief picket when the Asiatic Registration Office was (kept) open in Germiston, picketing having been a purely persuasive act."[327]

Not only some mosques, but also Hindu temples became centers for Gandhi's political propaganda. At the occasion of a Hindu festival, the Sanatan Veda Dharma Sabha organized a meeting. Gandhi's follower," *Ram Sundar Pundit explained how a Hindu who believed in God would never submit to the Asiatic Act.*"[328] The priest R. Sunder, who worked as a picket, supposedly belonged to be the first person, to be prosecuted in Nov. 1907, under the Asiatic act. He was arrested on November 8, for "unlawfully entering and remaining in the Transvaal", after the expiry of his temporary permit."[329] He had come to S.A. in 1905. He was connected to the Sanatan Dharm Society. In Oct. 1907, he was asked to leave the country. For not doing so he was arrested. Gandhi defended his case – "The accused knew the consequences of disobedience to the Registrar's order, but, in his own words, he had a call of higher duty in obedience to which he was before the Court to suffer imprisonment or worse."[330]

Pandit was sent to jail for one month. For propaganda sake "Indian Opinion" reported that "… Government had already laid violent hands on an Indian priest."[331] "Ram Sundar Pundit was arrested without any reason. *This was an attack on religion.*"[332] About R. Sundar's experience in jail, Gandhi wrote: "He was quite comfortable in gaol. He had all the facilities, such as a living-room, a bathroom, etc. As he himself says, he had fever when he went there. Now he is all right. Arrangements for his meals have been made by the community, and milk and fruits are being supplied to him every day. He did not wish to take anything else."[333] And further:

> "He received a number of telegrams in gaol, offering him congratulations and asking him to have courage. They were sent by the Natal Indian Congress, the Durban Anjuman-e-Islam, the Durban Memon Committee, the Hindu Dharma Sabha (Durban), the Parsi Committee (Durban), Mr. Vyas (Pretoria), and the Surat Hindu Association (Durban). In all the telegrams, Punditji was congratulated on going to gaol for the sake of religion and for the struggle of the Indian community."[334]

After the due time, R. Sundar was released. According to Indian fashion, as soon as he came out there was a shower of flowers. A meeting was held in the building of the Sanatan Dharma Sabha.[335] Gandhi called it the beginning of the struggle.[336]

It is very likely that a Muslim, M. Shah was asked to write a letter to a local newspaper to put the "Pundit" on the podium of the "non-violent" heroes. He wrote as follows:

> "I had the privilege of being present at the trial of my co-priest Ram Sundar Pundit. A thought struck me most forcibly, that there must be something radically wrong in the laws of the Transvaal. As everyone now knows, I struck Imam Kamali in the heat of the moment for what I considered was a breach of the Koranic injunctions. I was fined £5 for it, with the option of imprisonment. An unkind friend, who is good enough to describe himself as my disciple, paid the fine, and I escaped gaol. I struck again Mahomed Shahboodeen, who, in his evidence, admitted he had broken his *oath on the Koran*, and said my striking him

was as from father to son. An indulgent court, therefore, let me off with the warning that I may at any time be required to come up for sentence."³³⁷

After "Pundit's" arrest, people were told that if they do not follow his path, they are not men enough. And the struggle is not a children's game.³³⁸ About a week later, Gandhi once again pointed out the arrest of Sunder as *"an attack on religion" and laying "hands on a leader."*³³⁹

While the Pundit was in prison, Gandhi visited and interviewed him. The interview was intended to fulfill Gandhi's purpose to show the luxury and comfort in gaol. Only "essential" parts were produced in "Indian Opinion". In part it reads:

"It would have been better if the Government had awarded me hard labour. After my release, I shall be prepared to go to gaol again for the sake of the community. ....Please tell everyone that *there is no hardship in gaol. I see even women here.* No one should feel anxious on my account. *I feel as if I am in a palace.* I only wish that no Indian submits to the law. *The Governor and the Chief Warder look after me very well.*"³⁴⁰

After reading such statements and later comparing with Gandhi's own experience in gaol, one doubts, who lied more – Gandhi or the Hindu priest! It will not be exaggerate to say that Gandhi deliberately manipulated the facts. As we shall see later, in many letters the B.I.A. or Gandhi complained about food and living conditions in goal. Most of Indians had to work hard. This led to health problems. Pundit, who were arrested under the Peace Preservation Ordinance and the Asiatic Law Amendment Act for remaining in the Colony without a permit, after his permit was expired on Sept. 30, 1907, after living in jail for one month; was set free on Dec. 13, 1907.[341] He was told that if he wants to escape punishment in prison a second time, he should leave the colony within seven days. As he had been brainwash by Gandhi, at least according to "Indian Opinion" he stated: "*But a law higher than the laws of the Colony* dictates to me another course that, as a British subject, and as a preacher of religion in charge of the Hindu temple at Germiston, I should adhere to my duty, irrespective of all consequences. ...."[342] It seems that Smuts was asked to give special permission. He declined to give a new permit to the priest.[343] That was not the end of the story. Later R. Sunder left the city Germiston and decided to live in Natal. After that action, the holy priest was declared by Gandhi as a demon in the following words: "Whenever anyone has unworthy thoughts, let the memory of Ram Sundar startle him into self-contempt and let him turn to God in prayer. We frighten children saying, "Look! Demon!" We should think of Ram Sundar as a demon, and guard ourselves against being possessed by it."[344]

Why Struggle – Nobody Knows

In Gandhi's own words: "For the past twelve months, we have been writing something or other in this journal in reply to this question. In spite of that, the cause behind the struggle, we are afraid, has remained obscure to most Indians."[345] He explained as follows:

"To many it appears that there is a fight because of the objection to giving *ten finger-prints, to some, the only objectionable thing is submitting the names of mother and wife*; while others say that it is painful to think of the police making a house-to-house search. It is true that all these things are rather humiliating. Only thieves submit ten fingerprints; reference to *the sacred name of the mother, by way of insult, has called forth daggers from waist-bands*; when the police have asked for passes from people, presuming them to be suspects, they have had from the persons, enraged by the insult, a blow with the fist which sent them staggering to the ground."[346]

Now, all of sudden, he provided a new interpretation, why it is not insulting to give a mother's name and finger prints. He stated:

"..., if someone asks for finger-prints courteously, and without compulsion, and we comply, no serious resentment is felt. It is with great joy that we take the name of the mother in the same manner as we utter the name of *Ishwar* or *Khuda* while saying prayers with the rosary. That is to say, the things referred to above are objectionable because they have been introduced with a view to insulting us."[347]

Arrest of Railway Workers and Others

The first victims of the law, who refused to register and lost their jobs, were waiters and Indian railway workers.[348] *People were asked to fight for the honour of "Mother India."* They were told that B.I.A., N.I.C. and Gandhi would take care of them and their families. Once the people became active in struggle, soon they had to hear that "*if anyone suffers monetary loss before he is imprisoned, he will have to bear the loss himself.* The community can offer no help in such a case."[349] About the railway workers the "Indian Opinion" wrote:

> "There are about forty of them. No notice was given to them. … they were not even paid for the day on which they were dismissed. The balance of the month's rations that was given to them was taken away from them. Turning a deaf ear to the entreaties of the workers on behalf of their womenfolk and children, they removed the roofs of their rooms that very day with a view to driving them out."[350]

Why the workers did so? Gandhi wrote: "These poor workers have lost their jobs, relying on merchants and other leading Indians. If those merchants and leaders now yield at the last moment and embrace slavery out of fear of imprisonment or monetary loss, they will earn the curses of the poor Indians and their families."[351]

In general, strikes and protests last only a few days, as the workers and the employees are both financially dependant on there occupations. It seems that Gandhi's followers had similar thoughts, as his article from Dec. 1907, indicates. Gandhi wrote:

> "We observe that some Indians *in the Transvaal are getting impatient to see the end of the struggle.* But the end is not in sight just yet. *Great things are not achieved in a day.* Everywhere in South Africa people know that this is a *struggle for the honour of Indians.* … If we become impatient, that will mean that to that extent we are less in the right."[352]

As we shall see in the following chapters, people needed to show "patience" for ca. 7 more years. They had to sacrifice lives, health and money. However, before that Gandhi had his first experience in gaol as well as the first "political compromise" with General Smuts. That all ended in chaos and frustrations as discussed in the following chapter.

Notes and References

[289] Indian Opinion, 10-8-1907.

[290] Indian Opinion, 24-8-1907

[291] Indian Opinion, 24-8-1907.

[292] Indian Opinion, 24-8-1907.

[293] Indian Opinion, 14-9-1907.

[294] Indian Opinion, 21-9-1907.

[295] Indian Opinion, 21-9-1907.

[296] Indian Opinion, 28-9-1907.

[297] Indian Opinion, 27-7-1907.

[298] Indian Opinion, 19-10-1907.

[299] Indian Opinion, 26-10-1907.

[300] Indian Opinion, 30-11-1907.

[301] Indian Opinion, 30-11-1907.

[302] Indian Opinion, 30-11-1907.

[303] Indian Opinion, 9-11-1907.

[304] Indian Opinion, 3-8-1907.

[305] Indian Opinion, 27-7-1907.

[306] Indian Opinion, 31-8-1907.

[307] Indian Opinion, 14-9-1907.

[308] Indian Opinion, 21-9-1907.

[309] Indian Opinion, 28-9-1907.

[310] Indian Opinion, 28-9-1907.

[311] Indian Opinion, 19-10-1907.

[312] Indian Opinion, 17-8-1907.

[313] Indian Opinion, 7-9-1907.

[314] Indian Opinion, 7-9-1907.

[315] Indian Opinion, 26-10-1907.

[316] Indian Opinion, 26-10-1907.

[317] Indian Opinion, 2-11-1907.

[318] Indian Opinion, 9-11-1907.

[319] Indian Opinion, 16-11-1907.

[320] Indian Opinion, 7-12-1907.

[321] Indian Opinion, 14-12-1907.

[322] Indian Opinion, 28-12-1907.

[323] Indian Opinion, 11-1-1908.

[324] Indian Opinion, 23-11-1907.

[325] Indian Opinion, 21-12-1907.

[326] Indian Opinion, 8-2-1908.

[327] The Transvaal Leader, 12-11-1907.

[328] Indian Opinion, 7-9-1907.

[329] Indian Opinion, 16-11-1907.

[330] Indian Opinion, 23-11-1907.

[331] Indian Opinion, 16-11-1907.

[332] Indian Opinion, 16-11-1907.

[333] Indian Opinion, 16-11-1907.

[334] Indian Opinion, 16-11-1907.

[335] Indian Opinion, 16-11-1907.

[336] Indian Opinion, 16-11-1907.

[337] Shah M. to Editor, The Transvaal Leader, Nov. 23, 1907.

[338] Indian Opinion, 23-11-1907.

[339] Indian Opinion, 23-11-1907.

[340] Indian Opinion, 7-12-1907.

[341] Indian Opinion, 21-12-1907.

[342] Sunder R. to Sec. Colony, Dec. 14, 1907.

[343] Indian Opinion, 28-12-1907.

[344] Indian Opinion, 4-1-1908.

[345] Indian Opinion, 30-11-1907.

[346] Indian Opinion, 30-11-1907.

[347] Indian Opinion, 30-11-1907.

[348] Indian Opinion, 14-12-1907.

[349] Indian Opinion, 28-12-1907.

[350] Indian Opinion, 28-12-1907.

[351] Indian Opinion, 28-12-1907.

[352] Indian Opinion, 21-12-1907.

Gandhi's Sword "to pierce the violent, rock-like hatred in the hearts of the whites"

In Johannesburg, on Dec. 28, 1908, M.K. Gandhi, C.M. Pillay, P.K. Naidoo, M. Easton and M.E. Cadwa (Karwa) were charged under the Asiatic Registration Act. For not possessing documents, Gandhi was sentenced to two months' imprisonment without hard labour.[353] In the following we shall see:

- Why Gandhi agreed for a quick compromise with Smuts?
- What was the reaction of the members of the N.I.C.?
- What led to the revival of the political struggle?

The Quick Compromise

On 28 Jan. 1908, Gandhi, Leuing Quinn - Chairman of the Chinese Association and the Cantonese Club, and Thambi Naidoo - a Tamil businessman from Mauritius, wrote a letter to J.C. Smuts, Transvaal Colonial Secretary. They proposed the following compromise:

> "Our opposition has never been directed so much against the fingerprint requirements of the Regulations under the Act - in so far as such finger-prints were deemed necessary for the identification of Asiatics who could not very well be otherwise identified - as against the element of compulsion contained in the Act itself. On that ground we have repeatedly offered to undergo voluntary registration if the act were repealed."[354]

And further, they suggested:

> "That all Asiatics over the age of sixteen years should be allowed within a certain limited period, say three months, to register themselves, and that to all who so register, the Act be not applied, and that the Government take whatever steps they deem advisable to legalize such registration. Such mode of registration should apply to those also who being out of the Colony may return and otherwise possess the rights of re-entry."[355]

They continued:

> "In taking the registration of Asiatics we do not object that the requirements of the Act and the regulations be as nearly as possible complied with, provided the registration officials do not press for any information which *offends the religious sense of the applicants, and receive discretion to dispense with the finger-print* requirement in the case of those applicants who by reason of their education or property or public character are well known or can be easily identified other- wise. In those cases we urge that the officials should have discretion to accept the signature of the applicant as a sufficient identification."[356]

Two days later, Gandhi and General Smuts met in Pretoria. The outcome of the conversation was a compromise. On Jan. 30, 1908, a journalist from the newspaper "The Rand Daily Mail" wanted to know the details of the talk. Gandhi refused to disclose.

All in all, 220 persons were arrested during the struggle. They were released after the compromise. The duty of Gandhi and Co. was to explain the nature of the agreement to their countrymen.[357] In

Johannesburg, on Jan. 31, 1908, at a meeting of the B.I.A. Gandhi delivered a speech and praised the "great victory" of the Indians. About the compromise he stated as follows:

> "We will now register voluntarily for purposes of identification and the scrutiny (of our rights of domicile) and the Government has accepted this (offer). That means that the obnoxious law will die altogether. .... Under the proposed arrangement, the Government will accept signatures by educated persons and by owners of property, but *unlettered people have to give ten finger-prints* on the application forms. Though I am against this myself and will strive with the Government to the best of my ability to have the requirement waived, *I see nothing wrong in having to give finger-impressions* if the Government does not come round. For after all we shall be giving them of our own free choice. They must not be given if they are made compulsory. And the Government has allowed us a period of three months for the matter to be settled."[358]

Further:

> "Under the law, the Government wanted the compulsory registration of children, and this (provision) too, has now been dropped. The question of amending the law suitably will be taken up when Parliament meets in Pretoria. .... When Parliament meets, we shall be delivered from this law. That is, the Act will be repealed and the Immigration Bill will be suitably amended."[359]

Causes of Quick Compromise

In order to justify, why Gandhi made compromise without discussing with the community, he stated that[360]:

- He was told that people were losing courage.
- "The hawkers, ... wanted me to bring about a compromise as early as possible."
- "Those who went to gaol lost their nerve in a few days, and some of them hinted that they would not go to gaol again."
- General Smuts told me ... "that I did not have the slightest idea of the number of people who had wanted to submit to the law. A few people had already sent applications to him in secret. I even know the names of some of them."

He stated that he could not ignore these facts. However, he insisted:

"As far as I could judge, there was no objection to the voluntary provision of finger-impressions just as there was none to voluntary registration; and I knew that sensible persons in the Transvaal were not opposed to the idea, for they had no objection to finger-impressions as such, but only to the manner in which they were (required) to give them under the law. Since that situation no longer obtained, finger-impressions in themselves had become innocuous."[361]

Aftermyth of the Compromise - Finger-Prints Become a Hot Issue

Soon after the compromise, the Indian community in Transvaal was divided in two groups – Those who wanted to follow Gandhi and others who wanted to follow God. The later threatened the former with punishment, if they give finger prints. In "Indian Opinion" Gandhi wrote:

> "Some persons are threatening to resort to violence if the community agrees to give the ten finger prints. I must tell these persons that I myself gave my finger-prints twice while in gaol. If violence is to be used against anyone, let it be first used against me. *I will not lodge a complaint with the magistrate on that score.* Rather, I shall thank the person who assaults me, grateful for the blow from one of my brethren and feel honoured by it. The responsibility for whatever has happened is mine as it will be for whatever happens in the future."[362]

As we shall see below, soon Gandhi's desire was fulfilled.

Before going for registration, "Indian Opinion", once again taught its readers:

> "The main point having been secured, we are of opinion that everyone should give digit-impressions without the slightest hesitation. In any case, the leaders who have a right not to give fingerprints should be the first to waive it and offer to give those impressions, so as to facilitate the work of identification, and make the process easier for the

Government. We believe that the Indian community will show its real dignity by making as limited a use of the concession as possible. We understand that Messrs. Essop Mia, Gandhi, and others who have been closely identified with the struggle, have decided not to claim the concession."[363]

Again, "Indian Opinion" thematized the finger print issue as follows:

"(i) Those who know English well will not be required to give either finger-prints or thumb-impressions. (ii) Men of standing and those who own property can be exempted from the giving of finger-prints or thumb-impressions. (iii) Those who strongly object (on grounds of conscience) to giving ten finger-prints will be allowed to give thumb-impressions. (iv) The rest will have to give the ten finger-impressions."[364]

As we have seen above, in the compromise signing committee, none of the members was a Muslim. This lead to criticism, as some of the Muslims thought that their interests had been sold by Gandhi. In his defence, Gandhi wrote: "I have heard some Muslim brethren say in arguments about the compromise, "Gandhi has totally ruined the Muslims and has been doing so for the last fifteen years." It is most regrettable that any Indian should utter these words. I am sure those who say this themselves know that I have never even dreamt of harming anyone."[365]

Gandhi, who had promised the registration, was followed by two Pathans. About the incident he wrote:

"I do not remember the manner of the assault, but people say that I fell down unconscious with the first blow which was delivered with a stick. Then my assailants struck me with an iron pipe and a stick, and they also kicked me. Thinking me dead, they stopped. I only remember having been beaten up. I have an impression that, as the blows started, I uttered the words 'He Rama!'. Mr. Thambi Naidoo and Mr. Essop Mia intervened. Mr. Naidoo was hit as a result and injured on the ear. Mr. Essop Mia received a slight injury on a finger. As I came to, *I got up with a smile.* In my mind *there was not the slightest anger or hatred for the assailants.*"[366]

In the end of March 1908, in Pretoria, 5000 Indians in Johannesburg had applied for registration.[367] Gandhi was not quite happy with those who had stated either a wrong number of children or purposefully misstated names.[368] One point to be noted is that Transvaal had about 13000 Indians. Due to Registration Act 5000 left. Either they went to Natal or Cape Town or India. Only 8000 remained back.[369] Up to April 8, 1908, 7607 applications for registration were made, and the number of certificates issued was 4590.[370] While the registration was going on, still many were unsure about the difference between "voluntary- and compulsory registration as well as finger prints." Gandhi offered a simple solution: "My advice to everyone concerned is, "Give them." Since the giving of finger-impressions is voluntary, I see nothing wrong in doing so."[371] Further he stated:

"But no one should imagine, on the other hand, that he can avoid giving the ten impressions without reason. He must state the reason, such as religious scruple or (his right to) exemption on grounds of education or status. There are others who are reluctant to give even the thumb-impressions. This is improper. I think the thumb-impressions must be given, if demanded. I, however, advise those who have raised a sincere objection against the ten impressions to remain firm."[372]

By the end of April 1908, the registrations in Transvaal were complete. According to "Indian Opinion":

"Of the eight thousand odd applications made, six thousand have already been approved and passed. .... The Asiatics have, therefore, fulfilled their obligation, both in the spirit and the letter. It now remains for the Government to complete the performance of its duty, namely, to repeal the Asiatic Act, and to legalize voluntary registration in a manner acceptable to the Asiatics and satisfactory from the Colonial standpoint, which is to restrict the authorized influx of new-comers."[373]

Useless Voluntary Registration and Asking for the Repealing of the Act

The deadline set for the voluntary registration was May 9, 1908. Shortly after that Gandhi was informed by M. Chamney, the Registration Officer, that those who at the time of compromise resided outside the colony, and who are coming in after May 9th should be registered under the act. Gandhi was shocked to read the telegram as is evident from his letter of May 12, 1908, to Smuts. It states: "I am sure you do not mean this at all, in the face of the clear statement in the letter addressed by me from the jail. It has created almost a panic. I venture to hope that the necessary instructions will be issued, and that voluntary registration will be accepted from those who may now come in."[374]

As a reply to Gandhi's objection, Smuts' private Secretary E.F.C. Lane wrote on May 13, 1908, telling that Smuts' exactly meant, what Chamney said.[375] Gandhi who felt misunderstood wrote to Lane: "When the negotiations were going on, I could never have dreamed of accepting a compromise which would mean a differential treatment of Asiatics entering after the period of three month."[376] Pathetically he pleaded:

> "In order to make good my word, as also to assist the Government, it is within the General's knowledge that I very nearly lost my life, and this arose because, in the opinion of some of my countrymen, I had sold them, by reason of having agreed to the principle of ten finger-prints. Were the proposed registration under the Act of new arrivals persisted in, not only will suspicion be accentuated, but it will be justified, and I cannot help saying that those who may feel irritated against me will be entitled to my life. I should consider myself totally unworthy of the trust reposed in me by my countrymen, and to hold the position that they have allowed me to hold for such a long time,

were I ever to consent to the Act being applied to newcomers."[377]

The readers of the "Indian Opinion" were told that "If the officials violate the terms of the settlement, it will be possible to set matters right. Because the officials act contrary to its terms, the compromise itself should not be blamed."[378] Under the title "Foul Play", Gandhi confessed that his calculation had gone wrong; as General Smuts "categorically declaring in the end that Indians arriving after May 9 will be governed by the provisions of the obnoxious Act."[379] Gandhi was inquired to use his influence and asked the entrants to register accordingly.[380] He threatened with satyagraha.[381] At the same time he criticized his countrymen who after returning from India had registered under the new law. He sent a general "warning" not to register under the new law.[382]

Once again, some of Asiatics, in particular Pathans, felt betrayed by Gandhi and the Chairman of the B.I.A., Essop Mia. Both of them had preached against the finger-prints, and they were the first to go to the registration office. As we have seen earlier, Gandhi was attacked. Essop Mia, who gave evidence in the court, was attacked in a dinner party. His nose was broken.[383] Gandhi wrote: "If the Pathans believe that they can terrorize the poor Indians, they are mistaken. In the near future, if not today, the Indian community will learn to be courageous and defend itself."[384] To J.C. Smuts *he suggested to deport the most violent Pathans to their home country.*[385]

In a letter Gandhi informed Smuts about the attack on E. Mia. He lamented:

> "Your decision ... has created a turmoil amongst the Indians. ... I daily receive indignant letters saying that I have entirely misled the people as to the compromise and that the law is not going to be repealed at all. Can I not ask you, for the sake of those who *have helped the Government*, to do a very simple thing - to announce immediately that the Act will be repealed and that new arrivals may be voluntarily registered?"[386]

Smuts was determined not to make any promises. In protest, on May 26, 1908, Gandhi wrote to M. Chamney, Registrar Colonial Office, to return his registration documents.[387] Similar letters were written by Essop Ismail Mia, Chairman B.I.A.[388], Imam A.K. Bawazeer, Chairman, Hamidia Islamic Society[389], Leung Quinn, Chairman, and Transvaal Chinese Association.[390]

As seen above, Smuts refused the repealing of the obnoxious Act. Gandhi and Co. thought to restart political action. They wanted that the Government of Transvaal should fulfill the following demands:

> "(1) Those who hold valid registers from the Dutch period should be entitled to register voluntarily.
>
> (2) Those who have entered openly, but with permits, and have lived here for some time should be entitled to registration certificates.
>
> (3) Those who can prove to the satisfaction of a court that they are refugees should be permitted to enter.

(4) No laws should be enacted to deprive a subject of his personal liberty exclusively on the basis of the colour of his skin.

(5) Educated Indians should be allowed to come in even if they are fresh entrants."[391]

Though Gandhi blamed Smuts, the fact is that the latter was dependent on other political partners. He was not in the position to repeal the law without the support of the Progressive Party.[392] He admitted drawbacks in the Asiatic Registration law.[393] Gandhi demanded the following amendments in the Immigration Act:

"1. No position will ever be accepted by the Asiatic communities that does not put those who have not yet entered the country but are entitled to do so on a level with Asiatics who have voluntarily registered. .....

2. Refugees who have not yet received permits under the Peace Preservation Ordinance should be protected. There will be no objection to defining who may be termed a refugee - I suggest residence in the Transvaal for two years prior to the 11th day of October, 1899 - and a period may be fixed within which these applications may be received, say one year, and they should be entitled to prove their claim before a court of law.

3. Those who hold £3 Dutch Registration Certificates should also be protected, the onus being on them to prove that they are *bona-fide* holders thereof.

4. Those who hold Peace Preservation Ordinance permits or permits issued by Asiatic Officers should be protected.

5. Those who possess educational qualifications, whatever the test may be, should be free like the European immigrants.

6. There are applications being made which have not been yet decided by Mr. Chamney, or which he has refused. These should be decided finally before a court of law."[394]

Smuts was hoping that the Progressive Party might give him support. According to Gandhi's letter to him, of June 16, 1908:

"At the interview, General Smuts said that the new law would certainly be repealed and the Immigrants' (Restriction) Act amended. But he had still to consult his draftsmen in the legal department. He therefore advised (Mr. Gandhi) to wait for a week. He said, moreover, that the *British Indian Association did not represent the entire Indian community, and that he had received a petition from (some) Indians* requesting that the law be retained."[395]

On June 22, 1908, the hopes were shattered. After a meeting with Smuts, Gandhi told the press: "...General Smuts was, and still is, under promise to repeal the Act. But if he was willing to carry out the letter of the compromise, he wanted to break the spirit of it. For it will not be argued that the material position of the Asiatics was, under and after the compromise, to be lower than under the Asiatic Act."[396]

Gandhi continued:

> "Yet such was General Smuts' draft which I was today pained to study and, so far as I was concerned, to reject. The draft measure proposed to treat the following as prohibited immigrants:
>
> (a) Asiatics possessing educational qualifications prescribed by the Immigrants' Restriction Act.
>
> (b) Asiatics, whether in or out of the Colony, holding Dutch registration certificates under Law 3 of 1885, for which they paid £3.
>
> (c) Other Asiatics who were residents of the Transvaal before the war, and who could prove before a court of law their previous domicile.
>
> (d) Those Asiatics whose claims have been rejected by Mr. Chamney. (For these it is contended only that they should have the right to have their claims investigated by a judicial tribunal, not finally disposed of by an administrative official)."[397]

Further Gandhi stated: "In rejecting these claims for consideration and adjudication, not for admission *ipso facto*, General Smuts has misread the passive resistance struggle."[398] So far as the registration was concerned, he said:

> "The fact that over 7600 out of 9000 have already proved their *bona fides* disposes of the charge. It was in order to refute that foul charge that voluntary registration was tendered, and for no other reason. The Asiatics, therefore, approach the public with clean hands. .... General Smuts'

Act will be that of the Government and the Government's will be the white men's - mostly British."[399]

The Last Blow – Gandhi's Sword "to Pierce the Violent, Rock-Like Hatred in the Hearts of the Whites"

Gandhi had insisted, again and again, that Smuts breached his promise of repealing the law. By submitting affidavits, General Smuts (see Box) and M. Chamney proved that they never made such promises.[400]

"SMUTS' AFFIDAVIT

[PRETORIA,]

June 26, 1908

I, Jan Christiaan Smuts of Pretoria, Colonial Secretary, make oath and say:

1. 1 made no promise to Mr. M. K. Gandhi either on the 30th January or on the 3rd February, 1908 that Act No. 2 of 1907 would be repealed.

2. The Letter of the 30th January, 1908, copy of which is attached to the Petition in this matter, sets out all that I agreed to.

3. The matter is being laid before Parliament as stated in that letter.

J. C. SMUTS

Sworn before me at Pretoria, this 26th day of June, 1908.

J. H. L. FINDLAY

Justice of the Peace."[401]

In Supreme Court, the Justice Solomon said that Smuts' reply to Gandhi's *et al.* letter as well as the letter from gaol did not throw any light on the repeal of the Act. Gandhi wanted that the application for voluntary registration should be returned back. It was ruled out by the judge with the argument that under the law, a letter belongs to the person to whom it is addressed. Thus Indians cannot demand their registration applications. However, the government is bound to return the old registration and permits.[402]

After the case was lost, many Indians were disheartened. To console them, Gandhi came up with his irrational philosophy as follows:

> "*Khuda is the ultimate court of appeal for a satyagrahi,* and in that court false evidence does not avail. Moreover, our object in demanding that the applications be returned was to make certain that we were arrested as early as possible. *We must achieve the same object now by burning the registers.* This will appear a little difficult, but in fact it can be done easily."[403]

All of a sudden all whites became his opponents, who needed to be fought. He wrote:

> "*It is a conflict between the whites and the Coloured persons.* The whites want to ride roughshod over us, to keep us down always as slaves. We want to be their equals. ... *The sword of satyagraha* is not to be used for cutting dung cakes which is what the domiciliary rights of a handful of Transvaal Indians really are, but to pierce the violent, rock-like hatred in the hearts of the whites."[404]

"In a "do or die" mood they resolved to put up a fight. It was decided to fight a test case for the withdrawal of an application."[405]

Gandhi publically admitted that his opponent Pathans were right in disbelieving Smuts. He stated:

"Another of his fellow-religionists, or a fellow - Pathan, has assaulted me. He deserves every thanks for having assaulted me, because he believed that I was selling the community. He had no grudge against me, he was my client. He had a perfect right to do what he did, as I find now from the consequences that have been entailed on the whole of the Asiatic communities."[406]

Gandhi was motivating his followers to restart with the political struggle. Meanwhile he had developed his political ideas and tools. Most importantly the so-called "satyagraha" was taking firm form; as we shall see in the next chapter.

Notes and References

[353] Indian Opinion, 18-1-1908.

[354] Gandhi M.K., Quinn L., Naidoo T. to Colonial Sec., Transvaal, Jan. 28, 1908.

[355] Gandhi M.K., Quinn L., Naidoo T. to Colonial Sec., Transvaal, Jan. 28, 1908.

[356] Gandhi M.K., Quinn L., Naidoo T. to Colonial Sec., Transvaal, Jan. 28, 1908.

357 The Transvaal Leader, 31-1-1908.

358 Indian Opinion, 8-2-1908.

359 Indian Opinion, 8-2-1908.

360 Indian Opinion, 29-2-1908.

361 Indian Opinion, 29-2-1908.

362 Indian Opinion, 8-2-1908.

363 Indian Opinion, 8-2-1908.

364 Indian Opinion, 8-2-1908.

365 Indian Opinion, 22-2-1908.

366 Indian Opinion, 22-2-1908.

367 Indian Opinion, 21-3-1908.

368 Indian Opinion, 21-3-1908.

369 C.W.M.G. 8, 1907-1908, pp. 220-228.

370 Indian Opinion, 11-4-1908.

371 Indian Opinion, 25-4-1908.

372 Indian Opinion, 2-5-1908.

373 Indian Opinion, 9-5-1908. According to "Indian Opinion" of 9-5-1908: "About 8,700 applications for registration have been made and 6,000 applicants have already received their certificates."

374 Gandhi M.K. to Smuts J.C., May 12, 1908.

375 Lane E.F.C. to Gandhi M.K., May 13, 1908

376 Gandhi M.K. to Lane E.F.C., May 14, 1908.

[377] Gandhi M.K. to Lane E.F.C., May 14, 1908.
[378] Indian Opinion, 16-5-1908.
[379] Indian Opinion, 23-5-1908.
[380] Indian Opinion, 23-5-1908.
[381] C.W.M.G. 8, 1907-1908, p. 326.
[382] Indian Opinion, 23-5-1908.
[383] Indian Opinion, 23-5-1908.
[384] Indian Opinion, 23-5-1908.
[385] Gandhi M.K. to Smuts J.C., May 21, 1908.
[386] Gandhi M.K. to Smuts J.C., May 21, 1908.
[387] Indian Opinion, 30-5-1908.
[388] Mia E.I. to Chamney M., May 26, 1908.
[389] Bawazeer I.A.K. to Chamney M., May 26, 1908.
[390] Quinn L. to Chamney M., May 26, 1908.
[391] Indian Opinion, 30-5-1908.
[392] Gandhi M.K. to Cartwright A., June 6, 1908.
[393] Indian Opinion, 13-6-1908.
[394] Gandhi M.K. to Smuts J.C., June 13, 1908.
[395] Indian Opinion, 20-6-1908.
[396] Indian Opinion, 27-6-1908.
[397] Mia E.I. to Colonial Sec., July 6, 1908.
[398] Indian Opinion, 27-6-1908.

[399] Indian Opinion, 27-6-1908.
[400] Indian Opinion, 4-7-1908.
[401] C.W.M.G. 8, 1907-1908, p. 493.
[402] Indian Opinion, 11-7-1908.
[403] Indian Opinion, 11-7-1908.
[404] Indian Opinion, 11-7-1908.
[405] Indian Opinion, 27-6-1908.
[406] Indian Opinion, 4-7-1908.

Satyagraha – A Fatalist and Fanatic Ideology – "This is a fight on behalf of religion ..."

Most of the religions pretend to preach peace. Their believers think that their own religion is the only way to salvation. Most of the religious ideologies tell the followers that their good deeds will lead to better life after death. For bad deeds the followers will suffer. Directly or indirectly the believers are encouraged to degrade the opponents. Gandhi called his political ideology *"a universal religion."* As we shall see below:

- How the term "satyagraha" (stick to truth) was coined?
- Gandhi's "universal religion", that is, the "satyagraha" was like any other brutal religion.
- How he exaggerated this ideology, by calling it the master key to solve the world problems?
- How he exaggerated that for the success of his politics, "only one satyagrahi" is enough?

Coining the Term "Satyagraha"

In the Jan. 10, 1908 issue of the "Indian Opinion" readers were asked for a Gujarati term, which should be equivalent to "passive resistance" as coined by a journalist of "The Daily Rand Mail". A small amount of money was to be given to the winner. About the proposal of the term, Gandhi wrote:

> "I have received one which is not bad, though it does not render the original in its full connotation. I shall, however,

use it for the present. The word is sadagraha. I think satyagraha is better than sadagraha. "Resistance" means determined opposition to anything. The correspondent has rendered it as agraha. Agraha in a right cause is sat or satya agraha. The correspondent therefore has rendered "passive resistance" as firmness in a good cause. Though the phrase does not exhaust the connotation of the word "passive", we shall use satyagraha till a word is available which deserves the prize. Satyagraha, then, is at high tide at present. The Indian satya-grahi is getting world-wide publicity."[407]

After a struggle of more than two years people started criticizing Gandhi's philosophy of "sataygraha" as a useless instrument. However, like any religious "Founder" he was convinced that *"satyagraha is in no way to blame for this. The continued delay shows that the satyagraha is not as intensive as it should be."* He argued that in Natal only 13 had come forward to take part.[408] Why out of 150000 only 13 followed him? Was there a fault in the method? Were there financial, political and social reasons? He did not ask such a question. When he was asked to stop the movement, he stated that those who advise him, they: "do not understand the deep significance *and the marvelous power of satyagraha. .... If the Indian community can practise satyagraha even in a small measure, there is no reason why it* should have to leave this country."[409] Those who had been deported (detail later) they were told: "But, *even if it is obliged to leave the country, it will have already enjoyed the fruits of satyagraha."*[410] On the one hand, people were asked to offer their families and wealth to get rights, but at the same time they were told:

> *"That one can secure one's rights through satyagraha is not the reason why it is practised.* Securing one's rights is one of the results, *but satyagraha can be offered without thinking of the result.* As for efforts of other kinds, we count them wasted if there are no results. .... *In satyagraha, it makes no difference whether the result is achieved or not.* ... If on any occasion we fail to discover such a result, it will not be because of any imperfection in satyagraha as such, but because people might not have been steadfast in their satyagraha."[411]

For Gandhi, satyagraha was not a political ideology. It was a religion. Almost all religions console their followers to die for its cause to receive a good life in "heaven." That is what he told to his followers, in particular to his wife: *"If you die, even that death of yours will be a sacrifice to the cause of satyagraha. My struggle* is not merely political. *It is religious and therefore quite pure. It does not matter much whether one dies in it or lives."*[412]

In 1909, from a political point of view, the movement was a flop. Gandhi came up with the last card, which often works among fanatic religious people. The struggle was no longer a political issue but:

> *"This is a fight on behalf of religion, that is, on behalf of the (universal) religion which underlies all religions.* Had I not believed so, I would never have advised the community to invite grievous suffering on itself. I believe that sacrificing one's all in a struggle like this should in no way be difficult.

> It is the duty of every Indian *to forget all thought of relatives and friends, to sacrifice wealth and life*, in this struggle. *I pray to God, and beg of Indians that all of them fulfil this duty.*"[413]

So far his "religion" satyagraha was concerned, Gandhi remained blind to see faults in it. For, "if, on any occasion, we fail, we shall discover that the failure was due to some deficiency in the satyagrahi and did not argue the inefficacy of satyagraha as such."[414] His ideas were as much fanatic as today's Talibans or the Islamic State terrorists, where it is propagated by calling people to break with the family and die for Allah. Gandhi's "Allah" was his "satyagraha." Accordingly he preached:

> "A satyagrahi is obliged to break away from family attachments. This is very difficult to do. But the practice of satyagraha, if satyagraha is to be worthy of its name, is like walking on the edge of a sword. In the long run, *even the breaking away from family attachments will prove beneficial to the family.* For, the members of the family will come to feel the call for satyagraha, and those who have felt such a call will have no other desire left."[415]

Gandhi wrote: "A satyagrahi can make no conditions. *He stands ready to sacrifice himself, body, mind and possessions and, hence, is not afraid of losing wealth or life.* He has entered into *a pact with death itself.* There is no middle of the road line for him. …. *He will live on even after death.*"[416]

The "holy warrior", Gandhi, found smoking and drinking intolerable. He preached to his followers:

"It has come to my knowledge that some of the satyagrahi prisoners have learnt to resort to underhand ways in gaol. Formerly they would not eat anything which was not openly available for all or which others could not get; now they do so. Those who were not used to chewing tobacco or smoking have now learnt to do so. Such prisoners should be ashamed of themselves, ..."[417]

Who can be a Satyagrahi? In June 1909, Gandhi answered:

"In the Transvaal, satyagraha consists for the most part in going to gaol. But imprisonment is not the end of the matter. *Satyagrahis have had to mount the gallows, embrace a pillar of red-hot iron, suffer being rolled down a mountain, swim in boiling oil in a big frying pan, walk through a blazing forest,* suffer loss of a kingdom and be sold (as slave) in a low-born family and *stay in a lion's den.* Thus, satyagrahis have had to pass through different ordeals in different parts of the world."[418]

Evidently, the philosophy has a touch of fanatacism. And further:

"Every person, then, who wants to go to gaol must have, in some measure, the qualities which, as we have seen, are essential in a satyagrahi. But, in addition, he should have the following strong points:

(1) Freedom from addiction to harmful things.

(2) A well-disciplined body.

(3) Disregard for comfortable seat or bed.

(4) Extreme simplicity in food habits.

(5) Total freedom from false sense of prestige or status.

(6) Fortitude."[419]

For years Gandhi was saying that his struggle or satyagraha is for the sake of the rights of Indians. One is absolutely surprised or even annoyed when shown the following incidence. He was asked by a journalist: Why passive resistance? He told that it: *"was a harmless search for truth,* and he appealed to every Indian present to be prepared to die, if need be, for the truth."[420]

Satyagraha the Master Key

Gandhi for every silly instance or events used/misused the term "satyagraha". For instance, in Durban, Hindus bursted crackers at the occasion of "Diwali" festival. After complaint from some inhabitants, police arrested a leading Hindu. Members of the N.I.C. went to the Mayor and argued, as to why Hindus need special permission, while Christian can do so during Christmas. The arrested person was released. Gandhi boasted with his "satyagraha" as follows: "..., *satyagraha is the master-key to our innumerable hardships.* How much could be achieved if only all the Indians would use that key! *Satyagraha is not a difficult term to understand. It only means adherence to truth.*"[421]

How limited was his "master-key, satyagraha", he had to confess soon. For instance, after Gandhi had achieved a few social rights and was preparing for to leave for India; a reader advised him to make use of the opportunity and suggested:

"Circumstances will never again favour you with a similar opportunity, what with the support India has been giving you and the strong sympathies that have been aroused. *Nothing, therefore, should be left out from the full citizenship rights* which are to be achieved, so that our people may not have to endure hardships again. *Besides the matters in dispute*, there are the questions of *the right to own land, the Gold Law, the Township Act, freedom to hold licences in the Transvaal, the franchise, the prohibition on Indians putting up stores on new stations*, ... I have only mentioned this in passing. All that I mean is that the present opportunity will not come again and that, therefore, every right should be secured."[422]

Gandhi who had praised the wonder weapon satyagraha as the solution of the world's problems stated:

"*Like everything else, satyagraha has its limits. To understand how much may be achieved* through it is the first step to success in it. It needs to be understood, once and for all, that the path of truth is not meant for ends not consistent with truth. *It is our belief that raising our demands will amount to untruthfulness.* ... , Indians need to realize in all seriousness that it is the *first principle of satyagraha not to enhance our original demands.*"[423]

Once a reporter asked him: Do you want voting for Indians? Gandhi told: "No; ..., and my firm conviction is that *passive resistance is infinitely superior to the vote*. I have never asked for the vote. What I always have insisted on was *the removal of racial distinctions, not for equality.*"⁴²⁴

A Satyagrahi as a "Super and Selfless Creator"

Just imagine that you are lecturing to people for almost ten years about an ideology. They follow you day and night. Still they do not understand what the "teacher" wants? Is his method of teaching wrong? Or is there a flaw in the philosophy? In the beginning of 1914, Gandhi wrote:

> "Seen superficially, the difference between satyagraha and brute force is *so subtle that it escapes notice and both satyagrahis* and non-satyagrahis, i.e., those who believe in brute force, are misled. Some of our well-wishers and friends did not like our strike in Natal, as they thought we had overstepped the limits of satyagraha. *Others mistakenly imagined that the recent strike of the white railway men was satyagraha*, though the difference between their aim and ours in going on strike is as great as that between North and South."⁴²⁵

Gandhi criticised the violent attitude of the railway men, who wanted better salaries. For him, it was not a religious act. About his own action he stated: *"If we went on strike, it was not in order to harass the Government. We only wanted to suffer - do tapascharya (practice of austerity) - by going to gaol."*⁴²⁶ One should ask Gandhi and Gandhians, is it a sin to ask for better living conditions? Is it not satyagraha to ask money for the work? Further, Gandhi accused them: "They went on strike ... with the object of bringing pressure on the Government. If the latter were to use force against them, they, too, would, if they could, use force in return. If it were possible, they would even overthrow the Government and install themselves in power."[427] Was writing thousands of letters, petitions, memorials and articles by Gandhi and his organisations not putting pressure on the Government? Was it without harassment for the Colonial-Government, when Gandhi's supporters from U.K. and India were interfering from abroad?

Satyagraha - Does not Depend on the Number of Followers!

Gandhi often boasted that even a single man is enough for the movement. For instance, in Feb. 1909, he wrote: "All the Indians who fought for two years got a taste of this way of fighting. They realized something of its beauty. It is possible that they may give up fighting now. But even if a majority of Indians give up the fight, that will not mean the end of the movement. *It will go on so long as there is one single person to carry it on.*"[428]

Gandhi, who roared like a lion, saying that a movement does not depend on the number of persons, had to say in despair: "A task that needs a *thousand men cannot be accomplished* by ten, as it were. The struggle is being *prolonged because not enough men join it.*"[429]

He was never sure, how many would follow him. For example, once he wrote: "The active passive resisters who are likely to remain staunch to the last we count as *one hundred*."[430] Somewhere else:

"We trust that those who lack this spirit will not come forward for going to gaol. It is our firm belief that fifty Indians so inclined, *or five or even one, will be enough for winning our demands.*"[431] After seven days, he came up with absolutely new number, that is, "We hope, too, that the male members of the population will realize their own duty in the matter. It is largely in their hands to end the struggle at an earlier stage. *"The larger the number of passive resisters, the quicker the termination of the struggle" is a mathematical formula.*"[432]

In Sept. 1910, the movement was breathing its last. To motivate his followers, Gandhi made wrong promises. He wrote:

> "We hear it being said by many that the Transvaal agitation has no force left. We have repeated, time and again, that so long as at least *one person remains to continue satyagraha*, we may rest confident that *victory will be* ours. That is the only test of satyagraha. ... This support that we are getting should encourage us and strengthen the weak. But at the same time we should like to point out that satyagraha does not require encouragement from others. *It is like a razor's edge*. He who would walk on it does not pause to think of ways of securing help from others."[433]

In the beginning of 1911, Gandhi was daydreaming about the achievements of his satyagraha, and believed that struggle will end soon. He wrote in a letter: "Remember this as an axiomatic truth that *even if a single satyagrahi remains, he will win*. During this struggle many successes have already been achieved. Being idol-worshippers, *we shall recognize our victory only when the Act has been repealed and the colour bar removed.* But for this, the battle is already won."[434]

Oct. 1912, Gokhale asked him for the list of reliable passive protestors. Gandhi wrote *sixty-six names, but admitted that their number might drop to sixteen.* These he called his "army of peace."[435]

In Gandhi's "peace army" educated community, in particular, the South Africa born Indians showed little interest. In order to include them in the struggle, he thought of a clever method, namely, to ask the colonial Government to allow per year, six Indians to enter the colony. The details are given in the following chapter.

Notes and References

[407] Indian Opinion, 11-1-1908.

[408] Indian Opinion, 10-10-1908.

[409] Indian Opinion, 3-10-1908.

[410] Indian Opinion, 3-10-1908.

[411] Indian Opinion, 3-10-1908.

[412] Gandhi M.K. to Gandhi K., Nov. 9, 1908.

[413] Indian Opinion, 6-3-1909.

[414] Indian Opinion, 29-5-1909.

[415] Indian Opinion, 29-5-1909.

[416] Indian Opinion, 3-5-1913.

[417] Indian Opinion, 12-6-1909.

[418] Indian Opinion, 5-6-1909.

[419] Indian Opinion, 5-6-1909.

[420] The Natal Mercury, 23-12-1913.

[421] Indian Opinion, 28-10-1911.

[422] Indian Opinion, 11-2-1914.

[423] Indian Opinion, 11-2-1914.

[424] The Transvaal Leader, 15-7-1914.

[425] Indian Opinion, 4-2-1914.

[426] Indian Opinion, 4-2-1914.

[427] Indian Opinion, 4-2-1914.

[428] Indian Opinion, 13-2-1909. Similar results were reported in: Indian Opinion, 27-2-1909.

[429] Indian Opinion, 29-5-1909.

[430] Indian Opinion, 25-12-1909.

[431] Indian Opinion, 3-5-1913.

[432] Indian Opinion, 10-5-1913.

[433] Indian Opinion, 17-9-1910.

[434] Gandhi M.K to Gandhi N., Jan. 10, 1911.

[435] Fischer L., Gandhi – His life and message for the world, New American Library, New York 1954, p. 43.

The Magic of the "Soul Force" - "Your bonds will be loosened in ... less than 24 Hours"

Until the middle of 1908, Gandhi's politics were mainly for the interest of the traders. It was dominated by the leaders of N.I.C. and B.I.A. The B.I.A. was not comprised of more than a group of traders and the Hamidia Islamic Society. They offered Gandhi their mosque for political propaganda. In the present chapter we shall see:

- How Gandhi changed his strategy to attract the educated people?
- Why he was criticized by his countrymen?
- What he had achieved during the last 2-3 years?

"Devil" Smuts vs. "god" Gandhi – Wanting More and More – Entry for Educated Indians

The traders, who mainly supported Gandhi in the past, were not ready to go to prison again. This forced him to change his political strategy. This time the demands were very limited, namely, "*The fight is for (the rights of) those who hold the £3 Dutch registration certificates,* for those who are outside the Transvaal at present, but are in a position to prove that they are old residents of the Transvaal. It is also *for the sake of the educated Indians.*"[436] Similarly, he had clear-cut idea about the political struggle. He suggested the following steps to disobey the state's law:

"(1) When necessary, we should burn the certificates of voluntary registration.

(2) We must refuse to affix our finger-impressions or signatures (on any documents) or to give our names when asked for these by the police.

(3) We should tender the licence fee, but if the licence is refused, should carry on trade without one."[437]

The number of educated Indians was limited. In order to give boost to the movement, Gandhi made use of the "illiterate's" sentiments. He was determined for the confrontation. In Johannesburg, out of 800 Indian hawkers, 700 had taken out licences. They were suggested either to burn out or to lock up the documents. So that on controlling by the authorities, they are arrested for "illegal" working.[438] On July 28, 1908, Gandhi's son (Harilal Gandhi, who lived in Volksrust and came to Johannesburg) and five more were arrested. Gandhi pleaded them guilty in the court. They were sent to jail for seven days as they refused to pay one pound fine.[439]

Harilal Gandhi was just a pawn on the chess board of his father's "satyagraha." Why he sent his own son to gaol? His answer follows: "... I am afraid I cannot join myself since I am enrolled as an attorney. I therefore thought it right to advise my son to make his rounds as a hawker. I hesitate to ask others to do things which I cannot do myself. I think whatever my son does at my instance can be taken to have been done by me."[440] And further: "It will be a part of Harilal's education to go to gaol for the sake of the country."[441] Before proceeding further, it should be mentioned that poor Harilal could not fulfill his father's desires. He lost his wife, became alcoholic and converted to Islam. In India he publically denounced his father.

Gandhi boasted about his action as follows: "I want every Indian to do what Harilal has done. Harilal is only a child (At that time he was 20 years old). He may have merely deferred to his father's wishes in acting in this manner. It is essential that every Indian should act on his own as Harilal did (at my instance) and I wish everyone would do so."[442]

Gandhi promised to defend the "true Satyagrahis" free of charge.[443] About his way of defending he stated: "When I go to defend those who have been arrested, *I do not, strictly speaking, defend them but only send them to gaol.* If we have acquired real courage, there should be no need for me to present myself in Court."[444] The man who preached truth had the following to say: "I repeat that (1) those who are prepared for imprisonment should go to gaol without depending upon a lawyer or myself. *That is not to say that I go back on my promise of defending Indian satyagrahis arrested in connection with the campaign against the law.*"[445] According to my personal view, there cannot be a bigger contradiction or lie than this statement.

On Aug. 16, 1908, a mass meeting of 3000 Indians was held at Fordsburg Mosque. Gandhi suggested to burn certificates. Then he came with an old trick "oath", namely, reminding the audiences that they had taken vow not to submit to the Asiatic Act. He told them that if he himself takes a certificate:

> "I should call myself *a traitor to my countrymen, a traitor to God, a traitor to my oath.* I shall do no such thing, no matter what suffering may be imposed on you by reason of burning your certificates, but, if you do burn your

certificates, *please bear in mind that you are not to take advantage of the certificates at any time whatsoever until a proper and just and honourable settlement has been arrived at.*"[446]

He continued:

"I would pass the whole of my lifetime in gaol, and I say that in the House of God, in the House of Prayer, and I repeat it that I would far rather pass the whole of my lifetime in gaol and be perfectly happy than see my fellow-countrymen subjected to indignity and I should come out of the gaol. No, gentlemen, *the servant who stands before you this afternoon is not made of that stuff,* and it is because I ask you to suffer everything that may be necessary *than break your oath,* it is because I expect this of my countrymen, that they will be, above all, true to their God, that *I ask you this afternoon to burn all these certificates.*"[447]

Once again, Smuts tried to communicate with Gandhi. Gandhi, Cartwright (a journalist) and Quinn met General Botha, General Smuts, Sir Percy Fitzpatrick, Sir George Farrar, Lindsay, Hosken and Chaplin. After a three hour discussion, the Governmental representative agreed to the following terms:

"1. The Act shall not be applicable to Turkish Mahomedans.

2. Those who can prove that they had resided in the Transvaal for three years before the (Boer) War shall be permitted to enter.

3. For children under sixteen years registration shall not be necessary.

4. When taking out a licence, either a well-formed signature or a thumb-impression shall be given.

5. An appeal can be made to a magistrate (against the decision of the Registrar of Asiatics) and to the Supreme Court against the magistrate's decision.

6. The section relating to intoxicating drinks shall be deleted.

7. The obnoxious law will be retained, but only as a dead letter and it shall not apply to voluntary registrants or to those who may register of their own accord in future.

8. The deficiency in section 21 shall be rectified.

9. Those who have taken out registers under the obnoxious law shall be allowed to apply for new ones."[448]

From the forgoing we see that Smuts and Co. were ready to make compromises. They did whatever possible. With the offer Gandhi went to his men and a meeting was held. The results of the meeting were given to the private Secretary of Smuts as follows:[449]

"I placed before the meeting, for the third time today, the terms that I told them the Government were prepared to offer, and I told them further that these would form an acceptable compromise, if some provision was made for highly educated Indians and ...; but the meeting would not listen to anything short of repeal of the Asiatic Act and the recognition of highly educated Indians under the general clause of the Immigrants' Restriction Act. All I could persuade them to accept was that, the statutory right being recognized, there would be no objection to an administrative discrimination against educated Indians so that only the most highly educated Indians could enter."[450]

Gandhi continued:

"After much difficulty, I was able to persuade the meeting to unanimously agree to the following:

1. Mr. Sorabjee (Shapurji Adajania an educated Indian who entered Transvaal, who entered illegal and claimed his stay on the base of immigration law) to be re-instated, with full residential rights.

2. All prisoners to be discharged.

3. The Asiatic Act to be repealed.

4. A general education test, with discretionary power as to its severity regarding educated Indians.

5. The terms as per (Sir) Percy's notes to be embodied with the necessary changes in the new Bill.

6. Free re-issue of burnt certificates.

7. The essential clauses of the Asiatic Act, in so far as they may be necessary for a proper check over the Asiatic

population and for prevention of fraud, to be re-enacted in the new Bill.

8. The draft Bill to be shown to the Committee of the Association for suggestions as to details."[451]

After dictating Indians' demands he hoped that the Government would accept the conditions and the controversy will be closed.[452]

According to Gandhi's habits, all of sudden, other points were unimportant, but the issue of educated Indians was central. He wrote:

"*Surely then if we are restricting ourselves to the entry of highly educated Indians*, it is we who give up something and not the legislature that will give us a new privilege. It is, therefore, preposterous to say that we are setting forth a new demand. *The other points*, in what has been called the Asiatic Ultimatum, and what I would call the Asiatic submission, *are really not matters of law but of administrative act.* .... All I feel is that for these small matters an otherwise admirable Bill will be wrecked, so far as I can judge. My countrymen will not accept the benefit of the provisions of the new Bill until the wrong I have referred to has been redressed and passive resistance will, therefore, unfortunately, have to go on."[453]

On Aug. 21, 1908, in an interview Gandhi admitted that:

"The Bill, ..., is a vast improvement on the Validating Bill, which would undoubtedly have been a violation of almost all the terms of the compromise. ... It is a most unfortunate thing that the Government has not seen their way to grant the very limited concessions asked for by the Asiatic Conference-namely, *repeal of the Asiatic Amendment Act, and admission of highly educated Indians. The two points are most important for British Indians*, but in my opinion of little importance from the Colonists' standpoint."[454]

Once again the "devil" Smuts and "god" Gandhi were portrayed in the following words:

"If, therefore, the very moderate request of my countrymen is not embodied in the new Bill, I very much fear, though I am very sorry, that the passive resistance will be resumed. General Smuts calls it a state of anarchy, lawlessness, and a declaration of war. We call it a state of suffering, and pray to our Maker, our reliance being entirely on Him. It is indeed a declaration of war on the part of General Smuts against British Indians."[455]

After the bill was passed; on Aug. 23, 1908, a meeting was held in a Mosque. In protest about 525 certificates were consigned to the flames; as the Government neither repealed the bill nor considered the issue of the educated Indians.[456] Gandhi in his speech admitted: "I have no hesitation in making this admission, that the Validation Bill, is a vast improvement on the old Asiatic Act, *much of the irritating clauses have been removed, the great religious objection has been removed, our oath has been preserved, ...*"[457]

Somehow, Gandhi had determined to fight against all. For him it was battle of principles. Once again he attacked Smuts as the Act was not repealed and the status of the highly educated Asiatics was not placed on firm footing.[458] All of sudden the "native" became his playing ball. He stated: "I draw your attention to this fact, that General Smuts himself has told us now and told the world that the natives of South Africa, the Zulus and Bantus, get treated the same as the Europeans, if they possess the same educational qualifications as the Europeans, but the poor Indian and the poor Chinaman cannot do that."[459] In the "Indian Opinion" under the title: "What have we gained through the new bill?", he told the readers that:

> "*The Bill contains almost everything (we wanted). ..... But there are two things which the Bill does not contain. The obnoxious law will be repealed in effect; but it will remain as a dead letter. ....,* what is more important, (the rights of) the educated have not been safeguarded. *I am afraid that there is going to be a long-drawn-out struggle over this issue. It is the duty of the Indian community to put up a fight.*"[460]

Gandhi had still not defined - Who an educated person was? This was done in the end of Aug. 1908, in the following words:

> "In consequence, *only barristers and others of equal* (attainments) will be able to enter the Transvaal. *I do not see that we can do anything more.* What is important is that the educated should not be kept out altogether. As for those with a lower standard of education who may want to come in for business or professional reasons, the section which allows them to come in with a temporary permit

remains. In fact, there is no real difficulty about these persons."⁴⁶¹

In order to restart the movement, he assumed that 2300 persons, who burnt their documents might support. The majority of them were Tamil-speaking. He was sure that in the end, *out of them only 1000 will remain true to their word.*⁴⁶² His plan was to spare the traders and shopkeepers, who should support the struggle with money. In Gandhi's own words the *ways to harass the government* (we have seen earlier than Gandhi criticized the Railway workers for harassing the Government) were:

> "The first is for the hawkers to get arrested by going on their rounds without a licence. Since there can be no question of a hawker's goods being auctioned, he will only be fined. The second is to court arrest and imprisonment by refusing to give thumb-impressions or fingerprints or signatures at the border. .... They (the authorities) have started prosecutions against those who refuse to give thumb-impressions. It is easy therefore to get arrested. Only those who hold genuine permits may, however, enter the Transvaal now. Holders of Dutch passes, etc., must not come in for the present. Educated persons may not come in either - not just yet. If we carry on the fight in this manner, the climax may be reached in October (1908). The end may come even earlier if we pull with all our strength. If not, it may come in October."⁴⁶³

Meanwhile the Government was not passive. It has started punishing people and if they refused to pay a fine, their property was auctioned.[464] Many were sent to jails, mistreated and deported. To support the families of the passive registers and to make propaganda, money was needed. Gandhi was not earning anymore as he had suspended his legal practice. In a meeting it was discussed: From where he was to get money for the rent of office of the Association; to defraying Polak's expenses who was working in India on behalf of the Association; to meet the deficit due to the publication of the "Indian Opinion."[465] On the one hand people were being asked to support the movement, at the same time, Gandhi's loyal fellow, Abdul (Abdool) Gani, Chairman, B.I.A., gave his thumb-impression on his return to Volksrust.[466] When he was questioned in a meeting, he justified as follows: "Being in a hurry to get away, he had given it out of sheer nervousness. He promised not to repeat his mistake and to remain firm in his resistance while urging others to do likewise."[467] In spite of mass propaganda by Gandhi, to protest against the Asiatic Law Amendment Act, only 350 Indians went to jail in Transvaal.[468]

Fight for 6 Educated Indians

On the one hand Gandhi was making too much fuss for the entry of 6 educated Indians per year; on the other hand, against the poor indentured he said in a speech:

> "The better policy would be *to stop indentured labour entirely*; …. If I were an autocrat in Natal, I would fix not even three years, but stop it entirely. *This kind of labour has not done any good whatsoever to the Indians* who have emigrated under those conditions to Natal, *or to the*

Colonies themselves. ... If the Colony persists in that policy, I should admire General Smuts or anyone else using the steamroller (...) and compelling Natal to stop indentured immigration."[469]

In Oct., 1908, he repeated again: "..., *the main duty of Natal Indians in this matter is to start an agitation on a big scale, to adopt satyagraha, if necessary, and bring the system of indenture to an end.*"[470]

In a talk with Gandhi's supporters Cartwright and Hosken, Smuts was ready to give some concession on the issues of the refugees, but he was not ready to consider the right of educated Indians.[471] Gandhi who had suggested a ban on the immigration of indentured servants, wanted to "import" educated Indians. He stated: "The fight now is really *on behalf of the educated Indians.* ... How can the Indian community agree to this wrongful denial of the rights of educated (Asiatics to enter the Colony)?"[472] Smuts tried his best and hence he came up with a compromise. He was ready to accept all conditions expect one. Gandhi flatly refused Smuts' offer. In Gandhi's own words from a speech of July 20, 1908: "*We have been informed* through Mr. Cartwright that the *Government will agree to a settlement if we do not insist on the rights of educated* (Asiatics). But all of you resolved at a previous meeting that you would agitate for the cause of the educated. Your decision is commendable. We certainly cannot agree to the abolition of the rights of educated Asiatics."[473]

Before we proceed further, we need to ask: Why Gandhi insisted on the immigration of educated persons? Considering the fact that in

1911 *only one percent of* 244 million Indians in British Empire were literate in English.[474] Probably his idea was to bring his own lawyer friends from Indian as well as his own family members. Secondly, it was a clever strategy to involve a few of the second generation Indians in S.A. in the movement. Some of them were the sons of rich traders. This is evident from the following statement: "Mr. Dawad Mahomed's son is in England for his studies. Should he not be able to return after completing them? ... Mr. Joseph Royeppen is due to return in a few days. He was born in South Africa but he cannot come in either. How can the Indian community countenance all this?"[475]

In a confidential letter, Gandhi and Co., demanded the entrance of six educated Indians per year.[476] Gandhi's logic was: "*In law, all educated persons should have equal rights. ...* The law should be the same (for all), but it may be administered differentially; that is all that the demand means. *There is thus no difference between this demand and the one that was put forward at the mass* meeting and which was described by General Smuts as an ultimatum (...)."[477]

In an interview with "The Star" Gandhi argued:

> "Before the war, the immigration of Indians was free. After the conclusion of peace, immigration generally was regulated under the Peace Preservation Ordinance, under which new educated Asiatics were allowed to enter the country. The Asiatic Act of 1907 simply provided for registration of those who were entitled to reside in the country, but, according to the admission made by General Smuts, did not regulate immigration. The Immigrants'

Restriction Act replaced the Peace Preservation Ordinance, and laid down a general education test. The Asiatic (Registration) Act was then dishonestly, without even mentioning it, brought in to defraud Indians of their just rights, ..."[478]

Further, Gandhi was of the opinion that the Indian community never accepted the Asiatic Act.[479]

In Aug. 1909, Gandhi interpreted the introduction of educated Indians on an entirely new base, that is, racial equality, which he himself never supported. He accepted that the white race is "better" than others. In the U.K., as Gandhi was accused of coming with a new demand of the immigration of educated Indians, in order to clarify it, on Aug. 5, 1909, he wrote a letter to his supporter, Lord Ampthill as follows:

"I fully realise that the difficulty will be on the question of right. I have given many an anxious night to find out a solution without insisting on the "right", but I have failed because anything short of it, in my humble opinion, implies a record on the Statute-book of the Colony *of racial inferiority*, and this reply to your question is also the reply to Your Lordship's suggestion that, in the enumeration of demands, the status of educated Indians should be replaced by "the occasional admission of the few highly educated Indians", etc. Any such substitution is not possible *because the fight is not that of getting the few educated Indians admitted*, but it is essentially that of having the potential or *theoretical right recognised*."[480]

For Whom Was the Struggle – Violence of the "Non-Violents"

On Oct. 13, 1908, that is, just one day before his trial in a court, he sent a message, stating that *we are fighting for India*. "Those who do not realize this are not servants but *enemies of the motherland*."[481] Gandhi was charged with failing to give his thumb- or finger impression on demand; and for not furnishing his identity. The Magistrate found him guilty; and "sentenced him to pay a fine of £25 or go to jail with hard labour for two months."[482] On Dec. 12, 1908, he was released. He did not lose time to complaint against the rules in gaol.[483]

In the end of 1908, Gandhi had stated that *"This is really a movement on behalf of the traders - especially the hawkers. The latter can also ensure its early success."*[484] Soon, Gandhi ceased to believe not only the traders, but also hawkers. He called them cowards, who needed to be watched by pickets. He suggested: "Pickets should therefore be appointed in every town. They must mount guard outside the Licensing Office and see that no one goes there to take out a licence. To ensure this, the leaders of every community should set themselves up as watchmen. If that is done, hardly anyone would go there to take out a licence."[485]

As a politician, Gandhi was not a man of words but lofty promises. To the British Indians he said that: "..., your bonds will be loosened in eight days according to your Chairman, *but in less than 24 hours according to me.*"[486] How this "wonder" will happen? The answer was very simple: "*I am sure that we shall be free when God stirs their (our opponents') conscience.*"[487]

Balance Sheet of Struggle: Years 1907 and 1908

In the past three years, except deportations and sufferings, nothing was achieved. But for Gandhi, it was a victory. In a speech, which was delivered at the Hamidia Islamic Society, on Dec. 13, 1908, he proudly declared: *"We have won because of the sufferings of our people. A community, 1500 members of which have been to gaol, must certainly be considered to have emerged victorious. That out of a population of 7000 as many as 1500 have been to gaol must surely, I think, be counted as a victory."*[488] The facts were:

- The gap between the shopkeepers and traders had increased. For, the hawkers felt betrayed by shopkeepers and businessmen. Being afraid of them, they were unable to express their grievances in meetings. Gandhi did not publish their protest letters. He wrote: "The hawkers ought to see that they do not envy the traders. They should be satisfied if the traders go to gaol. To say that the traders have ruined them suggests that they think they themselves made a mistake in going to gaol."[489]

- To save their property some traders transferred their business to the name of their wives or whites.[490]

The "Indian Opinion" reported:

- *"...over 2000 Indians have undergone imprisonment, mostly with hard labour.*

- *Hundreds have been deported, only to-return immediately.*

- *Many families have been ruined pecuniarily.*

- *Many Indian merchants have suffered enormous loss.*
- *Some have even closed (down) their businesses.*
- The Chairman of the Association, in order to avoid confiscation of his property by the Government under fines imposed for trading without licences, has accepted sequestration of his estate.
- Some Indians have, no doubt, owing to their weakness accepted the Asiatic Acts, and more are likely to succumb;... "[491]

In May 1909 the B.I.A. was bankrupt.[492]

Continuation of the Struggle in 1909

The Fallen Indians: On Jan 23, 1909, the "Indian Opinion" reported that: "There is no doubt that some Indians have weakened. Many of them have given up the fight. Others, it appears, are about to do so." In order to stop Indians for registration, the *pickets dressed in khaki uniform were posted, who weared bands like soldiers*. Their function was to oppose Pathans, who were loyal to the Government. Pathans saw themselves as Gandhi's and Polak's bullies. They were of the opinion that "Not only does Gandhi always make derogatory remarks about our religion and pass insulting remarks; against our Prophets, but he is ever disturbing the peace (of the land). If the Government cannot remove him and his corps of volunteers from the Colony, we can do that much for the Government with all despatch."[493]

Now, businessmen from Transvaal were asked to support the satyagraha and "to sacrifice their money, as women were sacrificed (in the olden days)."[494] They were suggested to follow the example of Cachalia, who "accepted honourable insolvency for the sake of the community" and was serving a term of three months' imprisonment with hard labour in gaol.[495] Until now, mainly Muslim businessmen had subscribed. Gandhi said that "If the Hindu businessmen display even half as much strength, they can serve the movement."[496]

Out of fears and for family sake some of the British Indians registered themselves. The "Indian Opinion" wrote: "Those who have fallen in this way must not think of bringing down others. They can even inform the Government that they have surrendered owing to their weakness, ... This much they can certainly do. If they do not, it will be assumed that they did not give in out of weakness, but that *they deliberately turned enemies of the motherland.*"[497]

Probably to give impetus to the movement, Gandhi decided to go to gaol. Along with six other persons he was arrested on Feb. 25, 1909. For not producing identification documents they were asked either to pay a fine of fifty pounds for each person or to undergo imprisonment for three months with hard labour. They decided for the latter.[498]

Gandhi's Critics – The Natal Indian Congress

Gandhi was released on May 24, 1909. He delivered a speech at a Mosque in Pretoria.[499] Meanwhile, H.O. Ally had founded the British

Indian Conciliation Committee, with Haji Habib as Chairman and George Godfrey as Secretary.[500] On June 12, 1909, its meeting was held under the auspicious of the Hamidia Islamic Society. The participants were from Standerton, Pretoria, Krugersdorp and Johannesburg. Gandhi attended the meeting as a special invited guest. Hajee Habib said that:

> "In regard to the struggle, Mr. Gandhi had acted hastily at the time of the settlement. *Had he not done so and had insisted on having everything in writing from General Smuts, the community would not have had to go through so much suffering.* However, (he said) they were concerned at present with bringing about the end of the struggle itself. … It was not proper to call those who refused to go to gaol blacklegs. …. *Real satyagraha, it might be claimed, was offered by Mir Alam alone. He declined even to show his permit and had been deported for that.* "Indian Opinion" very often published tendentious articles and reports which, he thought, was not quite proper. … He also believed that it was necessary to send a deputation to Europe."[501]

H.O. Ally and Abdool Ganie "pointed out that, if the demands were not accepted by the Government, the question of people not going to gaol would not arise. Their duty was to extend as much support as possible to those who went to gaol."[502]

Second Unsuccessful Deputation to U.K.

J.C. Smuts and other white politicians decided to abolish the colonies and establish a country, the Union of South Africa. In this connection a meeting was planned in the U.K. It was evident that there cannot be a new State without the support of the Imperial Government. Gandhi thought to put pressure on the local politicians, through the Imperial Government. In this context, on June 16, 1909, a meeting was held in Johannesburg. Gandhi told that: "The European Committee that has been formed in the Transvaal, in order to sympathise with us and to help us in every legitimate way, has also advised that ... a deputation should proceed to England."[503]

For his "satyagraha" many had lost their existences, and Gandhi with his followers had written thousands of pages; thus is it surprising to read the following argument for the need of a new deputation to England: *"Our struggle is not properly understood either in England or in India. If it can be properly explained in both the countries, that by itself will surely mean much. It will lead to increased help from both countries, and to that extent the duration of the struggle may be shortened."*[504]

On June 16, 1909, in a resolution, in a mass meeting of the Transvaal British Indians, the B.I.A. proposed A.M. Cachalia, H. Habib, V.A. Chettiar, and M.K. Gandhi, as members of a deputation. N.A. Cama, N.G. Naidoo, E.S. Coovadia and H.S.L. Polak (Assistant Sec. B.I.A.), as members of the deputation for India.[505] The traders of Natal under the auspicious of N.I.C. sent their own deputation to England.[506] As most of the leaders of the B.I.A. were arrested, Gandhi remained the only person to represent the Association. He stated that "..., it is the opinion of all our European friends that I should go; the community desires it; the Committee in England is of the same opinion. I am therefore going along with Mr. Hajee Habib."[507]

Gandhi and H. Habib, on June 21, 1909, left for England.[508] They reached in Southampton on July 10, 1909, and were interviewed by "Reuter."[509] They explained that the demands of the deputation are as follow: "(1) Repeal of Act 2 of 1907 and (2) The status of highly educated Indians."[510] Whereas: "The Transvaal Government alleges that these two points are as good as granted, because - (1) Act 2 of 1907 is to be treated as a dead letter, and (2) Highly educated Indians can receive temporary permits to be indefinitely prolonged under a clause of the new Asiatic Bill."[511] Gandhi insisted:

> "If the Transvaal Government are willing to admit highly educated Indians, they might as well admit them under the immigration law; unless the Government intend to insult the whole Indian people, it must be a matter of indifference to them whether educated Indians are admitted under the Asiatic Act or the Immigration Act; to the Indians it is a vital principle. The manner of admission is everything to them."[512]

In the U.K. Gandhi met many influential persons who promised to help. At the same time, behind the back, he criticized them. He wrote: "The more experience I have of meeting so-called big men or even men who are really great, the more disgusted I feel after every such meeting. All such efforts are no better than pounding chaff. Everyone appears preoccupied with his own affairs. Those who occupy positions of power show little inclination to do justice. Their only concern is to hold on to their positions."[513]

Contrary to the first deputation in 1906, this time, Gandhi was getting bored in England. He was not getting information from the Imperial Government, which was dealing with Botha and Smuts. He wrote:

> "Lord Crewe has written to say that he has no further information to give "for the present", and that something will be known after General Smuts has had a discussion with the other members of his Cabinet. There is no information as to what General Smuts will propose to the Cabinet. If the proposal follows Lord Crewe's cable, that will mean our demand. If he proposes what is in his mind, that will mean the repeal of the Act and admission of a limited number of educated men as a matter of favour but on a permanent basis. If it is this latter proposal which he is thinking of presenting for consideration, we can be sure it will lead to nothing."[514]

As usual, then followed his irrational statement: "*If we have failed* to gain our demands so far, *it is because we have not employed that means, our soul-force*, in full measure."[515]

Smuts promised to meet Gandhi's men, but left U.K. without meeting them. He gave an interview to "Reuter", which reads:

> "I hope it is in a fair way to disappear from the horizon of Transvaal politics. The vast majority of Transvaal Indians are sick to death of the agitation carried on by some of their

extreme representatives, and have quietly submitted to the law. I have had repeated conversations with Lord Crewe and other important leaders interested in this matter, and I think it will be possible now to find a solution of this vexed question which all reasonable men will consider right and fair."[516]

One is surprised to read that even in the U.K., on the issue of the educated Indians, Gandhi felt misunderstood. One of the reasons could be that being a lawyer, he was able to interpret the laws far better than a "normal" reader. He wrote:

"If, ..., the Act is now repealed and permanent permits for six men are offered, *that will give further impetus to the fight.* Its real nature will come to be better understood. *Everyone will then realize that we have been fighting not for (the admission of) a particular number (of educated men), but for India's honour* (emphasis in original). *There must be legal equality with the whites; it will not matter then if, in practice*, not even a single Indian is able to get in. .... *It is not a fight on behalf of the educated or the highly educated, but for India's honour, for our self-respect,* for the fulfilment of our pledge."[517]

In England, Gandhi was still waiting to meet Crewe. On Sept. 11, 1909, he wrote: "We are just where we were. ... There has been no invitation from Lord Crewe so far."[518] Crewe was diplomatic enough to let Gandhi wait and deal with Smuts. After the meeting was over and Smuts left for Pretoria, Gandhi got an appointment on Sept. 16, 1909.[519]

After Smuts left, Gandhi and H. Habib met Lord Crewe. About the interview with Crewe, Gandhi wrote: "From what Lord Crewe said, I imagine that the negotiations still continue. I think he admits that the amendment that I have suggested is very reasonable and that he would press it upon General Smuts. I do not know what should now be done in the circumstances."[520] During the interview, Crewe told that Smuts is afraid that Indians will come with new demands. Gandhi was ready to give in written that it will not happen. If his countrymen do so, he will start passive resistance against them. Crewe said that he will discuss the question with Smuts. Gandhi suggested sending a cable; but the latter preferred to send a dispatch.[521] Gandhi informed to Ampthill: "He (Crewe) has promised to cable to General Smuts the result of our interview, and press upon him acceptance of the amendment submitted by me through you."[522] About a week had passed. Crewe did not informed Gandhi about Smuts' reaction. Gandhi noted: "There is no reason to believe that General Smuts will hurry to reply that he accepts Lord Crewe's advice. But of this I am sure, that, if General Smuts does not accept the suggestion, the fault will be entirely ours."[523] On Oct. 19, 1909, in a letter to the Colonial Secretary, Gandhi wanted to know about the results of negotiation between Crewe and Smuts. The latter stated:

> "I may add that a cablegram received from Johannesburg states that to a newspaper reporter Mr. Smuts said that he was waiting for a reply from the Earl of Crewe before he made any public statement regarding his proposals on the question. This cablegram adds to our difficulty as to the course we should adopt, so long as we are uniformed as to

the action which His Lordship proposed to take when the interview of the 16th ultimo was granted."

After waiting for weeks and without any achievement, Gandhi decided to leave on Nov. 13, 1909.[524] However before that on Nov. 3, 1909, he got a letter from Francis G.S. Hopwood, Colonial Office. In part it reads:

> "I am to inform you that the proposals in question were those put before you by His Lordship on the 16th of September as having been made by Mr. Smuts, viz., the repeal of Act 2 of 1907 and the admission of six educated Asiatics each year on certificates of permanent right of residence, which would involve, in your own view, a real step in advance and would, so far as their practical effect is concerned, provide a solution of the present difficulty. They were not, nor were they connected with, those made by yourself, and involving a theoretical claim for which His Lordship is not able to hold out any hope of obtaining recognition."[525]

And further:

> "Indeed, at the interview on the 16th of September, His Lordship explained to you that Mr. *Smuts was unable to accept the claim that Asiatics should be placed in a position of equality with Europeans in respect of right of entry of otherwise.* His Lordship cannot, therefore, admit that at the interview he undertook, as stated by you, to place your proposal before Mr. Smuts for his acceptance. His Lordship understood you to desire that he should

telegraph to the Transvaal Government that, though you admitted the practical advance involved in Mr. Smuts' suggestions, yet you could not consent to abandon your claim for theoretical equality, and this has been done."[526]

A disappointed Gandhi wrote back as follows:

"It is a matter for very deep regret that the Earl of Crewe is unable to hold out any hopes of obtaining recognition of theoretical equality as to immigration such as is claimed by British Indians in the Transvaal, and as has hitherto been accepted throughout the Colonies, and which alone, it is respectfully submitted, can justify the holding together of different peoples of the world under the same sovereignty."[527]

Before leaving, on Nov. 9, 1909, Gandhi gave an interview to a representative of Reuter's Agency. He "expressed disappointment at the failure of negotiations with Mr. Smuts. He paid a tribute to the efforts of Lord Crewe to effect a settlement of the Asiatic question with the Transvaal Government, but he said that the concessions which had been made did not touch the vital principle of legal equality."[528] After returning back, Gandhi stated that through Lord Ampthill we made clear that by law Indians *must be provided with equal rights of entry to all states*; and Governor be empowered to regulate the number of immigrants belonging to any community. General Smuts is "prepared to give permits of permanent residence to Indians, and also to repeal the obnoxious Act." But he is not willing to grant equal rights to white and coloured.[529]

What we see from the forgoing is that the rich Bombay Muslim community turned its back from Gandhi and his "satyagraha." He had no other choice but to find new partners for his "experiment" of satyagraha. His next "experimental objects" were indentured and colonial born Indians. The persons either degraded or neglected by him. The persons, who were branded by him "the cause of trouble." At the same time he needed people who should financially support the movement. This he achieved successfully as we shall see in the following chapters.

Notes and References

[436] Indian Opinion, 4-7-1908.

[437] Indian Opinion, 4-7-1908.

[438] Indian Opinion, 25-7-1908.

[439] The Transvaal Leader, 29-7-1908.

[440] Indian Opinion, 8-8-1908.

[441] Indian Opinion, 8-8-1908.

[442] Indian Opinion, 8-8-1908.

[443] Indian Opinion, 4-7-1908.

[444] Indian Opinion, 8-8-1908.

[445] Indian Opinion, 8-8-1908.

[446] Indian Opinion, 22-8-1908.

[447] Indian Opinion, 22-8-1908.

[448] Indian Opinion, 22-8-1908.

[449] Gandhi M.K. to Lane E.F.C., Aug. 20, 1908.

[450] Gandhi M.K. to Lane E.F.C., Aug. 20, 1908.

[451] Gandhi M.K. to Lane E.F.C., Aug. 20, 1908.

[452] Gandhi M.K. to Lane E.F.C., Aug. 20, 1908.

[453] Indian Opinion, 29-8-1908.

[454] The Transvaal Leader, 22-8-1908.

[455] The Transvaal Leader, 22-8-1908.

[456] Indian Opinion, 29-8-1908; The Transvaal Leader, 24-8-1908.

[457] Indian Opinion, 29-8-1908; The Transvaal Leader, 24-8-1908.

[458] Indian Opinion, 29-8-1908; The Transvaal Leader, 24-8-1908.

[459] Indian Opinion, 29-8-1908; The Transvaal Leader, 24-8-1908.

[460] Indian Opinion, 29-8-1908.

[461] Indian Opinion, 29-8-1908.

[462] Indian Opinion, 5-9-1908.

[463] Indian Opinion, 5-9-1908.

[464] Indian Opinion, 5-9-1908.

[465] C.W.M.G. 9, 1908-1909, p. 115.

[466] Indian Opinion, 12-9-1908.

[467] Indian Opinion, 19-9-1908.

[468] Mia E.I. to Sec. of State for the Colonies, Sept. 9, 1908.

[469] The Transvaal Leader, 21-8-1908.

[470] Indian Opinion, 3-10-1908.

[471] Indian Opinion, 18-7-1908.

[472] Indian Opinion, 18-7-1908.

[473] Indian Opinion, 25-7-1908.

[474] Copley A., Gandhi against the tide, Basil Blackwell Inc., Cambridge 1989, p. 39.

[475] Indian Opinion, 18-7-1908.

[476] C.W.M.G. 9, 1908-1909, p. 162.

[477] Indian Opinion, 26-9-1908.

[478] The Star, 17-9-1908.

[479] The Star, 17-9-1908.

[480] Gandhi M.K. to Ampthill L., Aug. 5, 1909.

[481] Indian Opinion, 17-10-1908.

[482] Indian Opinion, 17-10-1908.

[483] Indian Opinion, 19-12-1908.

[484] Indian Opinion, 26-9-1908.

[485] Indian Opinion, 26-9-1908.

[486] Indian Opinion, 19-12-1908.

[487] Indian Opinion, 19-12-1908.

[488] Indian Opinion, 19-12-1908.

[489] Indian Opinion, 9-1-1909.

[490] Indian Opinion, 9-1-1909.

[491] Indian Opinion, 30-1-1909.

[492] Indian Opinion, 29-5-1909.

[493] Indian Opinion, 23-1-1909.

[494] Indian Opinion, 23-1-1909.

[495] Indian Opinion, 6-2-1909.

[496] Indian Opinion, 6-2-1909.

[497] Indian Opinion, 13-2-1909.

[498] Indian Opinion, 27-2-1909.

[499] Indian Opinion, 29-5-1909.

[500] Sanghavi N., The agony of arrival - Gandhi, the South Africa years, Rupa Co., New Delhi 2006, online version, pp. unknown.

[501] Indian Opinion, 12-6-1909.

[502] Indian Opinion, 12-6-1909.

[503] Indian Opinion, 19-6-1909.

[504] Indian Opinion, 19-6-1909.

[505] Indian Opinion, 19-6-1909.

[506] The members of the "Natal deputation" were: Abdul Caadir, Anglia, Bhayat and Badat. Gandhi prepared a statement for them. Gandhi M.K. to Polak H.S.L., August 6, 1909. On Aug. 6, 1909, Gandhi wrote that the delegates will not achieve much, because: A) The delegates reached too late to do lobby work. B) Being holidays important supporters like Justice Ameer Ali are out of station. C) The issue which they raise is old. Indian Opinion, 4-9-1909. They were

told to restrict their representations to the following grievances: "The Dealers' Licenses Act, 18 of 1897; The Indentured Immigration Law of 1895; and the policy with reference to the Education of Indian children." C.W.M.G. 10, 1909-1910, p. 17. The out come of this deputation is not known.

[507] Indian Opinion, 26-6-1909.

[508] Indian Opinion, 31-7-1909.

[509] Indian Opinion, 7-8-1909.

[510] C.W.M.G. 9, 1908-1909, pp. 411-423.

[511] Indian Opinion, 21-8-1909.

[512] C.W.M.G. 9, 1908-1909, pp. 411-423.

[513] Indian Opinion, 21-8-1909.

[514] Indian Opinion, 6-11-1909.

[515] Indian Opinion, 6-11-1909.

[516] Gandhi M.K. to Ali A., Aug. 30, 1909.

[517] Indian Opinion, 2-10-1909.

[518] Indian Opinion, 9-10-1909.

[519] Gandhi M.K. to Ampthill L., Sept. 13, 1909.

[520] Gandhi M.K. to Ampthill L., Aug. 10, 1909.

[521] C.W.M.G. 10, 1909-1910, pp. 88-91.

[522] Gandhi M.K. to Ampthill L., Sept.16, 1909.

[523] Indian Opinion, 23-10-1909.

[524] Gandhi M.K. to Ampthill L., Oct. 29, 1909.

[525] Hopwood F.G.S. to Gandhi M.K., Nov. 3, 1909.

[526] Hopwood F.G.S. to Gandhi M.K., Nov. 3, 1909.

[527] Gandhi M.K. to Under Sec. Colonies, Nov. 6, 1909.

[528] Indian Opinion, 13-11-1909.

[529] Indian Opinion, 18-12-1909 and 25-12-1909.

Indians in the Union of South Africa – Gandhi's Opportunistic Approach

In the beginning of 1910, Gandhi's satyagraha was breathing its last. He needed reliable persons who were prepared to *"fight unto death."*[530] The contrast was happening. Many left Natal and were willing to cooperate with the officials.[531] He praised the Chinese, who had roused, and criticized Indians for sinking into lethargy.[532] He violently attacked his countrymen, who had returned from India, for loosing "sense of shame" as in Transvaal they had signed the documents. They needed to be saved. Like a missionary, he told his disciples that *"It will be a matter of rejoicing if even one Indian is saved...."*[533]

From the past Gandhi had learnt that:

(a) He cannot expect much from the Imperial Government.

(b) Traders were trying to establish their own lobby.

(c) For future work he needs money from sources other than traders in South Africa.

(d) He requires involving workers for the success of his political ideas.

(e) At the same time he needed to consider the changing local politics due to the formation of the Union of South Africa.

Indians in the Union of South Africa

Meanwhile the internal politics in South Africa was changing rapidly. According to the "Indian Opinion" of June 25, 1910: "So far, there were the Het Volk, the Union and the Bond parties in the Transvaal, the Orange Colony and the Cape Colony, respectively. Efforts are now being made by Mr. Botha and his friends to amalgamate the three under the name of the South Africa Party. The Progressive Party has been renamed the Unionist Party."[534]

Lord Galdstone became the Governor General of the Union of South Africa. Cachalia, Chairman B.I.A. requested him to meet a deputation of the Association. He declined, as in the past results were not positive.[535]

Before 1910 different colonies had their own rules and regulations. They were still in force. According to the "Indian Opinion": "The Transvaal continues its persecution of passive resisters. The Orange Free State keeps her gates closed against them. Silently but surely an agitation against Indians is being fostered at the Cape and the Natal licensing laws, in spite of the recently made amendment, still remain a standing menace to Indian merchants and traders."[536]

Gandhi informed his readers that before the elections are over General Botha would not take decision as he depends on others.[537] In Nov. 1910, they were going to the celebration for the foundation of the South Africa Union. Gandhi and his followers were not in the mood of a party. They sent the following telegram to General Botha: "If the struggle does not end in November, we must observe mourning."[538] A new state means the making of new laws. Gandhi protested as follows: "I learn that the Colonial Secretary will early in the session bring in a Bill which, in addition to modifying the existing Transvaal conditions, will, in a considerable degree, aim at the consolidation of the immigration laws of the Provinces of the Union."[539]

Smuts–Gandhi Correspondence and Gandhi's Role in the Union of South Africa

In March, 1910, a new immigration bill came out. "Indian Opinion" reported that it had the following:

> "(1) The Asiatic Act 2 of 1907 is to be repealed, save in so far as it protects the rights of minors.
>
> (2) Act 36 of 1908 is not to be repealed.
>
> (3) It seems, but it is not clear, that those who pass the language test can enter the Transvaal and not be liable to registration. (If this is so, it will stop passive resistance.)
>
> (4) The wives and minor children of domiciled Asiatics do not seem to be protected.
>
> (5) The granting of certificates of domicile to Asiatics in Natal and the Cape is at the discretion of the authorities.
>
> (6) The education test is of so drastic a character that not a single Indian may be allowed to enter the Union.
>
> (7) No facilities seem to exist for the protection of those who may be wrongly prohibited by an officer."[540]

Gandhi stated that he will withdraw the campaign: "If the Bill permits educated Indians to come in as fresh immigrants without requiring them to register, ..."[541] He was least interested about the educated Indians in Natal and Cape, who was going to loose by this compromise. They were told: "If the Bill passes into law, educated persons will not be able to come in as freely as they have been doing, and the rights of those who are already there will not be protected. Natal and the Cape need to take immediate steps."[542]

Gandhi was tired of the struggle and was wishing its end. On March 2, 1911, he wrote to Lane, Smuts' Sec.:

"... it seems to me that educated Asiatics who pass the test prescribed by the immigration officers will be able to enter and remain in the Transvaal, without being liable to take out registration under Act 36 of 1908. And, if such be the meaning of the first section of the Bill, the Transvaal struggle can happily end. But I venture to submit that such meaning should be clearly and unequivocally brought out in the Bill itself. May I also know under what clause of the Bill the wives of registered Asiatics are protected?"

After consulting with other lawyers, Gandhi came to know that he misunderstood some parts of the new bill. On March 4, 1911, he sent a telegram to the private Sec. to Minister of Interior. He told that according to the Council of his group to unless special mention is made in the bill regarding the education test these persons under certain circumstances will be prohibited; the wives and minors of the lawfully living Indians in Transvaal are not protected under common law. Gandhi promised to cease the passive resistance, if General Smuts would give assurance to alter these points in the bill. Also he sent a long letter to Smuts' private secretary regarding these points.[543] The matter was discussed with his friends J.J. Doke and H.S.L. Polak in private letters.[544-545]

Gandhi had stressed again and again that his struggle for educated Indians and the demand for the rights of wives and minor children is limited to Transvaal. If the demands are accepted the passive resistance will cease.[546] Botha and Smuts agreed to it under certain conditions. Soon he changed his mind. He reasoned in a letter to the missionary J.J. Doke saying that according to Ritch's telegraphs, the new Asiatic Ordinance will not apply to the Orange Free State and the colour bar will remain in the Immigration Law. Similarly educated Indians will not be allowed to enter into the state.[547] Smuts' compromise to let enter 12 educated Indians per year for the Union was called by Gandhi as absurd.[548] At the same time he did not lose time to roar about the "victory" of his satyagraha after some parliamentary opposed Smuts and asked to fulfill Indians' demand as follows:

> "For the present, the important point to note is that our demands have been met, more or less. Sir Percy Fitzpatrick, who at one time used to hold out threats against us, now says that General Smuts would do well to satisfy the Asiatics. The gentleman is afraid lest satyagraha should spread to the whole of South Africa. Mr. Duncan, the man who designed the obnoxious Act, now advocates its repeal, and says he will be happy if the proposed law sees the end of the satyagraha campaign. *We do not find a single member who has spoken against satyagraha. Can there be a triumph greater than this?*"[549]

Gandhi's optimism was due to the fact that it had been revealed to him that the Imperial Government would support the Indians' demand of educated Indians.⁵⁵⁰ On March 22, 1911, he sent a telegram to the Private Secretary to General Smuts and thanked him for his promise of relief regarding minors and wives. He reminded that the Secretary should draw General Smuts' attention to the General Botha's dispatch of 20th December, in which he assured to Lord Crewe that a limited number of educated Indians should be permitted to settle in the provinces of the Union. On the same day, that is, March 22, 1911, he informed L.W. Ritch via a telegram that Smuts attitude towards the question of minor and women is positive, but he considers that the attitude of Free State is quite unfair. The Asiatics never claimed to enter the state. This makes it quite difficult to reach a solution. Ritch was told that Smuts' offer is unacceptable.[551]

Gandhi was asked to meet Smuts. After the meeting he wrote about the conversation as follows: "I am giving you everything. I could have done so by regulation but now I am protecting wives and children in the Bill. I do not know why, but I know that everybody suspects me. I am also recognising domicile. But you are very unreasonable (about the issue of educated Indians). *Your point is absolutely new.*"[552]

Apart from that he mentioned his difficulty to convince members of the Orange Free State. *Gandhi on his side insisted that the law still have racial bar. He is fighting against it since five years.* According to new Asiatic Bill: "the educated Asiatics will be still prohibited from owning fixed property and from trading." Smuts told Gandhi that the interview notes are not for publication, but they are to be destroyed.[553]

After the talk, Gandhi wrote to E.F.C. Lane stating that General Smuts wants evidence for domicile, marriage and parental relationships, and they should be furnished to the Immigration Officer. According to my experience, it will lead to favouritism, corruption and bribery. Further, the delicate questions of marital and parental relationship should be left in the hand of the courts, not an administrative officer.[554] For Gandhi it was a matter of principles. He stated:

> "....There is little probability that a single British Indian of education will seek to enter the Free State, since the Indian population there is too sparse to support an Indian barrister or doctor. *Unless this racial bar is removed, passive resistance, I fear, must continue*, and I do not know but that its extent may be increased by the British Indians of Natal and the Cape joining it."[555]

Extending the Field of Struggle – Gandhi's-Smuts' Problems

Gandhi's follower L.W. Ritch prepared ground for agitation in Cape. Gandhi went there and delivered a speech on March 30, 1911. Once again he stressed on the entrance of educated Indians in the Free State. He stated: "We in the Transvaal and in Natal are firm in our opposition to it, and I am glad to know that the Cape Indians have also joined us."[556] Privately, to a relative he informed: "I do not feel that this time, too, we will be able to arrive at a settlement. Yesterday, I had a long talk with Smuts. He says that it can be done only next year. In the meantime, he does not want to arrest anyone.

How can we sit quietly the way he wants us to. I wrote to him a strong letter yesterday."[557]

On April 7, 1911, Gandhi wrote to L.W. Ritch:

"I told him (Lane) that I could not rest so long as women were taxed, *Indians could not hold landed property in the Transvaal*, & c. I told him pretty plainly that *if the Gold Law prosecutions in Klerksdorp were proceeded with, I would not hesitate to advise & raise passive resistance.* He tells me quite confidentially that the alternative solution will be accepted though he adds that J.C.S. is still in treaty with the Free Staters."[558]

A day later he wrote to Ritch that according to Botha's amendment, in the Free State there will be no change in laws.[559]

Smuts needed time to deal with his opponents from the Orange Free State. He requested Gandhi to postpone satyagraha. However, Gandhi had his own problems. On April 19, 1911, he told Smuts:

"If the question is not settled during the present session, the prospect of passive resisters remaining totally inactive is too appalling to contemplate. *There are men on Tolstoy Farm with their families who are pecuniarily ruined. There are others outside in the same position. If they are not to court arrest or are to avoid it, their movements must be hampered.* .... Some who are traders cannot trade because they will not produce their registration certificate(s) so long as the struggle lasts. I should have nothing to say about all this misery if we were conducting an active campaign. ... As you know *the campaign has cost us heavily*, and our monthly expenditure for supporting families, &c., is naturally great."[560]

Smuts felt sorry for Gandhi and wrote:

> "My advisers consider that your suggestion cannot be carried out. How can we keep out whites from the other provinces (?). Parliament will not pass such a bill. I therefore want to pass my bill which I like and which I consider is fair. I shall try but I may fail to pass it during this session. All the members want to go away. And the Free State members are still opposed to admitting any Asiatic. I think I can beat them in the Assembly but the Senate will throw out the Bill. I therefore want to pass the measure during the next session, if I cannot carry it this session. But meanwhile I want peace."[561]

He continued: "I do not want to harass your people. You know that. And I do not want you to bring people from India and elsewhere to fight. I want to help the Imperial Government & they want to help me."[562] Then he flattered Gandhi:

> "I know you to be high-minded & honest. I have told Imp. Govt. so. You have a right to fight in your own way. But this country is the Kaffirs'. We whites are a handful. .... I have read out your pamphlet. You are a simple-living & frugal race. In many respects more intelligent than we are. You belong (to) a civilization that is thousands of years old. Ours, as you say, is but an experiment."[563]

Smuts asked Gandhi to give him more time to solve political problems. Gandhi was not in such a mood. On April 20, 1911, he sent a cable to Lane and told that N.I.C. and B.I.A. refuse the suspension of the agitation as suggested by Smuts. Next day, that is, on April 21, 1911, he wrote to L.W. Ritch, who was in Cape Town as follows: "Lane showed me the confidential correspondence with the G(overnor-) G(eneral), showing that the bill could not possibly be brought up this session whether we stopped passive resistance or not. I thought therefore that we could suspend p(assive) r(esistance) if certain assurances were given. .... We have a chance of getting loaves & fishes for the passive resisters and I am trying."[564]

In a speech at Komberley, Gandhi informed the audience: "He had in his possession a letter from General Smuts which stated that the legitimate demands of the Indian community would be granted during the next session of Parliament."[565]

In a meeting on May 2, 1911, Gandhi was accompanied by his loyal workers, Ritch and Kallenbach. He explained the correspondence with the Government and advised the Indian community to accept the proposals made therein. "Abdul Rahman of Potchefstroom moved that the proposal as to suspension of passive resistance be accepted conditional upon fulfilment of the pledges given by General Smuts."[566] On May 23, 1911, in an interview with "Reuter", Gandhi told:

> "That the settlement contemplated the introduction next session of legislation repealing the Asiatic Act of 1907 and restoring legal equality as regards immigration. As a setoff to the suspension of the passive resistance the

Government recognizes the right of the passive resisters, numbering ten, to enter the Transvaal by virtue of their education, and reinstates the passive resisters who formerly had rights of residence, the Government also releasing the imprisoned passive resisters immediately...."[567]

While Gandhi was interested to finish the controversy, the members of the N.I.C. came up with new demands regarding the number of educated Indians. On May 15, 1911, D. Mahomed, D. Osman and M.C. Anglia, in the capacity of President and joint secretaries sent a memorial to the authorities on the entry of educated Indians. They argued that twelve Indians for the whole Union not enough, if we consider the fact that Transvaal with Indian population of not more than 8000 will take six. It is unfair for Cape and Natal with 15000 and 150000 Indians respectively. They wrote: "In proportion to the numbers, there should be for the whole of the Union 72 new Indian immigrants of culture, but your Memorialists would be satisfied if it were understood that 50 British Indians of culture in any one year would be allowed to enter under any education test that might be proposed."[568]

The Provisional Settlement

By the end of May 1911, Gandhi wrote an article and informed the readers that during a deputation to London, in 1909, two demands were stressed: (a) Repeal of Asiatic Act of 2 of 1907 and (b) "legal equality for immigrants to the Transvaal, ..., to the guarantee that at least six educated Asiatics in any one year should be able to immigrate to the Transvaal under any test that might be provided in the law...."[569] To show that Smuts was trapped, Gandhi cynically wrote:

> "General Smuts as a responsible Minister with a Parliamentary majority behind him has bound his Government to introduce the necessary legislation. If the Parliament does not accept it, it will amount to a vote of no-confidence entailing the resignation of the Ministry of which he is perhaps the most important member. But we are free to admit that General Smuts will not take any such heroic steps over an Asiatic question. Nevertheless the remote contingency of the Parliament rejecting his measure could not be allowed to stand in the way of our accepting the olive branch. Our quarrel hitherto was with General Smuts. He was the stumbling-block in the way of our reaching the goal. He has now softened his heart and is pledged to concede what only a few months ago he declared he would on no account give."[570]

As we have seen above, in South Africa Gandhi was talking big, but to his Indian friend G.A. Natesan, he wrote:

> "But we are by no means yet out of the wood. General Smuts has to translate his promises into legislation. This, however, there is little doubt, will be done unless General Smuts has no regard whatsoever for his reputation. The danger therefore lies not in the likelihood of his breaking his promise but in his passing other legislation affecting

adversely the position of domiciled Indians. His actions, therefore, will have to be closely scrutinized."[571]

The New Immigration Bill and Protest by the Indian Community

At last the promised bill came for the first reading in the Parliament. After getting a copy and reading it, on Feb. 1, 1912, Gandhi sent a telegram to the Private Secretary to Minister of Interior and complained about its drawbacks. He wrote that:

> "It does not quite fulfil the promise made by General Smuts. General Smuts has undertaken not to disturb the existing legal status throughout South Africa in any general bill designed to meet passive resisters. The existing legal position is among other things that, at any rate at the Cape and the Transvaal, domicile and the rights of minor children and wives of non-prohibited immigrants are dependent on a decision of the highest tribunal of justice; that British Indians of the Transvaal passing the ordinary simple education test can easily enter the Cape or Natal; and that Indians of Natal have until lately received certificates of domicile as a matter of right upon proving domicile."[572]

And further:

> "Under the New Bill the Immigration Officer constitutes the highest court of justice to consider the rights of domiciled Asiatics and their wives and children; educated Indians of the Transvaal have to pass the stiffer test under the new Bill on entering the Cape or Natal and the Natal Indians will

be unable to demand certificates of domicile as a matter of right. Now these are new disabilities which passive resisters cannot be expected to accept. ... There still remain general objections by Natal and the Cape."[573]

In Cape Town, on Feb. 4, 1912, the Cape British Indian Union held a meeting. It's President, E. Nordien and other speakers, disapproved the Bill. The Anglo-British Indian community asked the President and Secretary to send a petition to the Parliament to bring out the modification of the Bill.[574] The N.I.C. did the same.[575] Somewhat in hard tone, "Indian Opinion" wrote:

> "General Botha's declaration made in England, and repeated elsewhere: that the Union Government do not desire to molest the resident Asiatic population of South Africa, will be falsified. It is more an Asiatic Expulsion Bill than an Immigration Consolidation Bill, as its authors have entitled it. The rights of residence of domiciled Asiatics and those of their wives and children are very seriously threatened, and the movement of educated Asiatics as between Natal and the Cape as also the Transvaal on the one hand and the Cape and Natal on the other, is to be considerably restricted by the new Bill. .... *Moreover Natal and the Cape have a special grievance in that educated Indians of the status of clerks and assistants will be practically prohibited immigrants under the arbitrary education test now proposed.*"[576]

On Feb. 24, 1912, Gandhi wrote to Lane that according to the Gandhi's Counsel's opinion, the bill will curtail the regal rights of Transvaal Indians. He continued:

> "It may be that proof of domicile will be required of Transvaal Indians before they can bring their wives or children, although they may be duly registered, and apart from proof of registration. I am sure such is not General Smuts' intention. The matter should, in my opinion, be placed absolutely beyond doubt." He hoped that the defects will be remedied soon. After the second reading of the bill, Gandhi wrote to Lane: "General Smuts' speech ... leaves, I fear, the question of interprovincial migration in a somewhat unsatisfactory state. .... As I have already remarked, this will not satisfy passive resisters. I therefore, hope that the measure will be so amended as to leave the rights of Asiatics residing in the other provinces to enter Natal and the Cape in *status quo ante.*"[577]

By the end of July 1912, "Indian Opinion" wrote that Gandhi corresponded with the Union Government. According to "Indian Opinion":

> "Meanwhile, six educated British Indians will be permitted to enter the Transvaal Province as if the legislation had already been passed. ..... But there can be no peace so long as wives, recognized by Indian laws, are turned away, the Gold law and the Townships Act are administered so as to bring virtual ruin to Indian merchants, residents of long standing are being forced out of Locations pointed out

to them, residential title-deeds are disregarded, impossible proofs demanded as to marriages or domicile, and trade made well-nigh impracticable by a tyrannical administration of licensing legislation."[578]

It was a signal to continue the struggle. However, before that G.K. Gokhale, Gandhi's mentor came to South Africa (detail below). Though he was a "private" visitor, later Gandhi often used his name for political purpose as we shall see in the following chapters.

A New Turn – G.K. Gokhale in South Africa

Gopal Krishan Gokhale, who belonged to the so-called, moderate members of the Indian National Congress, was one of the influential Indian politicians. He supported Gandhi with money (detail later). Gandhi had spent some days with him in India, before he returned to South Africa. On Oct. 30, 1911, in a letter Gandhi asked him to visit S.A. to "bring the people here nearer to India, …" After getting consent, in the beginning of Jan. 1912, under the title: "Joyful News" Gandhi informed the Indian community about the visit and suggested a royal welcome.[579] To introduce the guest a short biography was published in the "Indian Opinion."[580] According to the drafted programme he had to arrive on Oct. 22, 1912. The estimated *cost for a meeting in his honour was about 1000 pounds.* He was to stay two days in Cape Town, one day in Kimberly, 10 days in Transvaal.[581] In a private letter Gandhi had proposed to meet different politicians.[582] He reminded the Indian community that Gokhale helped our struggle with money and "we can never thank him *enough for his work in regard to the abolition of indenture"* and he had helped Polak in India, while he was on deputation on behalf of the B.I.A. The cause of Gokhale's visit was to "*study the conditions of Indians here and he will meet local officials.*"[583]

Gokhale arrived on Oct. 22, 1912. In Cape Town, in his honour, a meeting was presided over by the Mayor Harry Hands. The Indian community was represented by Abdurahman.[584] A local newspaper reported about his visit to Kamberley.[585] In Johannesburg, he was welcomed by the Hamidia Islamic Society, the Tamil Benefit Society, the Patidar Association and the Pietersburg Indians; and Mayor of Johannesburg.[586] On Nov. 23, 1913, "Indian Opinion" reported his interview with a local newspaper. When Gokhale was asked: "*Is Mr. Gokhale the formally appointed representative of the Government of India in this matter?*" His answer was: "*No, he comes in his private capacity but with the full knowledge and approval of both the Indian and the Imperial Governments.*"[587] Before leaving he was to meet Ministers in Pretoria to know their political points of views.[588] The meeting was held on Nov. 14, 1912. Gandhi thanked the Europeans friends and the Deputy Mayor. General Botha, Abraham Fischer and General Smuts sent letters of regret for being unable to attend.[589]

The most important part of the visit is an article published in the "Indian Opinion", as it shows that *Gokhale was supposed to be a private man. As we shall see later, in the coming years, Gandhi insisted again and again that his passive resistance is being continued, while Smuts and Botha did not fulfil promises made to Gokhale.*

Aftermyth of Gokhale's Visit – Chaos Without End!

Unfortunately, the following information is based on Gandhi's opinions and the interpretation of the Indian newspapers. Not surprisingly they are more than positive. Still when reading between the lines it shows that Gokhale was under some criticism. Like Gandhi or any other politician of the world, Gokhale felt "misunderstood" at different issues (details below). Understandably, "English Newspapers" were responsible for publishing "wrong" information. How could it be other than the fact that "The Gujarati", a newspaper from Gandhi's state, defended Gokhale's speeches. The story was not different in S.A. to which Gandhi wrote: "In India, too, persons like our Mayor and Major Silburn misinterpreted Mr. Gokhale's speech. Such things have always happen, and will happen, to public men. No wonder, therefore, Mr. Gokhale's words were misconstrued. Not that Reuter's cables always report speeches correctly."[590]

Then Gandhi came with "his interpretation" of Gokhale's speeches as follows:

> "What this patriot then said was that, *if equality of rights in law is conceded under the Immigration Act,* India would not object to the prohibition of Indian immigration beyond what was necessary to meet our needs (here). *He also said that we did not want political rights for the present.* Replying to his critics in India, Mr. Gokhale has said that *India would not place any (upper) limit to (Indian) immigration* (into South Africa). About the franchise, he pointed out that that was contained in his demand that Indians in South Africa

should have *equal rights with the whites.* We shall see on reflection that this is not inconsistent with his speeches in South Africa."[591]

Now what about the banning of the indentured labour? Gandhi's remarkable interpretation was:

"Mr. Gokhale seems to have been charged with having bound India's hands and made her *responsible for ending immigration of Indians* into this country in excess (of the figure agreed upon). *This charge is not just,* because all that Mr. Gokhale has agreed to is only *that India would not object if the Union Government were to disallow further immigration of Indians.* Between this (statement) and saying that India herself has ended (emigration), there is a deal of difference."[592]

So far as there was questioning of the voting rights of Indians, Gandhi argued:

"The same is true of the franchise (issue). Between what Mr. Gokhale has said - that we do not ask for the franchise at present - and saying that India does not demand it, there exists a great difference and a contradiction. Accepting the latter proposition would make India a party to the disabilities inflicted on the Indians. Mr. Gokhale has further pointed out that he has not committed himself to the waiving of a single right. By arguing that the demands he put forward were the same as ours, Mr. Gokhale has shown that he has neither made new demands nor has he left out any from among those that we have been making."[593]

In another article Gandhi wrote that the Union Government assured Gokhale that "the immigration laws would not be applied inconsiderately." And *"Gokhale is convinced that the cruel £3 tax which the labouring class is made to pay will be repealed."*[594] However, he saw problems with the trade licences as told to him by the Union Government and European friends.[595]

On Feb. 14, 1913, Gandhi wrote to Gokhale and felt sorry for criticism in the newspaper. He was told about the attacks from the author Aiyer, whose article was reproduced in "The Advertiser." Gandhi said that the conflict between Botha and Hertzog may lead to the reorganization of the parliament; which means a prolongation in the satyagraha struggle.[596]

In U.K. the SABIC and its members informed the British community about Gokhale's visit. "Indian Opinion" wrote that Lord Ampthill, in the House of Lords moved a paper. "He was anxious that the good tone produced by the visit should be fully utilized for the purpose of securing legislation or administration of existing laws that might relieve the pressure that is continuously being put upon us."[597] In order to give credit to Gokhale's work in S.A., Gandhi wrote that "The Times of Natal" has published that the Union Government had decided to abolish the three pound tax from indentured Indians and their families. "The credit will be Mr. Gokhale's of this hateful impost is abolished this year"[598], wrote Gandhi. As we shall see later, this conclusion was too early. With Gokhale's visit, Gandhi's satyagraha entered into the new phase as shown in the next chapter.

Notes and References

[530] Indian Opinion, 29-1-1910.

[531] Indian Opinion, 26-2-1910.

[532] Indian Opinion, 5-3-1910.

[533] Indian Opinion, 5-3-1910.

[534] Indian Opinion, 25-6-1910.

[535] Indian Opinion, 2-7-1910.

[536] Indian Opinion, 13-8-1910.

[537] Indian Opinion, 3-9-1910.

[538] Indian Opinion, 29-10-1910.

[539] Indian Opinion, 5-11-1910.

[540] Indian Opinion, 4-3-1911.

[541] Indian Opinion, 4-3-1911.

[542] Indian Opinion, 4-3-1911.

[543] Gandhi M.K. to Lane E.F.C., March 4, 1911.

[544] Gandhi M.K. to Doke J.J., March 7, 1911.

[545] Gandhi M.K. to Polak H.S.L., March 7, 1911.

[546] Gandhi M.K. to Pretoria News, March 16, 1911.

[547] Gandhi M.K. to Doke J.J., March 17, 1911.

[548] Indian Opinion, 18-3-1911.

[549] Indian Opinion, 18-3-1911.

[550] Gandhi M.K. to Polak H.S.L., March 20, 1911.

551 Gandhi M.K. to Ritch L.W., March 24, 1911.

552 Gandhi M.K. to Schlesin S., March 27, 1911.

553 Gandhi M.K. to Schlesin S., March 27, 1911.

554 Gandhi M.K. to Lane E.F.C., March 29, 1911.

555 Indian Opinion, 8-4-1911.

556 Indian Opinion, 22-4-1911.

557 Gandhi M.K. to Gandhi C., April 5, 1911.

558 Gandhi M.K. to Ritch L.W., April 7, 1911.

559 Gandhi M.K. to Ritch L.W., April 8, 1911.

560 C.W.M.G. 11, 1910-1911, pp. 359-362.

561 C.W.M.G. 11, 1910-1911, pp. 359-362.

562 C.W.M.G. 11, 1910-1911, pp. 359-362.

563 C.W.M.G. 11, 1910-1911, pp. 359-362.

564 Gandhi M.K. to Ritch L.W., April 21, 1911.

565 The Diamond Fields Advertiser, 25-4-1911.

566 Indian Opinion, 6-5-1911.

567 The Times of India, 25-5-1911.

568 Indian Opinion, 20-5-1911.

569 Indian Opinion, 27-5-1911.

570 Indian Opinion, 27-5-1911.

571 Gandhi M.K. to Natesan G.A., May 31, 1911.

572 Indian Opinion, 3-2-1912.

[573] Indian Opinion, 3-2-1912.

[574] Indian Opinion, 17-2-1912.

[575] Indian Opinion, 10-2-1912.

[576] Indian Opinion, 10-2-1912.

[577] Gandhi M.K. to Lane E.F.C., May 31, 1912.

[578] Indian Opinion, 27-7-1912.

[579] Indian Opinion, 6-1-1912.

[580] Indian Opinion, 24-8-1912.

[581] Indian Opinion, 31-8-1912.

[582] Gandhi M.K. to Gokhale G.K., Aug. 4, 1912.

[583] Indian Opinion, 10-8-1912.

[584] Indian Opinion, 2-11-1912.

[585] The Diamond Fields Advertiser, 26-10-1912.

[586] Indian Opinion, 9-11-1912.

[587] Indian Opinion, 23-11-1912.

[588] Indian Opinion, 23-11-1912.

[589] C.W.M.G. 12, 1911-1913, p. 279.

[590] Indian Opinion, 4-1-1913.

[591] Indian Opinion, 4-1-1913.

[592] Indian Opinion, 4-1-1913.

[593] Indian Opinion, 4-1-1913.

[594] Indian Opinion, 21-12-1912.

[595] Indian Opinion, 21-12-1912.

[596] Gandhi M.K. to Gokhale G.K., Feb. 14, 1913.

[597] Indian Opinion, 22-3-1913.

[598] Indian Opinion, 25-1-1913.

The Final Phase of the Struggle – "They felt that the hand of God was upon their movement"

In the previous chapters we have seen that most of the traders and hawkers left Gandhi. The N.I.C. was going its own way. The colonial born Indians started fighting independently. To summarize: The Indian community was divided. In the following we shall see:

- What led to the revival of the struggle?
- Why the ignored groups like mine workers and indentured servants became the focus of Gandhi's interest?
- Which role was played by the Christian missionaries in making Gandhi's politics successful in S.A.?
- Why Gandhi's opponents criticised his "Magna Charta"?
- Why he left S.A.?

The three main events (detail below) which led to the revival of the struggle were:

(a) Indian marriages declared illegal by a judge.

(b) Three pound poll-tax from ex-indentures, though the indentured immigration was almost banished by law.

(c) The new immigration bill was worse than its predecessor.

Indian Marriages Invalid

The main event, which re-united the Indian community, was a decision in a court, in Cape Town. Justice Searle declared an Indian woman's marriage illegal as she was unable to produce documents.

According to his judgement, the marriages, which were either in accordance with Christian rites or were officially registered before a Marriage Officer, were in conforming to the law.[599] Consequently, Indian children had no legal status. It was demanded that for the recognition of wife and child status a certificate from the first-class magistrate had to be produced for registration.[600]

Gandhi asked Muslim and Hindu organisations to protest against the law. He demanded that the Government should immediately recognise Indian marriages, which were celebrated according to Indian religions. *For the honour of the religion and mother India, people were asked to "sacrifice all."*[601-602] On April 1, 1913, a letter was sent by Gandhi to the Minister of Interior, Cape Town, saying that Justice Searle's decision regarding the validity of Indian marriages "have created great consternation among my countrymen." So far the children were concerned; Gandhi argued that in general, in India only a few births are registered. Thus, practically it is impossible to produce birth certificates. He suggested consulting the leaders of the community regarding the proof of marriages or sonship of boys.[603] On April 9, 1913, he wrote to E.F.C. Lane: "It cannot for a moment be denied that the Searle judgment shakes the existence of Indian society to its foundation." Gandhi requested him to show the letter to General Smuts and asked for support. The advocate Alexander came up with a new idea, that is, the re-registration of marriages in India. Gandhi rightly said that it is impossible as such institutions did not exist in India. "Indian marriages are accompanied with great solemnity and elaborate ceremonial, lasting for days, and in some cases even months.

Indeed, there is much greater publicity and ceremonial rites within ordinary Indian marriages .... This in itself acts as a perfect safeguard better than any system of registration that could be devised", wrote Gandhi.[604] Later he stated: "As a matter of fact, a recent arrival from India endeavoured to obtain a certificate of marriage from a magistrate at Bombay, who refused to issue it, on the ground that he was not authorized by law to do so."[605] The official argument from the side of the Union Government was that Indians are bringing "undesirable women." To which Gandhi encountered: "..., it is a well-known fact that there is hardly a case on record during the past thirty years or more of an undesirable Indian woman having been introduced, although Indian women have entered until lately, on the mere verbal statement of their husbands."[606]

On Sept. 29, 1913, in an interview he confessed that the number of passive resisters is small. When he was asked for the reasons, he replied: "Many who had experienced the discomforts of Transvaal prisons had no wish to return." He also admitted that he is financially not well-off as at the occasion of last campaign.[607] On Oct. 2, 1913, the first batch of twelve women left for Maritzburg to be arrested. They were accompanied by H. Kallenbach. Two more were arrested for hawking.[608] In the middle of Oct. 1913, Gandhi reported about the state-of-the-art of the movement as follows:

> "..., Indians started passive resistance on September 15 by 12 men and four women setting out from Natal to court imprisonment .... There are already in gaol 35 passive resisters - .... Numbers of men and women are coming

forward daily to seek arrest. Several of the women have taken their babies with them, as they have not yet been weaned or are incapable of being looked after otherwise."[609]

With time the passive resistance was gaining more members. But not all were able to walk long distances on foot. Gandhi told Kallenbach that about 40 men and women, who could not or would not walk, should be entrained if they want to go to gaol. He was suggested: "As much as possible, please *discourage movement to Phoenix*. If you have sufficient accommodation there, the women should be kept and fed there so long as possible as you have plenty of rations there ...."[610]

The New Immigration Bill, Worse Than its Predecessor

After all instances in the Parliament the bill was passed in April 1913. Gandhi, in the "Indian Opinion" called it "disappointing" and "worse than its predecessor." He stated:

"The Bill plays with words regarding the Free State difficulty and is quite on a par with the Immigration Act of the Transvaal in unscrupulous subtlety. The immigration law of the Transvaal, as we have pointed out so often, has created a legal racial bar without anyone, save those well versed in the Transvaal laws, knowing it. .... Unless the Government yield and amend the Bill materially, passive resistance must revive, and, with it, all the old miseries, sorrows and sufferings."[611]

Gandhi in a letter to Gokhale wrote that if the struggle started, it will bring more suffering; he will collect money from the Indians in South Africa; he will not ask for money from India, but if someone wants to send, who knows him personally, it will be welcomed. In the end he disclosed that this time women, in particular his wife, will be involved in the movement.[612]

In spite of opposition by the Unionist Party, the Immigration Bill was read a second time.[613] During a debate the Minister Fischer told that Indians have declined to accept a Marriage Officer as they want the recognition of polygamy in South Africa. Gandhi warned him that *"even if this question is the only one left unsolved, revival of passive resistance is a certainty."*[614] On June 5, 1913, Gandhi sent a telegram to the Minister of the Interior, and he came to know that many members of the parliament had the intention to remove the three pound tax only on women; whereas during Gokhale's visit, it was promised to be abolished for all.

In an interview with a local journalist, Gandhi said:

> "I well remember the great meetings of Indians which Mr. Gokhale addressed at Lord's Ground, Isipingo, and, as the Hon. Marshall Campbell's guest, at Mount Edgecombe. Fully 10000 indentured and ex-indentured Indians were present at Mr. Campbell's estate. Over 5000 were present at Lord's. They were assured that, as Mr. Gokhale had met with no opposition from the Europeans to the removal of the tax, it would very probably be removed at an early date. *Subsequently, after his interview with the Ministers, he declared that he had received assurances that the tax*

would be removed. This information was passed on to these thousands of helpless men and women."[615]

At last General Botha reacted. In a speech of Nov. 1, 1913, he stated that he never made any promise to Gokhale in 1912.[616]

Improved Immigration Regulation Act and Gandhi's Objections

On June 28, 1913, Gandhi thanked the Minister of Interior, Johannesburg, for the improved original bill. However, he was disappointed as it failed: "to carry out the provisional settlement of 1911 in at least four important particulars", namely,

> "(1) According to the definition of the term "domicile", those indentured Indians who arrived after the Indian Immigration Law Amendment Act of 1895 and their descendants appear to become prohibited immigrants.
>
> (2) The descendants of this class, although born in South Africa, will, if the above interpretation be correct, be unable henceforth to enter the Cape Province.
>
> (3) Women married in South Africa according to the rites of Indian religions, and going to India, and returning with their husbands will not be on the same footing as those (married) in India. Nor are the hundreds of women married according to non-Christian faiths provided for by the amendment.
>
> (4) The Free State difficulty (entrance of educated Indians) seems to remain as it was before."[617]

Somewhat in different form, Gandhi told the Indian readers that according to the new act:

> "1. Indentured labourers who arrived after 1895 seem to lose their right of settling down (in Natal) on the expiry of their term of indenture.
>
> 2. The right of entry into the Cape which all Indians born in South Africa have enjoyed seems to disappear.
>
> 3. Indian marriages celebrated in South Africa must be recognized as valid. Moreover, the term "monogamous" used in the Bill must not be interpreted by the Government to imply that any woman intending to immigrate should be the only wife of her husband in India. So long as the husband does not have another wife in South Africa, there should be no objection to the entry of such a woman. Further, if any of those who are already resident in South Africa have married twice in India, or here, both the wives should be free to leave and return (to South Africa).
>
> 4. An Indian entering the (Orange) Free State as a fresh immigrant should not be required to sign the declaration that he has to at present.
>
> 5. Particulars about the admission of Indians this year must be settled."[618]

No Settlement - New Plan of the Satyagraha

In the beginning of September 1913, the Indian community was informed that there was no settlement at all. Gandhi poured out his frustration against the "white community" as follows:

> "*The real object of our fight must be to kill the monster of racial prejudice in the heart of the Government and the local whites*. We feel the presence of this monster in the Government's administration of the Gold Law in the Transvaal and the new immigrant law, in its insistence on the collection of the £3 tax from poor, miserable, helpless Indians, and in its attitude towards our women."[619]

Somewhat arrogantly he wrote that a microscopic Indian minority is *fighting not only against the "white Europeans" but also the "mighty British Empire."*[620]

On Sept. 22, 1913, Gandhi wrote to the Secretary for Interior that the Government has not given much thought to the Indian marriages. As a result of it, Indian wives have recieved the status of concubines and their children are not lawful heirs of their parents. Further, he stated that he did not ask for the legal recognition of polygamy; but suggested the admission of plural wives already married to Indians.[621] A.M. Cachalia, Chairman, B.I.A., in an interview threatened the Government that the passive resistance will be continued until the following demands are fulfilled:

"(1) A racial bar disfigures the Immigration Act;

(2) The rights existing prior to the passing of the Act are not restored and maintained;

(3) The £3 tax upon ex-indentured men, women, and children is not removed;

(4) The status of women married in South Africa is not secured."[622]

Gandhi and B.I.A. decided to protest. Contrary to the previous years, this time Gandhi's plan was concrete. The method of protesting against the law was, to go for hawking without licence.[623] The advantage of the method was that trader's property could not be auctioned.[624]

Three Pound Tax and the Involvement of Indentured Indians in Resistance

In fact to fight against the three pound tax was not Gandhi's "invention." The authors, S. Bhana and G.H. Vadeh wrote:

"Newly created bodies such as N.I.P.U. (1908) and C.B.I.A. (March, 1911) made the tax an important issue. In the forefront was P.S. Aiyar who used his *African Chronicle* to highlight abuses against the indentured laborers. He had convened a meeting in October 1911 at Parsi Rustomjee's Field Street residence to discuss the tax. The group created a £3 League with Vincent Lawrence as secretary. While N.I.C. stalwarts like Abdulla Hajee Adam and M.C. Anglia were present, most of the others in attendance were colonial-born. Aiyar established the South Africa Indian Committee (S.A.I.C.) in October 1911 whose sole purpose was to secure the abolition of the £3 tax. Gandhi showed little interest in Aiyar's endeavors. If not much came out of such attempts, it was, as S. Chetty was to reveal in 1913, the committee had suspended possible action on the advice of "friends" in India. If this was so, Gandhi may well have been privy to this "friendly" advice which perhaps suggested to him that the tax would be abolished in due course before the slate of other issues in the campaign were resolved."[625]

They further stated:

"Others like Bernard Gabriel and K.R. Nayanah were not only peeved that Gandhi should have upstaged them on the tax issue, but seemed to imply that Gandhi had an ulterior motive. How was it, asked (Bernard) Gabriel, that the tax was taking up so much of his time when he had paid no attention to the £3 Tax Committee when it was first created? "The fact is," said Nayanah, "that during the last twenty years of Mr. Gandhi's political career in this country, I am not aware of any systematic and organized effort made by him to give due prominence to the question of this £3 tax." When the *African Chronicle* started this movement, Gandhi did not raise "a single finger to help," he stated. John L. Roberts simply thought of passive resistance to be a "Hydra-headed blunder" that would have serious consequences."[626]

Surprisingly Gandhi's autobiography and articles in "Indian Opinion" say nothing about their work.

Some historians believe that:

"If they (indentured) responded to Gandhi's call to strike, it was because they saw the £3 tax as part of the same set of grievances they felt against employers who were seen to be working closely with the government. There are numerous instances of complaints by indentured Indians against their employers. The Indian immigration files in the Natal Archives Repository contain case after case from the 1880s to the 1900s about abuse by overbearing Indian sirdars or owners, overwork, inadequate rations, Sunday work, withheld wages, and late payment, to mention a few."[627]

How and why this tax was introduced? Gandhi told that the original plan of the government was to impose an annual tax of 25 pound on ex-indentured Indians. Due to protest from the Government of India it was reduced to three pound. In 1895 a bill was passed. According to it the tax was to be charged from "free Indian" (husband and his wife), who wished to settle in Natal. The first collections began in 1900.[628] "Gandhi's logic" was they if the system of indentured is abolished, then this tax should be removed.[629] He was not ready to listen that this tax is paid by other citizens, in different form. He asked his countrymen to *"go and fight for the removal of this tax even unto death."*[630] Now, all of sudden, he became a leader of workers. He told them: "*So far we could ask nothing of the thousands of ex-indentured Indians.* Now, they too can join the fight with all their heart."[631]

On Sept. 28, 1913, Gandhi informed to the Secretary for Interior that the campaign has started. Twelve men and four women are already serving three months' imprisonment with hard labour. He knows the movement might spread and might be difficult to control. This step is necessary to protest against the payment of £3 tax by indentured, as the Government has not kept its promise. He asked him to appeal to General Smuts to reconsider the decision.[632]

We have seen earlier that Gandhi was too optimistic about the abolishing of three pound tax after Gokhale left S.A. A few weeks later he had to tell to the readers: "The Government do not intend to introduce this session a Bill to repeal the £3 tax required, under Act 17 of 1895, of ex-indentured Indians who remain free in Natal at the expiry of their contracts."[633] Then he attacked Botha as follows:

> "General Botha has adopted the attitude that he is fighting his opponent in the interests of the Empire. He does not seem to realize the inconsistency of that attitude with his inability to keep *his unwritten pledge* to the Hon. Mr. Gokhale to repeal this tax at an early date. It is an open secret that the only reason why no public announcement of the intentions of the Government was made during Mr. Gokhale's visit was because Ministers desired, before definitely committing themselves, to ascertain the feeling of the Natal members."[634]

The B.I.A. held a meeting on April 27, 1913, and passed the following resolution against the Government: "..., inasmuch as *it affects the honour, the religious sentiment* and the very existence of the Indian community in South Africa, ..., passive resistance, ..., be revived and continued, ..."[635] According to the new strategy everyone was supposed to support the struggle either monetarily or by helping the families whose members are in prison.[636] Johannesburg had to lead the struggle. Gandhi said: "It would be shameful, however, if the Cape and Natal sit back. From there, too, people should come forward to go to gaol, and meetings should be held in both these provinces similar to the one in Johannesburg. The Government may treat us as if we are separate, but we can demonstrate our "union" by our actions."[637] Those with "sheer weakness" were asked to "dip their hands into their pockets" and give money for the struggle.[638]

Involving the Mine Workers – "The Movement is Bound to Collapse"

Before we proceed further, let us see the views of M. Campbell - a sugar baron and one of the wealthiest men in Natal.[639] He was known for his sympathy for natives and Indians. He observed:

> "If anything, it, in my opinion, aggravates the unfortunate blunder of your policy. More than this, no movement can be successful, however high the ideals of its founders, *if it involves the suffering of innocent and guilty alike; the inherent injustice of such an effect must work its ruin*, and you will pardon me if I say quite frankly, though as a friend, that many of *those you lead are realizing the weakness of your policy more and more every day,* and are coming to the conclusion that to use a large body of, in the main, contented but ignorant people, namely, *the indentured laborers, by inflaming their passions with high words, false hopes incapable of realization,* and violent threats, as a tool

for procuring political rights by which most of them will never benefit, even if they are ever attained, to put it very mildly, is not a policy dictated by wisdom and far-sightedness."[640]

Gandhi who was always convinced of his idea on Jan. 1, 1914, wrote to M. Campbell:

"I see that recent events have caused a breach between my friends and myself which must be left to time and future uniform conduct on my part to heal. I can only give you my assurance that I know of no agent who has been permitted to encourage or advise violence. It is the essence of passive resistance to be free from violent methods even under circumstances the most provoking. ... The strike and the subsequent courting of imprisonment were not intended to be a protest against the general treatment of indentured Indians, but against the Government's breach of promise given to India's greatest representative, and the injustice of perpetuating a cruel tax which has been so universally condemned."[641]

In the letter Gandhi defended his "wonder weapon satyagraha" with is usual arguments such as it is the only way to solve the Indians' problem. M. Campbell in a letter told Gandhi that indentured "were only induced to *come out by grave threats of personal violence* made by persons whom I believe to *be your agents*, two of whom were arrested and fined."[642]

In a telegram to the Press, on Oct. 23, 1913, Gandhi wrote: "We are advising the strikers to leave the mines and court arrested, and failing arrest, to march to Volkrust. We consider it improper to live on mine rations when we don't work."[643] On the first instance, Gandhi's statement gives the impression that as if, for him it was "immoral" to live on the cost of others. I personally find it difficult to believe as he himself was living on money, either given by Kallenbach or he got from India. Even after his return to India, from 1914 onward, until his death in 1948, he did nothing to earn his livelihood. In the above case, his aim was to get persons, the mine workers, for his "dying satyagraha." It is evident from the following private letter to his friend H. Kallenbach, which he wrote on Oct. 23, 1913. In part it reads:

> "Just now it seems to me that *a solution has been found* for the building proposal. *The strikers must leave the mines.* Otherwise the strike is bound to collapse. *I am therefore inviting them to come out.* If they do, one of us will march with them to the Transvaal border to court arrest. *We should be arrested on the way. This avoids the difficulty of lodgings, etc., and keeps the men going.* The situation is certainly difficult and serious. The strike is now having its effect. *But unless some such thing like the above is done, the movement is bound to collapse.*"[644]

While talking about the strike, Gandhi told journalists:

> "*I personally felt that the strike was weak so long as the men did not actually leave the mines.* …. According to my estimate there are nearly 3000 on strike. The effect of this is not entirely to stop work as they have a certain amount of Kaffir labour, and with this Kaffir labour and the Europeans they are able to do some work, though the bulk

of it is certainly at a standstill. *I saw it reported that we might even ask the Kaffirs to strike. But such is not our intention at all. ..... .* I may state also, that no intimidation of any sort was used against non-strikers, and the strike is absolutely a voluntary act, and in so far as I have been able to *see, quite spontaneous.*"[645]

Some historians believe that *if Indian passive resisters would have joined the British workers, it would have been devastating to Botha and Smuts. In contrast, Gandhi suspended his satyagraha. He was not willing that it should be made public.*[646]

The Struggle at its Peak

With the involvement of women, mine-workers and colonial-born Indians and the support of European friends, the movement reached a peak in Nov. 1913. Gandhi stated: "He contemplated moving 1500 men to the Transvaal to court arrest, and if not arrested they would proceed further, and would probably settle down on Mr. Kallenbach's farm at Tolstoy, near Lawley."[647] Proudly he told his mentor, Gokhale, that 5000 workers are on strike. Out of them 4000 (including 300 women and 600 children) needed to be feed. 300 have been arrested and 200 are in jails.[648] Gandhi successfully managed to move the masses, but he was not aware of the clever politics of Botha and Smuts, namely, they did not arrest the protestors. Consequently, they needed to be feed by Gandhi. Not only that, it was a matter of their hygiene and health care. In despair he sent a telegram to Gokhale saying that monthly expenses are more than 7000 pounds. The local contribution expected every month is about 1000 pounds.[649]

After Gandhi was arrested, on Nov. 7, 1913, he sent a telegram to the Minister of Interior saying that among the marchers there are 122 women and 50 children. They have limited food and shelter provisions. As he is responsible for the march, it was not wise from the Government to arrest him without informing his people. He requested either to let him continue the march or bring the protestors to the Tolstoy Farm with trains and provide ration for them.[650]

After the arrest, on Nov. 11, 1913, he had trial in court at Dundee. The Magistrate found Gandhi guilty for: a) Inducing others to leave the Province; b) Advising Indians to strike as he told them that Government had broken faith, which is not so; c) "The defendant was, by his threatening conduct, only bringing ruination to the men and harshness upon themselves."[651] As punishment, Gandhi was asked either to pay a fine or accept three months' imprisonment with hard labour. Gandhi decided for the latter. Most of the resisters did not get proper food and complained again and again (detail later). *Gandhi recieved special treatment like a king.* He wrote to a relative: "*Right from today the doctor has ordered fruits, etc., for my diet. I shall have no difficulty, therefore. ....I took a pledge yesterday that I would live on one meal a day till a repeal of the tax was promised. .... The pledge this time will permit my taking lemon or orange squash.*"[652]

Meanwhile the "Indian Inquiry Commission" (The Commission's personnel consisted of Sir William Solomon as Chairman) was set up by the Union Government on December 11, to inquire into the causes of the strike and the disturbances in connection with it. On Commission's recommendation, Gandhi, Polak and Kallenbach were brought to Pretoria *and released unconditionally on December 18, (1913).*"[653] Gandhi was against the appointment of Esselen and Col. Wylie in the Indian Inquiry Commission as in the past, the both had expressed anti-Indian views.[654] In a speech he showed his disappointment about the appointment of the commission. He declared that he, Polak and Kallenbach will decide later whether they should work together with the commission or not.[655] On Dec. 21, 1913, Gandhi addressed a meeting of the Natal Indian Association, which was presided over by Abdul Kadir. About six to seven thousand persons were present. One of the resolutions passed was:

> "That the community may not, in honour, give evidence before the Commission recently appointed by the Government because the community has not been consulted as to the choice of the members of the Commission, and because it does not include any members specially representing the community, whose interests are to be vitally affected by the finding of the Commission."[656]

On Dec. 24, 1913, Gandhi sent a confidential telegram to Gokhale and informed him that seven representatives of different religions have asked for Government intervention. If our demands are not accepted they will protest publically. He wrote a letter to Senator Marshall Champbell and told that he is negotiating with Smuts; and "if you have the leisure and could interest yourself in the negotiations, and if you would appoint a time and place, I would come over and discuss the situation."[657]

Gandhi's Work in Past 20 Years "not only worthless but highly injurious to the Indian community"

At this stage Gandhi was quite sure that the trader community would support him. However, on Oct. 22, 1913, he suffered a set-back as reported by "The Rand Daily Mail":

> "There certainly was a disturbance at the meeting, …, and one of the secretaries, at the time of tendering his resignation, made a long statement consisting of an attack upon Mr. *Gandhi and upon his work during the past 20 years which he characterised as being not only worthless but highly injurious to the Indian community. So much so that, in his opinion, Mr. Gandhi was instrumental in having enticed the Indian community into slavery.*"[658]

To avoid further confrontation among the members, the meeting was abruptly closed.

"The African Chronicle" reported about a mass meeting of the N.I.C. in Durban. The two secretaries, Anglia and Dada Osman, submitted their resignations over the way money was being handled. The decision to accept the resignations was deferred.[659] Gandhi reacted immediately by establishing a new body, that is, Natal Indian Association, with Mr. Dawad Mohamed as president and Omar Haji Amod Jhaveri as secretary. They promised to support the passive resisters.[660] To the journalist he tried to give impression that it was a minor confrontation. However, his private letter to Kallenbach gives different impression. It reads: "Anglia and Dada Osman are making much mischief. I have written Cachalia to that effect. He and the others are required to counteract the mischief."[661] The news about the split in the community was published by "Reuters" in India. In a telegram, in the end of Oct. 1913, Gandhi demented and wrote to his friend G.A. Natesan that the report is false. ... Presently nearly *100 men and women* from different sections, who *support the movement are in gaol.*"[662]

Taking Christian Missionaries as Political Partners – "They felt that the hand of God was upon their movement"

Gandhi began his political carrier as defender of rich traders' interests. As we have seen above his Guajarati friends (some Muslims and rich traders) supported him for a long time. After about 15 years most of them left him as their businesses were ruined. Jews, like Polak, Kallenbach, Sonja Schlesin stood on his side for the last 4-5 years. They not only supported him with money but also intellectual output such as organising work for the passive resistance.

Not Gandhi, but Gokhale realised that to deal with conservative Christian politicians, persons from the same religion would be the right partners. In 1914, Revs. C.F. Andrews and William Winstanley Pearson[663], both belonging to Christian Missions in India, were sent by Gokhale to Durban. Andrews was a man of interest, as he had close contact with Lord Hardinge, Viceroy of India, between 1910 and 1916.[664] On Jan. 2, 1914, Gandhi informed Gokhale that they have been cordially received by the Indian community. To give a "religious touch" and probably to win the sympathy of the Christians in S.A., Gandhi wrote: *"When the announcement was made in the papers of their coming, it gave a new hope to them in a time of darkness. They felt that the hand of God was upon their movement."*[665] Immediately after the arrivals, Gandhi's missionary started their work. It is reported that Gandhi "accompanied by C.F. Andrews, arrived in Pretoria on the morning of January 9, for negotiations with Smuts."[666] On Jan. 16, 1914, Gandhi met Smuts and laid before him a proposal and asked for definite assurances. The content of the interview was as follows:

> "(a) The £3 Tax: General Smuts enquired whether he would be satisfied if the payment of the licence money were abolished, but the licence retained and no further alteration made in the provisions of Natal Act 17 of 1895. Mr. Gandhi thought that this solution would meet his requirements, but he urged that if the licence were retained, it should be made a standing licence not subject to annual renewal.
>
> (b) The marriage question: He did not make it quite clear what precisely he desired, but General Smuts gathered that his expectations were not unreasonable, and that they would probably be satisfied if statutory recognition of *de facto* monogamous wives were accorded.
>
> (c) The admission of South Africa-born Indians into the Cape Province: Mr. Gandhi did not press for legislation on

this point but only for an assurance that the law would be so administered that the education test would not be applied to such Indians seeking to enter the Cape. This was to be subject to the understanding that only a small number would thus seek admission, and that if large numbers came forward, the education test should be applicable. I cannot vouch for the actual wording of the stipulation, but I believe that this was its substantial effect.

(d) The declaration said to be required under the Orange Free State Law: General Smuts pointed out that the Government had already in Mr. Gorges' letter of the 19th August (Cd. 7111, page 51) signified their willingness to accept Mr. Gandhi's suggestion on this point. Mr. Gandhi said that he did not so understand the relevant passage in that letter, but that a slight verbal amendment of its terms would meet the difficulty."[667]

Gandhi wrote to Kallenbach that: "General Smuts now knows my domestic position and he may hurry forward if he likes. In any case it cannot be long delayed now *seeing that the industrial crisis is now practically over. Meanwhile Mr. Andrews is moving forward.* He has got a wonderful grasp of the central position and he is pushing it forward with *all the spiritual force he possesses.*"[668]

It is a matter of great interest to note that Gandhi with his "satyagraha" could not convince Smuts and Botha; but two Christian missionaries, achieved the results within two weeks. Was their "spiritual force" better than Gandhi's "satyagraha"? On Jan. 25, 1914, Gandhi sent a cable to inform Gokhale about the "wonders of the Christian missionaries" as follows: "Provisional agreement reached. .... Suspending passive resistance pending legislation which government promises after commission. Principle of Indian consulation acknowledged. .... Prisoners being released. Opportunity for settlement now more favourable."

In the end of Jan. 1914, Gandhi informed the readers of the "Indian Opinion" that a meeting was held by the Natal Indian Association. The President in Chair was Imam Abdul Cadir Bawazeer. The aim was to discuss the provisional agreement between Gandhi and Smuts:

> "..., the Government should grant the community's request in terms of Mr. Cachalia's letter, namely, the five points (1) the repeal of the £3 tax; (2) the restoration of the status of Indian wives as it existed before the Searle judgment; (3) the restoration of the right of South Africa-born Indians to enter the Cape; (4) the removal of the little difficulty that still exists with reference to the racial bar regarding the Orange Free State; and (5) the question of the just administration of existing laws with due regard to vested rights. The last three points could be dealt with administratively; the first two only by amending legislation, and he had ventured to submit to General Smuts the easiest and the quickest way in which the matter could be dealt with. General Smuts had said that he would consider the matter, and after he had considered and conferred with the Cabinet, he said, in the presence of Mr. Andrews, that the Government were willing to grant these things, ..."[669]

The things were not running smooth as Gandhi wanted. He told Gokhale that N.I.C. held a meeting. It was engineered by those who opposed the passive resistance.[670] However, there was another reason, that is, the issue of more than one wife. On Feb. 2, 1914, Gandhi wrote under the title: "Views on the marriage question" in which it was stated that:

> "No Hindu or Mahomedans will be able to take to himself more than one wife, but it will not preclude him from taking a number of women whom he calls his wives, but who, in the eyes of the law, *will be considered as concubines*. ....
> *In the case of a past marriage,* a man can have only one wife before he can make the declaration that she is his only wedded wife."[671]

As to be expected, Gandhi's opponents were critical of the settlement. In "The Indian Views" (which was established by Anglia *et al.*) they called:

> *"The settlement "farcical" and questioned Gandhi's claim to be speaking for all Indians.* They pointed to the large numbers who opposed passive resistance, and they reproduced the names of people who sent telegrams opposing the settlement. Its July 24, 1914, issue stated that the one lesson that Indians could learn from Gandhi's twenty-one years was to resolve *issues "in a calm and constitutional manner and not to resort to passive resistance, strikes and other cut-your-nose-off-to-spite-your-face method."* It referred to the N.I.A. as a "relic of Gandhism.""[672]

Leaving South Africa - "Ours is a notorious family, ..., we are known to belong to a band of robbers"

More or less, Gandhi politically achieved what he wanted. During the struggle his work as a lawyer was suspended. Obviously, he could have continued it after the political settlement. Why he decided to leave S.A.? In "Indian Opinion" he told that it is "my desire to return to India to fall at the feet of my brother's widow and to take charge of the domestic cares of five widows in my father's family, in which the hand of death now leaves me the responsible head, according to the Hindu usage."[673] A few months later, he came up with an entirely different statement: "For me there can be no deliverance from this earthly life except in India. *Anyone who seeks such deliverance must go to the sacred soil of India.* For me, as for everyone else, the land of India is "the refugee of the afflicted". I am therefore longing to return to the motherland."[674] However, the following paragraphs suggest that he wanted to save his life as he was threatened to be assassinated.

The end of his stay was nearing. On Feb. 27, 1914, Gandhi wrote to Gokhale that if a settlement is signed in March, he is thinking to leave for India in April 1914. He said that he will come with 20 persons. However, after visiting relatives in India, the number may increase. The group was supposed to live at the Servants of India quarters in Poona, which was founded by Gokhale. Now, Gandhi had planned to leave with more than 20 persons. What will be their future in India? From what will they live? Gandhi had the following solution: "If I am enabled to leave for India in April, I propose to use the funds you have sent for our passages which shall be all deck. I have no means of my own and Phoenix can hardly supply funds now. It is drained totally dry."[675] On March 8, 1914, Gandhi sent a letter to his relative Maganlal Gandhi, which had the name of potential persons, who might follow him and leave South Africa.

Gokhale had suggested Gandhi to keep quiet for some time after his arrival in India. Regarding it Gandhi wrote: "I shall scrupulously observe the compact of silence for one year after my arrival in India. The vow of silence as I have understood it does not include the South African question and may be broken at your wish for furthering any project about which both of us hold the same view."[676] Gandhi considered himself as a great healer and medicine man. He told Gokhale: "My present ambition you know. It is to be by your side as your nurse and attendant. I want to have the real discipline of obeying someone whom I love and look up to."

It will not be exaggerate to assume that Gandhi decided to leave S.A. as he was afraid of his opponents. For instance, in a letter to C. Gandhi he wrote: "Medh writes to say that they *are plotting again in Johannesburg to take my life*. ... In case I die suddenly, be the reason this or any other, I want to set down here certain ideas which I have thought out and which I have not so far placed before you. The life of service or political work which we have followed so far seems to me of the lowest order."[677]

It is not quite clear, whether someone in the family threatened his life. About his own family he stated:

> "*Ours is a notorious family*, that is, *we are known to belong to a band of robbers.* Without disparaging *our elders*, we may say that they have possibly done service to the

people, but only incidentally, *while they pursued their selfish interests.* Judged by common standards, it would seem that they have acted with a fair measure of justice. That is, they treated people to a smaller measure of oppression. *At present, the family has fallen on evil days.*"[678]

"The Relief Bill"

The things were not running as planned. On March 6, 1914, Gandhi wrote to Sir Benjamin Robertson:

"... Now the Highest Court has reversed the decision of the Lower Court and the children of *de facto* monogamous unions (are) declared illegitimate and, therefore, prohibited immigrants. Now, such children and the children of wives to be administratively allowed to enter the Union are to be protected under the proposed settlement. Will you kindly go into this matter and secure, pending settlement, the non-deportation of the child? As I am writing to you, I am not myself writing to the Government in this matter."[679]

In May 1914, the draft bill was still not passed. It was possible that a final settlement might not be reached at all.[680] In order to know more, on May 19, 1914, he sent a telegram to the Minister of Interior and asked: "Could I know for satisfying inquirers when Indian Legislation likely be introduced."

In the beginning of June 1914, under the title "The relief bill" Gandhi told the readers of the "Indian Opinion" that: "The Bill removes the marriage difficulty and restores the status as it existed before the Searle judgment. It repeals the £3 tax and remits the unpaid arrears. Lastly, it validates Natal certificates of domicile, if the owner can establish his identity with the certificate by proving that the thumb-impression on it is his own."[681]

On June 5, 1914, Gandhi informed Gokhale that: "The Indian Bill has passed through the first stage. It is quite satisfactory and I am about to have another interview with General Smuts about the other points. There is, therefore, every prospect of the struggle being finally closed. In that event I should leave for London about the middle of July and even earlier if I can."[682]

"The Cape Time" published an article telling that some Indian agitated against the settlement. Gandhi wrote to M. Campbell:

> "*I do not know of any such Indian agitation as is referred to in the wire. I* am sure that no responsible Indian has taken exception to the Bill. I do not believe for one moment that the Bill makes the Indians, affected by it, prohibited immigrants - a result never contemplated by the Imperial Government, the Government of India or the Indian community or, I feel sure, by the Union Government."[683]

Due to criticism from different quarters, on June 30, 1914, Gandhi wrote to E.M. Gorges, a Minister, and told that my countrymen want me to go further as:

> "They are *dissatisfied that the trade licences laws* of the different provinces, *the Transvaal Gold Law, the Transvaal Townships Act*, the Transvaal Law 3 of 1885 have not been

altered, so as to give them full rights of *residence, trade and ownership of land*. Some of them are dissatisfied *that full inter-provincial migration* is not permitted, and some are dissatisfied that, on the marriage question, the Relief Bill goes no further than it does. *They have asked me that all the above matters might be included in the passive resistance struggle.*"[684]

He hoped that the Union Government will consider these issues in the future. In July 1914, the final round, that is, the making of law out of a bill, took place. Gandhi appreciated the help given by different parties and persons as follows:

"General Botha, it must be admitted, has done much for us, seeing that, for the sake of a community as docile as the Indians, he threatened to resign if the Bill was not passed. .... We are thankful, too, to the Imperial Government and to Lord Hardinge, that noble Viceroy of India, for their help. The help which India gave us under the leadership of Mr. Gokhale and the invaluable help from Mr. Andrews - each I of these surpassed the other and it is thanks to them that we have this final and satisfactory settlement today."[685]

Speeches at Farewell Meetings

Meanwhile it was clear that Gandhi would leave. After keeping mum for two decades, just a few days before leaving for the U.K., Gandhi showed sympathy for poor and colonial born and contemned his Gujaratis and rich Indian friends as follows:

> "Indians from Bombay are often rude to those hailing from Calcutta and Madras and indifferent to their feelings. The term 'colcha' has still not gone out of use in our language. .... it is necessary that we show them due regard. Even good Indians show contempt for Colonial-born Indians. I have believed, and still believe, that they are wrong in doing so. Colonial-born Indians do have some defects; but, then, who has not? They have also many fine qualities. It is worth noting that, if the satyagraha campaign has been a glorious performance, it was because of the sacrifices of Indians born in this country."[686]

In a Gujarati's meeting, he praised the colonial-born Indians for their contribution. He suggested them "to preserve their national characteristic, to learn their mother-tongue and study the history and traditions of their Motherland, ..."[687] In Durban to the Colonial-born Indians he said: "For Indians born here, this is their motherland. They have a better right here than other Indians. Their future is bound up with that of this country. I would ask them to be vigilant. They would do well to turn their attention to land instead of crowding lawyers' or other offices."[688]

In Verulam he said to indentured:

> "I came only to pay homage to my indentured brothers and to explain to them the facts under the new law. Moreover, a visit to this place is for me like going on a pilgrimage, for the Indian friends here played a great part in the recent strike; ... When all the so-called leaders were resting in their private rooms or were busy making money, the

indentured brethren of this place, the moment they happened to hear that a strike was on in Charlestown and elsewhere about the £3 tax, struck work too. They looked for no leaders."[689]

They were told:

"Free Indians who remain here for three years will be treated as domiciled here. After completing three years, anyone who wants to go to India and return will be able to do so. Such a person should go to India at his own expense, and not approach the Government for the purpose. But those who have made up their minds not to return here will be able to claim from the Government the expenses for the journey to India."[690]

About "his" property Gandhi said that "Indian Opinion" and "Phoenix farm" are property of the community.

"Those who have settled there have not done so with the intention of making money. They draw only as much as they need for a simple and plain life. It will be so much of a loss to the community if it does not utilize the services of those who are working in this spirit. Mr. Omar Hajee Jhaveri and Parsee Rustomjee are now the owners of the Phoenix lands and its managing trustees in South Africa. The community can get all information about Phoenix through them or even directly."[691]

The Transvaal Indian Women's Association was asked: "To continue the work they (women) had commenced, and that the work they had done was noble. They should hold together as one woman, and, if the call to duty came again, they should not fail to respond and should not fail to do even as Valliamma had done."[692] On July 15, 1914, in a meeting from Tamils, Gandhi appreciated them highly. He stated:

> "The largest number of deaths that passive resistance had taken had been from the Tamil community. .... The deportees had been Tamils. The last to fight and come out of gaol had been Tamils. Those who were ruined hawkers were all Tamils. The majority of the passive resisters at Tolstoy Farm had been Tamils. .... The majority of women to go to gaol were Tamils. ... the Tamils had sustained the struggle for the last eight years and had shown of what stuff they were made from the very beginning."[693]

He was critical to the Gujarati community:

> "..., I wish the Gujaratis to learn a lesson from the Tamils. Though I do not know their language, they have given me the greatest help in the fight. On the other hand, though I can explain my aims best to Gujaratis because I know Gujarati, they have failed in their duty. They cared (more) for money. It makes me very unhappy to hear that some members of the community have fallen a prey to drink. .... Some are engaged in smuggling gold. ...."[694]

In the Den of Lions - Speech at the Hamidia Islamic Society

As we have seen in previous chapters, the Hamidia Islamic Society had supported Gandhi's struggle. Before leaving for London, he was invited by it. The meeting was held in Society's hall, which was full to the capacity. Essop Ismail Mia presided. "The Rand Daily Mail" of July 16, 1914, reported that E.I. Mia asked Gandhi to speak on the following issues:[695]

- On whose authority the settlement was made with the Government?
- What became of funds of the plague hospital and the Indian Association?
- Four points were put forward in demands; he gained only one and a half. He is leaving them to fight the battle all over again.
- The compromise affects Mahommedans' marriages.
- What merchants have gained from eight year's struggle?

H.O. Ally, who had in 1909 accompanied Gandhiji on a deputation to England, raised a number of issues, such as:

- "...In his speech ... , Mr. Gandhi had admitted that the colonial-born question was not settled.
- Many things were not settled, and yet with what right or face could any Indian organisations apply to General Smuts in the future, and say there were certain disabilities and grievances that were killing their people - in the face of Mr. Gandhi's expressions here of the 'final honourable settlement'?"[696]

And further:

> "What they wanted him to explain to them was how they were going to live in future. They had trusted Mr. Gandhi. He (the speaker) was one of his admirers. He (Mr. Gandhi) knew that it was his elder brother that was talking to him. It was not one who was jealous of him. .... But he (the speaker) never knew that Mr. Gokhale cabled to Mr. Gandhi that it was a mistake not to submit to the Commission the real grievances of the Indians throughout the Transvaal. He now understood that Mr. Gandhi had received such a cable and had spent about £200 on sending a lengthy cable to Bombay about the oath to continue passive resistance until the four points were settled."[697]

About the settlements Ally stated:

> "No sensible man expected the Union Government to legalise polygamous marriages. But Mr. Gandhi ought to know very well, because a message was sent to him from that Hall, that it was impossible for Mussulmans to break one syllable out of their holy Koran. He was told that, whatever he did with regard to the marriage question, not to bind the *Mussulmans with regard to one man one wife, because they would be transgressing the law of God.* And the Koran said that 'Whosoever transgresses the statutes of God will be cast into hell fire for ever.' Therefore they could not accept the law and would remain in the country as unmarried. *Not a single Mussulman had accepted the*

Cape law of 1860. In fairness it was his duty to call a public meeting before talking of an honourable final Settlement."[698]

According to newspaper: "*He challenged Mr. Gandhi to call a mass meeting and produce the minute books of the British Indian Association.*"[699]

Other members asked Gandhi:

"How Mr. Gandhi could say he represented Indian opinion, when the *Hamidia Islamic Society and the Hamdad Society* passed a resolution on March 31 saying that he and his friends had no authority to act for them? He had been deliberately repudiated by the two societies. Mr. Gandhi received certain funds for the passive resistance movement, and it was up to him to give an account of them." Another member, Habib Motan, asked "if Mr. Gandhi did not take £1200 for the Phoenix newspaper."[700]

Gandhi replied:

"The first question was on whose authority he had accepted or arranged this settlement with the Government. It was on the authority of the general body of the Indians throughout South Africa, because when the final letter of Mr. Cachalia was sent, it was sent in the name of the British Indian community. He was the secretary and carried on the negotiations, and when he found that there was nothing he had to abandon but that he could get all, he did not consider it necessary to come to them again. It was not possible for any public man to do otherwise....."[701]

The next question was what had he done with the hospital money? There had been some misunderstanding about this. Gandhi stated that the origin of this fund was as follows:

"The stands in the old location had been expropriated, and he acted on behalf of certain claimands against the Town Council. He did not charge the full legal fees, which, taxed, would have amounted to £40 or £50. He agreed to charge so much a stand, and told them that he did not want it all for himself. £5 he would use for his own purposes, and set the balance aside as the nucleus of a hospital fund. …. The whole of that fund had been used up in the course of the passive resistance movement for public purposes and South African public purposes; but he was unable to hold himself responsible to the public in connection with those funds; but even a child could come and look at his public dealings."[702]

With regard to the accounts of the British Indian Association, Gandhi said:

"Every time they had held a committee meeting, he had submitted accounts of disbursements. Later on he had several funds—the anti-Indian law fund, the passive resistance fund, and the funds from Bombay. All these he had accounted for, some in the columns of the Press. He was not taking the books away, and at any time they could ask Mr. Polak as to the disposal of the funds."[703]

The next question was how many points had been gained. "The points in Mr. Cachalia's letter were the marriage question, the £3 tax, the Orange Free State and the Cape entry question, and the administration of the existing legislation with due regard to the Indians' feelings. They had got these five points, and a little more."[704]

Now what had the merchants gained? Gandhi replied:

"The merchands (merchants) had gained everything that the community had gained, and had gained probably most of all. The Indian community had raised its status in the estimation of Europeans throughout South Africa. They could no longer be classed as coolies by General Botha and others. The term had been removed as a term of reproach, silently but effectively. If they had not fought for the past eight years, no trace would have been left here of Indians as a self-respecting community. They might have been able to live in the Locations and eke out the miserable existence of coolies and dogs. If they had asked for more they would not have got it, and would have been hounded out of court and been regarded as a community not to be trusted."[705]

As for the future, Gandhi said that:

"The Settlement was final in the sense that passive resistance was closed. His own letter to General Smuts had left the door open. The Settlement was that of the passive resistance on the questions that were on the board for which they had fought and bled and suffered. It did not close anything else. It did not prevent them from holding mass meetings, passing resolutions and taking up new passive resistance."[706]

Further Gandhi said:

"The inter-provincial immigration was an open question yet. That was not in the terms of the Settlement, and it was a fair matter for agitation on the part of the Indian community. The Settlement did not bind himself or the Indian community not to restart passive resistance if they came to the conclusion that they had grievances which would justify it. Take the Free State question, the licensing laws, the gold laws, and the township laws."[707]

On marriage and religion issue Gandhi rebutted as follows:

"... The Settlement did not violate one iota of the Holy Koran. He had admitted that they did not expect a Christian community to legalise polygamy, so that there was no point at issue. …. He did not think the letter he had received was representative of Mahomedan opinion. It was their duty if they wanted a meeting at that time to call it and invite him."[708]

"With regard to the £1200, he pointed out that "Indian Opinion" was a public Indian property - it was only nominally registered in his name. The money was expended on behalf of the public, and he had rendered the accounts and had published them."[709]

Magna Charta – Farewell Letter – "A Confidential Circular" to Serve the Empire in WWI

Gandhi summarized his achievements as follows: "As I understand it, the Settlement which has taken place is a charter of our freedom. ... More it is not possible to secure at present."[710] He hoped that: "If the Indian community is strong and itself enterprising, if it maintains unity, truthfulness and courage, the following expectations may be realized in 15 years:

1. Complete freedom of trade.

2. Full rights of ownership of land in all Provinces and

3. Freedom of movement from one Province to another.

In order to bring all this about, it will be necessary to have the Licensing Acts, the Gold Laws, the Township Act, Law 3 of 1885 and the Immigration Act amended, for which purpose public opinion will have to be cultivated among the whites of South Africa. This is not difficult to do."[711]

Historians have different views about Gandhi's achievements. His contemporary and opponents like Aiyar had been quoted by authors as follows:

> "He accused Gandhi of being arrogant and a false patriot who did not interest himself in the welfare of the people. Gandhi was quick to attribute failure to the government, according to Aiyar, a "slippery customer" who "unblushingly" called the settlement a Magna Charta when it was simply a "farce". Gandhi said that only a "minority" opposed the settlement. Aiyar commented bitterly that the

"minority" did not get money from India, or organize crowds for shouting down opponents, or have the support of the "Junta" (public) at Field Street."⁷¹²

Gandhi's general "Farewell letter" was published in the "Indian Opinion". About the settlement he wrote:

> "..., it is the Magna Charta of our liberty in this land. *I give it the historic name, not because it gives us rights which we have never enjoyed and which are in themselves new or striking,* but because it has come to us after eight years' strenuous suffering, that has involved the loss of material possessions and of precious lives. I call it our Magna Charta because it marks a change in the policy of the Government towards us and establishes our right not only to be consulted in matters affecting us, but to have our reasonable wishes respected. It moreover confirms the theory of the British Constitution that there should be no legal racial inequality between different subjects of the Crown, no matter how much practice may vary according to local circumstance."⁷¹³

More importantly: "..., the Settlement may well be called our Magna Charta, because it has vindicated passive resistance as a lawful, clean weapon, and has given in passive resistance a new strength to the community and I consider it an infinitely superior force to that of the vote, which history shows has often been turned against the voters themselves."⁷¹⁴

To show his superiority over other Indian leaders and opponents, he told that their number is very small to be considered seriously. Their criticism is wrong that we have achieved too little. According to Gandhi's opinion, we achieved "all", what was demanded in Cachalia letter, written last year. He was afraid that we would have achieved nothing if we had demanded more. Further he argued that the present settlement does not preclude them from agitation against the Gold Law, the Townships Act and Trade Licences Laws in different stated. He wrote: "… , but these laws are in themselves defective, and can be, as they have been, turned into engines of oppression and instruments by indirect means to drive the resident Indian population from South Africa."[715]

What we note in the forgoing farewell letter and speeches is that he thanked Indians and "European friends." *There is not even a single word about the natives, to whom, the country belonged.*

Arrival in London

In the middle of July 1914, Gandhi left for London. He was accompanied by his wife and H. Kallenbach.[716] "A batch of some twenty-five Phoenix students, a few teachers and Maganlal Gandhi left for India in the first week of Aug. 1914, to join Tagore's Santiniketan."[717]

Gandhi *et al.* reached London on Aug. 4, 1914. At Cecil Hotel their Indian friends gave a reception. Some of these friends were either already known politicians or were going to play important role in future. Some of them to be mentioned are: Sarojini Naidu, Lala Lajpat Rai, M.A. Jinnah, Bhupendra Nath Basu.[718]

Then WWI had begun. In the past, Gandhi was loyal to the Imperial Government. In his reception speech of Aug. 8, 1914, he boasted of his "Magna Charta."[719] However, his main concern was the present political situation. He stated: "I would make the briefest reference to the tremendous crisis which has overwhelmed the Empire. Since we reached England and heard the news, I have been reading and thinking about it. I think of husbands and sons who have gone to fight, of mothers, wives, and sisters left weeping behind."[720] Like in previous wars, he imposed question to the audiences: "What is my duty?" Shortly after that "A Confidential circular" - "Indian offer to assist the British Government during the War", dated Aug. 13, 1914, was prepared. It was signed by Gandhi, Kasturba (Gandhi's wife), Sarojini Naidu and fifty others. It reads:

> "We, the undersigned have, after mature deliberation, decided for the sake of the Motherland and the Empire to place our services unconditionally, during this crisis, at the disposal of the Authorities. We advisedly use the word 'unconditionally' as we believe that, at a moment like this, no service that can be assigned to us can be considered to be beneath our dignity or inconsistent with our self-respect."[721]

Gandhi wanted to play the role of "Chairman of the Volunteer Corps" but was unhappy that due to bad health, he could not continue to support the mission. Before leaving London, in a farewell party, on Dec. 18, 1914, he gave a long speech and told: "The whole idea of the Corps arose because he felt that there should be some outlet for the anxiety of Indians to help in the crisis which had come upon the Empire."[722]

For supporting the British Empire in wars Gandhi was awarded the title of Sergeant Major as well as the Kaiser-i-Hind Gold Medal. In response to this honour he wrote to H. Kallenbach: "I understand that the Kaisar-i-Hind Gold Medal has been awarded to me. I have no official intimation as yet. My difficulties here are of a different type altogether and some of them most trying. When I have greater leisure, I shall describe them to you."[723] Gandhi was not entirely satisfied with the honour. He wrote: "*The medal has worried me.* It was announced without consultation. To refuse a medal would have been churlish. I therefore said nothing about it. I wrote a note to the Viceroy when at length a formal letter conferring the medal came to me. *It is not considered the same as a title.* It was presented last week at a Government at-home."[724]

In the previous chapters we have seen that Gandhi needed money for political activities. In the next chapter, we shall see who were his supporters? What were their interests?

Notes and References

[599] Indian Opinion, 22-3-1913.

[600] Gandhi M.K. to Registrar of Asiatics, April 11, 1913.

[601] Indian Opinion, 22-3-1913.

[602] Indian Opinion, 29-3-1913. "Another case of the same nature, regarding one Bai Janubie, has come to our knowledge. This lady is

a widow, whose husband has left her his property by a will. The Master of the Supreme Court, however, refuses to execute the will. He states that Bai Janubie's marriage cannot be recognized as valid."

[603] Gandhi M.K. to Minister of Interior, April 1, 1913.

[604] Indian Opinion, 31-5-1913.

[605] The Natal Mercury, 3-6-1913.

[606] Indian Opinion, 31-5-1913.

[607] The Transvaal Leader, 30-9-1913.

[608] Gandhi M.K. to Gandhi M., Oct. 2, 1913.

[609] Indian Opinion, 15-10-1913.

[610] Gandhi M.K. to Kallenbach H., Oct. 30, 1913.

[611] Indian Opinion, 12-4-1913.

[612] Gandhi M.K. to Gokhale G.K., April 19, 1913.

[613] Indian Opinion, 17-5-1913.

[614] Indian Opinion, 24-5-1913.

[615] The Natal Mercury, 11-6-1913.

[616] C.W.M.G. 13, 1913, p. 403.

[617] Gandhi M.K. to Minister of Interior, June 28, 1913. On June 16, 1913, on behalf of the B.I.A., A.M. Cachalia sent a telegram to the Governer-General, Pretoria, and pointed out these four issues.

[618] Indian Opinion, 19-7-1913.

[619] Indian Opinion, 13-9-1913.

[620] Indian Opinion, 20-9-1913.

[621] Indian Opinion, 29-10-1913.

[622] The Rand Daily Mail, 15-9-1913.

[623] Indian Opinion, 20-9-1913.

[624] Indian Opinion, 20-9-1913.

[625] Bhana S., Vadeh G.H., The making of a social reformer – Gandhi in South Africa 1893-1914, online, http://www.mkgandhi-sarvodaya.org/social_reform/social_reform.htm, Feb. 5, 2015.

[626] http://www.mkgandhi-sarvodaya.org/social_reform/social_reform.htm, Feb. 5, 2015.

[627] http://www.mkgandhi-sarvodaya.org/social_reform/social_reform.htm, Feb. 5, 2015.

[628] Indian Opinion, 24-9-1913.

[629] Indian Opinion, 24-9-1913.

[630] Indian Opinion, 24-9-1913.

[631] Indian Opinion, 24-9-1913.

[632] Indian Opinion, 29-10-1913.

[633] Indian Opinion, 26-4-1913.

[634] Indian Opinion, 26-4-1913.

[635] Indian Opinion, 3-5-1913.

[636] Indian Opinion, 3-5-1913.

[637] Indian Opinion, 3-5-1913.

[638] Indian Opinion, 3-5-1913.

[639] Marshall Campbell was "one of the wealthiest and most influential sugar barons, controllingthe vast Natal Estates as well as successfully promoting Natal sugar interests through his political career as Member of Legislative Assembly in Natal from 1893, and later as a Union Senator. Although Campbell believed they should never have been brought to Natal, he did employ Indians on his estates in Inanda when he entered the sugar business in the 1870s. An advisor to both Dube and Gandhi on matters of political organisation and strategy, he encouraged gradual social change and favoured careful control from a leadership which would use its influence to maintain order." Hughes H., 'The coolies will elbow us out of the country': African reactions to Indian immigration in the colony of Natal, Labour History Review, 72, 155-168, 2007.

[640] C.W.M.G. 14, 1913-1915, p. 19.

[641] The Natal Mercury, 5-1-1914.

[642] C.W.M.G. 14, 1913-1915, p. 18.

[643] Indian Opinion, 29-10-1913.

[644] Gandhi M.K. to Kallenbach H., Oct. 23, 1913.

[645] The Natal Mercury, 27-10-1913.

[646] Wolpert S., Gandhi's passion - The life and legacy of Mahatma Gandhi, Oxford University Press, Oxford 2001, p. 80.

[647] Indian Opinion, 12-11-1913.

[648] The Times of India, 5-11-1913.

[649] The Times of India, 7-11-1913.

[650] Indian Opinion, 12-11-1913.

[651] Indian Opinion, 19-11-1913.

[652] Gandhi M.K. to Gandhi M., Nov. 11, 1913.

[653] C.W.M.G. 13, 1913, p. 414.

[654] The Natal Mercury, 22-12-1913.

[655] Indian Opinion, 24-12-1913.

[656] The Natal Mercury, 22-12-1913.

[657] Gandhi M.K. to Campbell M., Dec. 26, 1913.

[658] The Rand Daily Mail, 23-10-1913.

[659] http://www.mkgandhi-sarvodaya.org/social_reform/social_reform.htm, Feb. 5, 2015.

[660] The Rand Daily Mail, 23-10-1913.

[661] Gandhi M.K. to Kallenbach H., Oct. 27, 1913.

[662] The Times of India, 25-10-1913.

[663] For a short biography of W.W. Pearson, see, Nauriya A., William Winstanley Pearson - The Natal experience, Natalia 44, 70 – 78, 2014.

[664] Copley A., Gandhi against the tide, Basil Blackwell Inc., Cambridge 1989, p. 33.

[665] Indian Opinion, 7-1-1914.

[666] Indian Opinion, 14-1-1914.

[667] C.W.M.G. 14, 1913-1915, pp. 33-35.

[668] Gandhi M.K. to Kallenbach H., Jan. 18, 1914.

[669] Indian Opinion, 28-1-1914.

[670] Gandhi M.K. to Gokhale G.K., Jan. 30, 1914.

[671] C.W.M.G. 14, 1913-1915, pp. 53-54.

[672] http://www.mkgandhi-sarvodaya.org/social_reform/social_reform.htm, Feb. 5, 2015.

[673] Indian Opinion, 18-3-1914.

[674] Indian Opinion, 15-7-1914.

[675] Gandhi M.K. to Gokhale G.K., Feb. 27, 1914.

[676] Gandhi M.K. to Gokhale G.K., Feb. 27, 1914.

[677] Gandhi M.K. to Gandhi C., March 11, 1914.

[678] Gandhi M.K. to Gandhi C., March 11, 1914.

[679] Gandhi M.K. to Robertson B., March 6, 1914.

[680] Gandhi M.K. to Gokhale G.K., May 6, 1914.

[681] Indian Opinion, 3-6-1914.

[682] Gandhi M.K. to Gokhale G.K., June 5, 1914.

[683] Gandhi M.K. to Campbell M., June 20, 1914.

[684] Gandhi M.K. to Gorges E.M., June 30, 1914.

[685] Indian Opinion, 8-7-1914.

[686] Indian Opinion, 29-7-1914.

[687] Indian Opinion, 9-9-1914.

[688] Indian Opinion, 22-7-1914.

[689] Indian Opinion, 22-7-1914.

[690] Indian Opinion, 22-7-1914.

[691] Indian Opinion, 29-7-1914.

[692] Indian Opinion, 5-8-1914.

[693] Indian Opinion, 5-8-1914.

[694] Indian Opinion, 5-8-1914.

[695] C.W.M.G. 14, 1913-1915, p. 245.

[696] C.W.M.G. 14, 1913-1915, pp. 247-248.

[697] C.W.M.G. 14, 1913-1915, pp. 247-248.

[698] C.W.M.G. 14, 1913-1915, pp. 247-248.

[699] C.W.M.G. 14, 1913-1915, pp. 247-248.

[700] C.W.M.G. 14, 1913-1915, pp. 247-248.

[701] The Rand Daily Mail, 16-7-1914.

[702] The Rand Daily Mail, 16-7-1914.

[703] The Rand Daily Mail, 16-7-1914.

[704] The Rand Daily Mail, 16-7-1914.

[705] The Rand Daily Mail, 16-7-1914.

[706] The Rand Daily Mail, 16-7-1914.

[707] The Rand Daily Mail, 16-7-1914.

[708] The Rand Daily Mail, 16-7-1914.

[709] The Rand Daily Mail, 16-7-1914.

[710] Indian Opinion, 29-7-1914.

[711] Indian Opinion, 29-7-1914.

[712] http://www.mkgandhi-sarvodaya.org/social_reform/social_reform.htm, Feb. 5, 2015.

[713] Indian Opinion, 29-7-1914.

[714] Indian Opinion, 29-7-1914.

[715] Indian Opinion, 29-7-1914.

[716] The Natal Mercury, 20-7-1914.

[717] C.W.M.G. 14, 1913-1915, p. 277.

[718] C.W.M.G. 14, 1913-1915, p. 280.

[719] Indian Opinion, 30-9-1914.

[720] Indian Opinion, 30-9-1914.

[721] Indian Opinion, 16-9-1914.

[722] Indian Opinion, Jan. 27, 1915.

[723] Gandhi M.K. to Kallenbach H., June 7, 1915.

[724] Gandhi M.K. to Kallenbach H., July 2, 1915.

Gandhi, Satyagraha and Money

Gandhi's biographer, the missionary, J.J. Doke, whose only source of information was personal contact, has exaggerated about Gandhi's family. For instance, "Gandhi's doors were open for all – a Brahmin or Shudra. Every morning there were 20 to 30 poor siting before the door, who were helped. Gandhi's mother house looked like a Closter in middle ages and the mother as a holy Elisabeth."[725] How lofty are such statements can be judged from the fact that for study in London, he had to borrow money and sell the jewelry of his wife. In his autobiography Gandhi said that his father as a "Prime Minister" was earning not more than 300 rupees a month.[726] The salary of a "Prime Minister" seems to be quite low, if we see that Gandhi applied for a job as English teacher, where he had to teach one hour a day to get 75 rupees per month. He did not get the job as he was not a graduate.[727] For his first case in court he charged 30 rupees as fee. The case was a flop. Gandhi recalled:

> "This was my debut in the Small Causes Court. I appeared for the defendant and had thus to cross-examine the plaintiff's witnesses. I stood up, but my heart sank into my boots. My head was reeling and I felt as though the whole court was doing likewise. I could think of no question to ask. …. I sat down and told the agent that I could not conduct the case, that he had better engage Patel and have the fee back from me. Mr. Patel was duly engaged for Rs. 51. To him, of course, the case was child's play."[728]

Due to his brother's contact, Gandhi was asked by Sheth Abdul Karim Jhaveri a partner of Dada Abdulla & Co to help them for a case in South Africa, which was worth of £40000. He was told: "We have big Europeans as our friends, whose acquaintance you will make. You can be useful to us our shop. Much of our correspondence is in English and you can help us with that too. You will, of course, be our guest and hence will have no expense whatever."[729] He had a contract for one year, which included a first class return ticket and a salary of 105 pounds.[730]

Gandhi and Financial Affairs

Until the end of the 19th century, the main source of the N.I.C. was membership fees or donations from traders. In 1905, Gandhi was of the opinion that: *"In the modern world, money is needed at every step*; and if it runs short, one has to face disappointment in the end, however great and noble one's hopes and aspirations might be. *Just as man needs food, so does public work require money.*"[731]

As we have seen above, the mass political movement began in 1907. In order to discuss the planning of the political movement and the money required for that, in March 1907, a mass meeting was organized. The "Indian Opinion" suggested to collect more funds.[732] In June 1907, referring to the report of the Women Association, U.K., Gandhi stated that they are spending 100 pounds per week.[733] He told his countrymen that to get their rights "they had to spend £13000 and 13000 Indians had to go to gaol. Till now Indians have not spent even £2000 all told, and no Indian has so far suffered imprisonment. And yet to believe that we could get our rights is, it would seem, a patent mistake."[734] His organisations, the N.I.C. and B.I.A. were not well off. In Sept., 1907, the latter had only 100 pounds[735], whereas the former had debt.[736] Gandhi's rescue was the rich Jew H. Kallenbach, who had sympathy for the Indians' cause. Gandhi's expenses were paid by him.[737]

In Feb. 1908, Gandhi told Muslim businessmen that they had to donate money as: "It is they whose interests are most heavily involved. …. Therefore it is they who especially feel the disgrace of the Act. …, if they have any iota of decency left in them, can join the movement."[738] The first biggest donation from India was due to the Indian industrialist R.J. Tata, who in Dec., 1908, sent 25000 rupees (1630 pounds) "for his countrymen in South Africa."[739] It was too little. Gandhi asked the businessmen to "lighten their pockets" as their "generosity will be justified; *it will also please God.*"[740] As their reaction was not quite positive, once again he appealed: "*They will have to sacrifice their money*, as women were sacrificed (in the olden days). *If not, they will be dishonoured and find their money as bitter as poison.* No religion believes it possible to worship God and Mammon at the same time. *Every religion teaches that if one wants to devote oneself to God, one must forsake wealth.*"[741]

They were not convinced. They were of the opinion that in the past they have done enough. Gandhi had no argument against it. In Dec. 1909, he wrote a letter to Gokhale and told about the pathetic situation of his "satyagraha and followers" as follows: "*The strongest have ruined themselves pecuniarily*, and they simply go to gaol as often as the Government arrest them. *Their families have also to be supported.* When this struggle commenced, I bore the whole of the expenses of the office, as also the rent of offices, which were really for my practice, but, *for the last two years, I have done very little legal work.*"[742]

Once again, Ratanji Jamshedji Tata of Bombay gave 25000 rupees.[743] Gokhale contributed 400 pounds.[744] In the end of Dec. 1909, Gandhi summed up the financial loses during the three years as follows: "The struggle has cost already, I think, no less than £10000. In this I include the expenses of all sub-committees, which are not found in the advertised accounts of the Central Association, but *I exclude the enormous losses that individuals have suffered.*"[745]

As the money was coming from abroad, in particularly India, it led to questions that Gandhi's movement was being engineered and controlled from abroad. Gandhi agreed that the struggle was being financed from India and England.[746] Meanwhile, due to awareness in India, the support was increasing. In the middle of Feb. 1910, Dr. Mehtra, Secretary of the Transvaal Satyagraha Fund Committee, said that 250 pounds have been received from Rangoon. In total there were 3923 pounds.[747]

As less was known about the management of funds, Gandhi was once questioned about it. He replied that the Passive Resistance Fund Account is being operated by him. The money is meant for the maintenance of indigent satyagrahis and their families. Gandhi wrote:

> "The rest is being used for financing the satyagraha campaign, that is, to meet the expenditure of the British Indian Association office here and in England and the expenditure incurred in India and also to pay off the debts incurred for the satyagraha campaign. Mr. Cachalia and

other satyagrahis are being consulted about all this expenditure and accounts of the same are forwarded to Prof. Gokhale and to the Secretary of the Fund, Mr. Petit."[748]

So far as his farm and the weekly "Indian Opinion" were concerned, Gandhi told:

"The Phoenix debt represented a personal debt incurred by me from European friends and clients by reason of the necessity of having to continue "Indian Opinion" under somewhat adverse circumstances and at a loss in the interests of the struggle. I have devoted to the continuance of "Indian Opinion" and the establishment of Phoenix *all my earnings* during my last stay in South Africa, that is, *nearly £5000.*"[749]

About the support of satyagrahis' families he stated: "The monthly expenses for relieving distress have, however, ..., gone forward, and, whereas, in the month of December only £25 was paid, on the present basis it comes to nearly £160 per month, over fifty families receiving support. ..... The expenses for supporting distressed families are bound to increase as time passes. I, therefore, put them down at £200 per month."[750]

With his calculations he showed that in the end of this year, no money will be left. In Sept., 1910, Gandhi had good news for the readers. Polak, who went to India on deputation, had collected over 6000 pounds for the passive resistance.[751] Gandhi's friend M.K. Natesan convinced the Maharaja of Bikaner, Maharaja of Mysore and Nizam of Hyderabad, who donated 1000, 2000 and 2500 rupees respectively.[752] On Dec. 9, 1910, Gandhi wrote to him:

> "Many thanks for the cable remitting £400. .... The unexpected difficulties about the landing of the returned deportees have cost over £500 leaving nothing for current expenses. I was therefore obliged to cable to you for funds. A similar cable was sent to Mr. Petit also. The same day that brought your cable brought also a letter from Mr. Ratan Tata enclosing a cheque for Rs. 25000."[753]

In Sept. 1912, Tata once again donated. Gandhi wrote:

> "At the Sheriff's meeting held at Bombay on the 31st ultimo and presided over by Sir Jamsetji, it was announced that Mr. Tata had given a third contribution of Rs. 25,000 to the Transvaal passive resistance fund. The total given by Mr. Tata therefore amounts to £5,000 - a fortune in itself. Mr. Petit has already cabled to Mr. Gandhi £1,500. Mr. Tata's munificence shows not only his large-heartedness, but also his keen appreciation of the struggle."[754]

From the forgoing we see that Gandhi had enough money for the movement. In June 1913, he informed Gokhale: "The struggle is expected to last a year but if we have more men than I anticipate, it may close during the next session of the Union Parliament. .... It is difficult to answer what amount will be required to see the community through the crisis. At the lowest calculation made by me, nothing in cash will be required."[755]

Gandhi had made calculations without considering the politics of Generals Botha and Smuts. Gandhi successfully managed to move the masses, but the generals refused to arrest them. Consequently they had to be fed by Gandhi. In despair he sent a telegram to Gokhale telling that monthly expenses are more than 7000 pounds. The local contribution expected every month is about 1000 pounds.[756] In Dec. 1913, nearly 1500 pounds were received from India. Out of them 660 pounds came from an influential Muslim leader, the Aga Khan.[757]

We have seen above that many families were ruined. Gandhi as a lawyer, knew – How to save his own property? He wrote to H. Kallenbach:

> "*If I am arrested, you should immediately transfer the Johannesburg balance in your name* and open a separate account called Agency Account. *I may be fined. I shall make a statement to the effect that I have nothing I can call my own*, that I have given up everything and that even in those things which are in my name I have no interest of my own. You and others should likewise say and return '*nulla bona.*' In order to avoid technicalities the accounts may be transferred. *The account at Durban should be withdrawn and it should be redeposited in the names of West and Maganlal,* either having the power to operate upon it severally. The paper too should be transferred in the names of West and Maganlal and the trustees may transfer it and the Press to them at pepper-cornrent."[758]

The Interests of the Supporters

As stated before the traders had their reasons to support Gandhi. So far as H. Kallenbach is concerned, he can be seen as a philanthropist, who was convinced by Gandhi's life philosophy. Neither politically nor financially had he benefited from Gandhi. Gokhale's support had the political and patriotic touch. What about Tatas or Sultan Muhammad Shah Aga Khan (who, in 1924, had to compete with Gandhi for the Peace Nobel Prize nomination[759])? Both families had already migrated from the Persian area. Tatas and Khan had no problem to support the Empire with money. The amount sent to Gandhi (due to Gokhale's connection) was even less than "peanuts." Thus Tata's support can be seen as a tactic to keep good contact with pro-British Empire political leaders like Gokhale. After Gandhi settled in India, he was financed by Birla's, the textile baron. India's political history tells us that even today both families dominate India's economy. So far Gandhi is concerned, for good reasons, he neither protested against Tatas or Birlas. He could not, as he had "sold his soul" for some thousands rupees. Gandhi's other supporter, Aga Khan, at the age of eight was awarded the title of His Highness by the British Empire.[760] He was a supporter of the Turkish ruler. Thus his support to the pro-Turkish Muslim community in S.A. Gandhi, Khan and R.J. Tata supported the British in WWI. The financial support 200 Pounds and 50 Pounds came from Khan and Tata respectively.[761]

In general, to convince others to get money, Gandhi manipulated their religious and patriotic sentiments. This is the same case as when he wanted them to go to jail or sacrifice their lives and health (detail later).

Notes and References

[725] Doke J.J., Gandhi in Südafrika – Mohandas Karamchand Gandhi – Ein indischer Patriot in Südafrika, Rotapfel Verlag, Erlenbach-Zürich 1925, p. 40.

[726] Gandhi M.K., An autobiography or the story of my experiments with truth, Navajivan Publishing House, Ahmedabad 1940, p. 48.

[727] Gandhi M.K., An autobiography or the story of my experiments ..., 1940, p. 48.

[728] Gandhi M.K., An autobiography or the story of my experiments ...., 1940, p. 48.

[729] Gandhi M.K., An autobiography or the story of my experiments ..., 1940, p. 52.

[730] Gandhi M.K., An autobiography or the story of my experiments ..., 1940, p. 52.

[731] Indian Opinion, 25-2-1905.

[732] Indian Opinion, 23-3-1907.

[733] Indian Opinion, 29-6-1907.

[734] Indian Opinion, 29-6-1907.

[735] Indian Opinion, 7-9-1907.

[736] Indian Opinion, 11-5-1907.

[737] Indian Opinion, 19-9-1908.

[738] Indian Opinion, 6-2-1909.

[739] Doke J.J., Gandhi in Südafrika – ...., 1925, p. 194.

[740] Indian Opinion, 29-5-1909.

[741] Indian Opinion, 23-1-1909.

[742] Gandhi M.K. to Gokhale G.K., Dec. 6, 1909.

[743] Indian Opinion, 4-12-1909.

[744] Indian Opinion, 25-12-1909.

[745] Gandhi M.K. to Gokhale G.K., Dec. 6, 1909.

[746] Gandhi M.K. to Gibson J.C., Jan. 6, 1910.

[747] Indian Opinion, 12-2-1910.

[748] Indian Opinion, 5-3-1910. See also, Indian Opinion, 7-5-1910.

[749] Indian Opinion, 7-5-1910.

[750] Indian Opinion, 7-5-1910.

[751] Indian Opinion, 10-9-1910.

[752] Gandhi M.K. to Natesan G.A., Dec. 9, 1910.

[753] Gandhi M.K. to Natesan G.A., Dec. 9, 1910.

[754] Indian Opinion, 10-8-1912.

[755] Gandhi M.K. to Gokhale G.K., June 20, 1913.

[756] The Times of India, 7-11-1913.

[757] http://www.mkgandhi-sarvodaya.org/social_reform/social_reform.htm, Feb. 5, 2015.

[758] Gandhi M.K. to Kallenbach H., Oct. 30, 1913.

[759] For more detail, see Singh R., Mahatma Gandhi – Sex scandals and the missed Nobel Peace Prize, Shaker 'Verlag', Aachen 2015, pp. 55-72.

[760] For a short biography of Aga Khan, see, http://www.ismaili.net/histoire/history08/history820.html, Aug. 17, 2014.

[761] C.W.M.G. 14, 1913-1915, p. 322.

Prison as a "Palace" – Tales of Suffering

In Sept., 1906, people were asked to take an oath and go to jails. Gandhi had told them that it is like living in a palace! Albeit at that time, he had never been in jail. In the beginning of 1907, Gandhi asked his countrymen: "... Will they emulate the *manliness shown by English women* and wake up? *Will they choose to find happiness in prison taking it to be a palace*, or will they submit to oppression when the Transvaal Government starts it? In a few days our mettle will be tested." [762] In fact, Gandhi's "mettle-test" was too hard. In 1907 there were ca. 9000 Indians in Transvaal. After the movement started, many left the state. A year later, the number was reduced to less than 6000.[763]

In 1907, after Lord Elgin gave assent to the immigration act. Gandhi asked his countrymen: "..., never to accept such a law. And, if it is enforced, *he will rather go to gaol than carry a pass like a Kaffir. True victory will be won only when the entire Indian community courageously marches to the gaol* - when the time comes - *and stays there as if it were a palace.*"[764] As we have seen earlier, one of the first resisters, Pandit R. Sunder, sent an exaggerated positive report. He felt as if he is in a palace; and he is being looked after by the Governor and the Chief Warden of the prison.[765] Was it really so, or was it Gandhi's interpretation who visited the priest. In the following we shall see:

- How were the living conditions in gaol, which was called "palace" by Gandhi?
- How the families were ruined during the struggle?

- How many persons died and ruined their health?

- How many persons were deported?

Living Conditions in Prisons

In general, Gandhi had no positive opinion about the natives. While writing about his experience in gaol, he stated:

> "There are some dangerous murderers among the Kaffir prisoners in gaol. We find these prisoners constantly engaged in disputes. After they are locked up in the cell, they quarrel among themselves. Sometimes, they openly defy the warder. One warder was twice assaulted by the prisoners. Indian prisoners are obviously in danger when locked up in the same cell with these."[766]

Gandhi's observation was not quite wrong. A prisoner Syed Ali told about his experience at Boksburg as follows:

> *"When I was admitted, a Kaffir came to me and asked me to strip myself naked.* I did so. I was then made to walk, in that condition, barefoot, some distance. *I was then kept, together with Kaffirs, in cold water, for twenty-five minutes.* I was then taken out and taken to an office. I was then given some clothes to wear, but I did not get any sandals. I, therefore, asked the gaoler for some. At first, he said 'no', and then he gave me torn sandals. *I asked for socks and he used abusive language.*"[767]

S. Ali continued:

"On the 20th August, the work given to me was that of carrying and emptying closet buckets. I complained to the gaoler about this work, and I *received a kick and slaps*. I still persisted in my complaint, and told him that I would be glad to break stones but would like to be relieved from the work of carrying and emptying these buckets. *I was then kicked again*. I became helpless and I had to carry those buckets."[768]

And further:

"On the 22nd August, Saturday, I was again kept in cold water for nearly half an hour. It was extremely cold. .... I then became, feverish. My chest became bad. On the 25th, I was discharged. The gaoler, on discharging, said 'You may come again, if you wish to die' and I retorted, 'All right, you may kill me if you can.' .... *And ever since I have been ill, and I have been discharging blood from the chest,* and am under medical advice."[769]

In a complaint, the Chairman of the B.I.A. wrote to the prison's director that: "I may add that the correspondent, as his name implies, is a direct descendant of the Prophet, and I need hardly comment upon the resentment that would be bitterly felt by Mahomedans, when they understand that such a person has been called upon to perform the dirtiest work at the Boksburg gaol."[770] While the Chairman of the B.I.A. protested about the mistreatment; Gandhi, who had lost smelling sense thus had no problem in cleaning toilets, wrote the following: "..., *we will carry buckets and suffer kicks. We will regard this as an expression of our nobility. Our* bonds will be loosened (only) when we (learn to) enjoy carrying buckets. Only then may we claim that we understand the meaning of satyagraha."[771] After some time Gandhi had to "change the meaning of satyagraha." On April 7, 1909, he sent the following bitter cable to the SABIC, London:

> "...HEIDELBERG PRISONERS STATING CONDITION STARVATION IMPROPER DIET FILTHY SURROUNDINGS UTTER INSANITATION NO WASHING BATHING FACILITIES NOR CHANGE CLOTHING. INDIAN PASSIVE RESISTERS TREATED WORSE KAFFIR CONVICTS. MANY HOSPITAL DYSENTERY FEVER HYSTERIA. GAOL AUTHORITIES BRUTAL. GOVERNMENT ENDEAVOURING BREAK DOWN MOVEMENT BY TORTURE."[772]

In 1910, one of the resisters, named Shelat had refused to clean toilets. For that he was mistreated. After his second arrest, Gandhi "hoped that this time, with the past experience to fall back upon, the authorities would let the matter rest and not force the issue by requiring Mr. Shelat to do that particular work."[773] In a letter the Director of prison was asked to grant him relief. It was declined. Instead of convincing his "satyagrahi", Gandhi complained: "To order lashes in order to compel a man to do anything against his conscience would be the height of barbarity. As a passive resister, Mr. Shelat will, no doubt, suffer cheerfully even the penalty of lashes. But for the authorities to persist in their brutal course can only add to the tension that already exists among Indians."[774]

Physically broken Indians: Many of the so-called satyagrahis were traders. They were not used to physical work. Not surprisingly they had to suffer in gaol. One such person was, Abdul Kadir Bawazeer, Chairman of the Hamidia Islamic Society. From prison he "returned almost a physical wreck."[775] In the case of Parsee Rustomjee, Vice President, N.I.C., a doctor wrote the following report: "I now find him very much reduced in weight and size, and that his health has greatly suffered from his late imprisonment, …. I find that his heart is affected, …. His eyes have also suffered from constant exposure to the sun, and are now in a state of congestion. There is distension of the flanks of the abdominal wall, …. He is also subject to delayed and difficult micturition."[776] Gandhi wrote in "Indian Opinion": "*Mr. Rustomjee is undergoing special medical treatment, Mr. Bawazeer can scarcely walk, Mr. Aswat is a cripple and Mr. Shah spits blood.*"[777] He attributed the cause of trouble to a lack of Indian food in prison.[778]

Joseph Royeppen, a barrister-at-law, belonged to a few educated South African born Indians, who followed Gandhi. In order to get arrested he went on round as hawker, going from place to place selling goods.[779] He was arrested and ordered for deportation.[780] In May 1910, "Indian Opinion" published his letter as follows:

> "*How they were kept standing barefoot on a cold stone floor, how they were kept undressed in a draughty passage,* how they were handcuffed and how brutally certain warders dealt with them, … Such treatment, instead of unnerving them, has, *we are glad to notice, strengthened them in their resolve to vindicate the national*

> *honour. ... We trust that the lead given by Mr. Royeppen will infuse a new spirit into the colonial-born and other Indians who have their work cut out before them if they wish to take part in the making of the future South African nation.*"[781]

As we have seen earlier, in 1913, the movement was at its highest point. Accordingly the prison's authorities were becoming harsher. On Oct. 9, 1913, a letter was sent to Gandhi by a prisoner. In part it reads:

> "They were asked to strip themselves entirely bare in the presence of other prisoners, for medical examination. They respectfully submitted to the doctor that it was contrary to their moral scruples and to their notions of decency, and they added that they were prepared to submit to the examination in a separate cell. Dr. Visser grew angry over this request and used most insulting language."[782]

So far women were concerned, Gandhi sent a telegram to the Minister of Interior, telling: "Goal director forcibly vaccinated passive resistance female prisoners by removing blouse and holding arm."[783] In Maritzburg prison *"P.K. Desai, was assaulted so violently that the blow sent him reeling to the ground and from there he was dragged to his cell. The treatment of the injuries kept him in the hospital for eleven days. ...* Rustomjee and his fellow-prisoners had to resort to a *fast to secure him* (permission to wear) *his shirt and sacred thread.*"[784] In another case: "*A youngster was beaten for standing out of line. On one occasion, several passive resisters went on a fast to register a strong protest against such treatment. At the end of four days of complete fasting, the boy referred to *above was forcibly fed while he kept shrieking in protest all the time.*"[785]

Food Problem

Compared to others, Gandhi had far better conditions but as soon as he entered the "palace", he was the first to write a petition on Jan. 21, 1908, and complained against the breakfast, as the food served was not "Indian", but that of the Kaffirs.[786] On Sept. 17, 1908, A.M. Cachalia, Chairman, B.I.A. sent a telegram to the Director of Prisons, Pretoria, and asked for better food for Indian prisoners. As many Indian prisoners became sick. Gandhi was of the opinion that it was due to the food. The government took action and made some changes but for Gandhi it was simply not enough. He wrote:

> "It is undoubtedly a matter for thankfulness that beans are added to the scale when Indians do not take meat. But the minute takes no note of the fact that, whilst beans are an admirable substitute for meat, they are no substitute for ghee (a clarified semifluid butter). We cannot, therefore, help saying that the civilized Government of the Transvaal must labour under the charge of wanton cruelty to the passive resisters so long as they callously continue to partially starve them."[787]

At some stage, instead of animal fat, the Government started supplying ghee. However, it was later stopped as Gandhi's article shows: ""The discharged passive resisters also *complained that there was no ghee or any vegetable fat supplied with their meals*, as used to be the case before. *Their meals, my Committee understands, consist of rice, mealie meal, vegetables, and a little bread.*"[788] As far as women's food was concerned, Gandhi sent a telegram to the Minister of Interior, saying: "Ladies not supplied with ghee, request investigation, prompt relief."[789] In Jan. 1914, the food condition became worse. "Indian Opinion" wrote that resisters have told: "The food was poor and was served, half cooked, in rusted tin bowls, ... *Cockroaches and insects were found in the food,* and, when the matter was reported to the officer, his reply was that a prison was no hotel and that even in a hotel one found insects in food."[790]

Gandhi – "They lived a most unnatural life" – "If anybody should have died it was Mrs. Gandhi"

Swami Nagappan, an eighteen years old young man took part in the movement and was prisoned. In the "palace" he had the following luxuries: "Early each morning he was taken to work on the roads, where he contracted double pneumonia. He died of this after he was released (on July 7, 1909)."[791] Just as Nagappan died of ill-treatment in jail, so also the hardships of deportation proved to be the death of Narayanswami (...)", wrote the author C.F. Andrews.[792] About the hardships, "Indian Opinion" wrote as follows:

> "... A. Narayansamy, was one of those who returned with Mr. Polak from India and who was not allowed to land in Durban. He proceeded, together with 31 others, to Port Elizabeth, and thence to Cape Town, where his landing, as also that of others, was prevented, and he was obliged to

return to Durban, with the prospect of being ultimately sent back to India. ... he and the other passive resisters were left without boots, hats, and even without sufficient clothing for the body, their clothes having been stolen at Port Elizabeth. But for the charity of the local Indians at Cape Town, they might have gone back to Durban without food. These men have been continuously on board now under exceptionally severe circumstances for nearly two months. It is not at all surprising, therefore, that poor Narayansamy has succumbed. I do not consider this a death in the ordinary course. It is undoubtedly a legalised murder."[793]

Even, women and children had to suffer. J.J. Doke wrote that a 20 year old girl died from exhaustion and other Indian women struggled with death for months.[794] A child died of bad weather.[795] Whereas Gandhi talked about the death of two babies during the march.[796] The most active members of the community were Hindi and Tamil speaking. Gandhi stated: *"Some of them have even lost their lives, killed by the bullets of the white soldiers.* As a tribute to their memory, we have decided to give Hindi and Tamil news in this paper."[797] The first woman to die for Gandhi's cause was Valliamah Moonsamy.[798] The cause of her death was "a prolonged illness in gaol."[799] In a private letter, Gandhi wrote to a friend:

> *"My first disappointment was that not a single Gujarati had died. Even I was left alive when those that did not want to die had gone. I then became conceited and felt that those that had died had done so because they had lived a most unnatural life. If anybody should have died it was Mrs.*

Gandhi. There is no guarantee even now that she will live. But she seems to be rallying and would certainly have succumbed under the orthodox treatment. And yet the desire in me to die is overpowering. I am unable to stare a Tamil in the face when I recall these deaths."[800]

In the memory of the dead resisters, Gandhi wished to construct a memorial. On March 2, 1914, he wrote to H. Kallenbach: "I think that if there is a settlement there will be a large surplus left. A part of it may be used for building Valliamma Hall in Johannesburg attached to which may be a school building or which itself may be a school, etc. There may be an outhouse for guests, etc. It should stand on a stand by its(elf). .... We shall have plenty of money for the purpose."[801]

Deportations

In 1907 the Transvaal Government passed a law of deportation.[802] Under the law, in 1908, twelve[803] and sixty-one persons were ordered to leave the state in September and October respectively.[804-805] In Feb. 1909, same was done with Dawad Mahomed, President N.I.C.[806] In the beginning, the deportees were sent to nearby colonies. Later the Government entered into an understanding with the Portuguese Government, which allowed using its territories to deport persons to India.[807] Gandhi lamented: "It cuts me to the quick, to hear of *a lad of sixteen being deported to India*, while his father remained in gaol at Volksrust."[808] In Aug. 1909, while Gandhi was on deputation in London, he told Earl of Crewe that he got a cable, which shows that about 100 Indians are likely to be deported to India. He requested the Imperial Government to interfere.[809] At the same time, Gandhi was expecting that deportation would "rouse the whole of India to protest."[810] In April 1910, "Indian Opinion" wrote: "Some of the young Indians who have been sent away were born in this country, some have lived here from their childhood and some have left their families here. Some, moreover, are residents of Natal or, being educated, are entitled to go over there. It is the extreme limit of tyranny that all these men have been sent away to India."[811]

In May 1910, 23 Indians were deported.[812] Under the Asiatic Act not only Indians but also Chinese were sent out. However, their Government safeguarded their interest. The Chinese Consul made good arrangements for their food, accommodation and transport from Colombo to China. A protest letter was sent to Lisbon.[813]

Once, twenty-six passive resisters were returned back from Bombay. On their arrival in Durban they claimed to be domicile of the Colony. Only thirteen were allowed to land and the rest were sent back. Gandhi "proudly" wrote: *"... the men who have been forced to go back have that stuff in them of which heroes are made."*[814] Little is known about the dignity of those who landed in India. At least, once "Indian Opinion" thanked G. A. Natesan of Madras, who rendered assistance to the homeless deportees.[815] In part, it was Gandhi's fault that colonial born Indians were deported, as he had told them that they cannot be deported.[816]

A balance of Gandhi's struggle is to be found in his letter of Sept. 12, 1913, to the Secretary for Interior, Johannesburg. In part it reads: "As is well known, *over 3500 imprisonments were suffered by my countrymen during the struggle, over 100 deportations to India took place,* and *even two deaths occurred*, owing to the suffering gone through during the crisis. *Several families were rendered homeless*, and they had to be supported from public funds."[817]

Ruined Families

Gandhi had advised his Satyagrahis that they should not pay fines. Consequently, in Boksburg a Magistrate allowed the confiscation of two houses (worth 550 pounds) from two Indians for not paying the four pound fine.[818] Gandhi said that there was some misunderstanding among the Indians, if they believe that the Satyagrahi Committee will stand for their loss. *"All satyagrahis have to bear (their own) losses."*[819] All of sudden, help was *"out of the question."* Gandhi's logic was: *"Those who have been fined should be proud* that, being reduced to poverty, *they will now be able to fight with all their strength. ...."*[820] Earlier, if the decision of the court was against the law, Gandhi had suggested to appeal. Now, he told: *"The days for such appeals are over."*[821] The fact is that due to Gandhi's struggle, *1000 Indians were completely ruined.*[822]

How far the complaints of Indians were correct and justified needs further investigation, as here they tell stories from Gandhi's point of view. What we see from the forgoing is that Indians, even though they were living in S.A. for more than three decades refused to accept the local food and culture. They did not try to integrate into the new country. They formed their own "ghetto." They lamented against the "white community." Why the white community reacted "hard" against Asians? The reasons are given in the following chapter.

Notes and References

[762] Indian Opinion, 23-2-1907.

[763] Doke J.J., Gandhi in Südafrika – Mohandas Karamchand Gandhi – Ein indischer Patriot in Südafrika, Rotapfel Verlag, Erlenbach-Zürich 1925, p. 210.

[764] Indian Opinion, 2-2-1907.

[765] Indian Opinion, 7-12-1907.

[766] C.W.M.G. 9, 1908-1909, p. 289.

[767] Indian Opinion, 26-9-1908.

[768] Indian Opinion, 26-9-1908.

[769] Indian Opinion, 26-9-1908.

[770] Cachalia A.M. to Director of Prisons, Pretoria, Sept. 19, 1908

[771] Indian Opinion, 26-9-1908.

[772] Gandhi M.K. to SABIC, April 7, 1909.

[773] Indian Opinion, 11-6-1910.

[774] Indian Opinion, 11-6-1910.

[775] Indian Opinion, 19-2-1910.

[776] C.W.M.G. 10, 1909-1910, p. 425. Indian Opinion, 5-3-1910.

[777] Indian Opinion, 26-2-1910.

[778] Indian Opinion, 26-2-1910.

[779] Indian Opinion, 29-1-1910.

[780] India, 18-2-1910.

[781] Indian Opinion, 7-5-1910.

[782] Indian Opinion, 22-10-1913.

[783] Gandhi M.K. to Minister of Interior, Telegram, Oct. 30, 1913.

[784] Indian Opinion, 7-1-1914.

[785] Indian Opinion, 7-1-1914.

[786] Indian Opinion, 21-3-1908.

[787] Indian Opinion, 26-2-1910.

[788] Indian Opinion, 22-10-1913.

[789] Gandhi M.K. to Minister of Interior, Oct. 30, 1913.

[790] Indian Opinion, 7-1-1914.

[791] Andrews C.F., Mahatma Gandhi's ideas – Including selections from his writings – Mahatma Gandhi: His own story – Mahatma Gandhi at work – His own story continued, The Macmillan Company, New York 1931, pp. 295-296.

[792] Andrews C.F., Mahatma Gandhi's ideas – ..., 1931, p. 295.

[793] India, 18-11-1910.

[794] Doke J.J., Gandhi in Südafrika – ..., 1925, p. 158.

[795] Doke J.J., Gandhi in Südafrika – ..., 1925, p. 165.

[796] The Times of India, 7-11-1913.

[797] Indian Opinion, 31-12-1913.

[798] Indian Opinion, 25-2-1914.

[799] Indian Opinion, 25-2-1914.

[800] Gandhi M.K. to Kallenbach H., Feb. 27, 1914.

[801] Gandhi M.K. to Kallenbach H., March 2, 1914.

[802] Indian Opinion, 24-8-1907.

[803] Indian Opinion, 5-9-1908.

[804] Indian Opinion, 17-10-1908.

[805] Indian Opinion, 17-10-1908.

[806] Indian Opinion, 13-2-1909.

[807] Indian Opinion, 26-3-1910.

[808] Indian Opinion, 29-5-1909.

[809] Gandhi M.K. to the Pvt. Sec. to Lord Crewe, Aug. 11, 1909.

[810] Indian Opinion, 16-4-1910.

[811] Indian Opinion, 23-4-1910.

[812] Indian Opinion, 28-5-1910.

[813] Indian Opinion, 28-5-1910.

[814] Indian Opinion, 18-6-1910.

[815] Indian Opinion, 16-7-1910.

[816] C.W.M.G. 11, 1910-1911, pp. 197-200.

[817] The Rand Daily Mail, 15-9-1913.

[818] Indian Opinion, 5-3-1910.

[819] Indian Opinion, 5-3-1910.

[820] Indian Opinion, 5-3-1910.

[821] Indian Opinion, 5-3-1910.

[822] Doke J.J., Gandhi in Südafrika – ..., 1925, p. 213.

Clash of Cultures – Social, Political and Religious Differences

In general, in South Africa, the laws were not always against Indians only. "The Immigration Restriction Act in Natal" was to prohibit "the immigration of lunatics, criminals, prostitutes, paupers."[823] The reason for such a law was the social problems, which were caused by new industry, such as mining. To work in coal and gold mines, mainly male workers were needed. Not surprisingly, in:

> "Johannesburg a gross imbalance in the ratio of the sexes, *a lack of a stable family life* within a male-dominated society of whites and blacks alike. *The flourishing sale of alcohol* was one way of controlling the unstable labour force; .... In 1896, for example, *ten per cent of all white women over 15 years of age were prostitutes.* Indian landlords in Durban were but one of many groups who had profited from organized vice. In time both Boer and Briton sought to check the consumption of alcohol and the spread of prostitution, one more vigorously than Smuts, the young Attorney-General of the South African Republic, in 1899."[824]

The white community induced new laws against Asians. The list of such laws is long (see Appendix A). The problem with such lists is that they do not tell us the background, under which conditions these laws were made? Why were they needed? In the following sections we shall see:

- Why the "white community" opposed Indians?

- How Colonial born vs. Indian immigrants; Hindus vs. Muslims; "free" vs. indentured Indians; N.I.C. vs. Gandhi reacted to each other?

Why was the White Community against Indians?

As we have seen in previous chapters, Indians supported the British during the Anglo-Boer War. Due to the British policy of scorched earth Boers lost half of their child population under the age of sixteen as one fourth of their population was eliminated. Though the Boers lost the war they won the election. It practically gave them political power. From their point of view – Gandhi and other Indian traders were detractors. Other points to be noted are:

(1) During the war Indians lost neither money nor lives.

(2) Most of the Indian stretcher-bearers were paid workers.

(3) During Boers's regime in Natal, Indians were treated fairly.

Gandhi had shown that the new laws are worse than the previous laws. Thus the foundation of anti-Asian institutions and strict immigration laws is understandable from Boers' point of view. However, the general public opinion is given and produced not by laws, but by different societies founded within and by the public. Such societies were founded by a number of whites as we shall see below.

The White League: In Pietersberg "The White League" was founded. Its executive committee had influential politicians.[825] The objectives of the League were: "To make a united stand by all the white inhabitants of this country against the Asiatics, to promote legislation to regulate and control the issue and renewal of licences to Asiatic traders, and to force them to vacate the towns and country districts and to reside and trade in bazaars specially set aside for them."[826] After Asians' shops were attacked during a demonstration, on March 14, 1905, A. Gani wrote a letter to the Colonial Secretary, Pretoria, and complained about the anti-Asian demonstration. He told that "the demonstration was led by the President of the Potchefstroom Chamber of Commerce. The demonstrators, in violent speeches protested not only against the traders but also the making of the planned mosque."[827]

Anti-Asiatic Vigilance Association: After the Anglo-Boer War the Anti-Asiatic Vigilance Association called for a boycott of Indians in Potchefstroom.[828-829] In 1907, a Member of the local Legislative Assembly had stated "that the law should be regarded as having been passed to establish the doctrine that there can be *no equality between the whites and the Indians.*"[830] Another example to be quoted is that in Natal before 1907, railway tickets at concession were available for all priests. Later Indian Hindu, Muslim and Christian priests were devoid of this right.[831] Gandhi often called the status of Indentured Indian as slaves. If a master was not satisfied, often he mistreated his worker. One such example was reported by "Indian Opinion", stating that a European cruelly beat up his Indian worker, who later died. For his deed, the European was prosecuted and fined 10 pounds.[832]

In 1907, a new law was passed for workers. It provided "for payment of *damages to workers and their families in case of disability suffered during performance of duty by workers employed in the various factories. This law is to apply to the whites only.*"[833] In the same year "Indian Opinion" reported: "A Bill has now been introduced in the Natal Parliament providing that Indian landlords, who have been cultivating their lands themselves and who let them now to other Indians or Kaffirs, *shall pay on those lands double the tax that the Europeans pay.*"[834]

Indian vs. White Traders

Indians who came as indentured or traders, within a short period of less than fifty years, in 1907, possessed 5 per cent of the total value of the land in the country.[835] Not surprisingly, whites got cold feet. At the occasion of the twelfth annual meeting of the Chamber of Commerce of South Africa a resolution was passed that the immigration of Indian traders should be stopped. One of the members said in a speech:

> *"That great harm was done by Indian trade as the whites could not compete with Indian traders. The whites had struggled hard in South Africa for a hundred years. How could Indians be allowed to oust them? Conditions in Standerton, Heidelberg, Potchefstroom and other places had deteriorated very much. If the influx of Indians could not be stopped forthwith, he said, they should be so heavily taxed that they could not afford to stay on. According to him, it would be better to drive out the existing traders, even after paying them compensation, if necessary."*[836]

The argumentation of the White traders regarding "the competition" was not quite wrong. Most of them were religious Christians. To work on Sunday's was not even imaginable to them. Also, they were used to work for a limited number of hours per day. In contrast, a newspaper reported the Indians' way of working and trading as follows: *"All the seven days in the week are working days for the Indians and they work from sunrise to sunset. On Sundays they write up their account books and hawkers settle their accounts. Others either keep the shop open on holidays blatantly or station a man outside to smuggle customers in."*[837] However, there was a tint of prejudices: *"The Indians know nothing about making payments on time. …. Ninety-five percent of all Indian trade is corrupt. An Indian will not lose a customer and will sell him goods even at a loss, for the loss is to be suffered not by him, but by his creditor."*[838] It was suggested that following the example of the Orange River Colony, Transvaal, Indians' shops should be closed down, with or without compensation.[839] Apart from the envy of White traders, the other reasons to protest against Indians were, as Gandhi noted:

"(1) Lack of cleanliness.

(2) The bad state of account books.

(3) The location of residence and shop in the same premises."[840]

Indians with the Wrong Identity

How some Indians tried to bring their own relatives to S.A. by illegal means, is shown by U. Dhupelia-Mesthrie in: "False fathers and false sons - Immigration officials in Cape Town - Documents and verifying minor sons from India in the first half of the twentieth century."[841] The fact is that this problem was well-known during Gandhi's time. A Registration Officer complained that *"boys come in dressed as women, others, sons take shelter under borrowed parents and women under borrowed husbands."*[842] In 1907, four Indians were alleged to have entered with manipulated permits. Three of them admitted that they have bought them in Bombay.[843] Also, old certificates were fraudulently duplicated and sold by Indian Agents in Durban, Johannesburg and Bombay.[844] Not surprisingly, the Government wanted to have new registrations.

Indians Way of Living – "Some Don'ts"

From the history we know that due to infectious diseases spread by the European colonialists, millions of natives died on the American continent. Not surprisingly, whites were afraid of Indians. In May 1905, "Indian Opinion" reported: "Smallpox has made its appearance in Johannesburg. It is said to have entered through passenger steamers. It started with the Malay Location. The first case was a Malay one, followed by another of a white. …. According to Dr. Porter, five Indians have also been affected."[845] Though Indians were suggested to cooperate with the authorities; they did not strictly follow the instructions. A doctor wrote: The greatest obstruction is caused by Asiatics and Somalis. The Asiatics resist anyone entering their houses (for purposes of inspection or treatment). They obstruct the isolation of patients and measures to prevent infection."[846]

There can be no dispute on the fact that any group, which migrates from one place to another, brings its social way of living with it. Many of the habits can be displeasing for the host country or state. Gandhi though suggested his countrymen to make their "ghettos", that is, stick to their religion, language and country; still asked them to avoid some activities in public, such as: "washing and chewing tobacco, betel-leaves or nuts."[847] In order to instruct British Indians, "Indian Opinion" published an article, entitled: "Some Don'ts -

"1. Avoid, as far as possible, blowing your nose or spitting on swept or paved walks or in the presence of others. ...

2. One should not belch, hiccup, break wind, or scratch oneself in the presence of others. ...

3. If you want to cough, do so holding your handkerchief against the mouth. ...

4. Even after a bath, in many men, some dirt remains in the ears or under the nails. It is necessary to pare one's nails and keep them as well as the ears clean.

5. Those who do not grow a regular beard should, if necessary, shave every day. An unshaven face is a sign of laziness or stinginess.

6. One should not let mucus accumulate in the corners of the eyes. One who allows this to happen is considered slothful and a sleepyhead.

7. Every act of cleaning the body should be done in privacy.

8. The turban or cap and the shoes should be clean. ...

9. Those who chew betel-leaf and nut should do so at fixed hours, as with other kinds of food so as to avoid giving the impression that we are eating all the time. Those who chew tobacco have a lot to think about. They disfigure every spot by spitting. Addicts to tobacco, as the Gujarati proverb goes, spoil the corner of the house where they chew tobacco, the whole house if they smoke and their clothes if they take snuff."[848]

About seven years later, Gandhi wrote about passengers:

"There seems to be no limit to the *filthiness of deck passengers*. Even though facilities for bathing are provided on the ship, *many of them rarely take a bath.* They feel they cannot bathe in brine from the sea. *This is only superstition, but they have clung to it.* Some of them bathe only once in a week due to sheer laziness. .... Many spit right where they happen to be sitting. ..... *The deck is so covered with leavings and spittle that one shrinks from walking barefoot over* it, and if one does, *there is every danger of slipping.* .... *They foul the latrines by using them so carelessly* that even those who observe the minimum of cleanliness cannot but feel revulsion."[849]

Shortly before Gandhi left S.A., once again he came to the topic, stating that: "*Whites had reason to feel disgusted.* Because in our community, many people sleep in small rooms in which food-grains and fruits are stored; many rarely clean lavatories; sleeping, cooking, bathing and relaxing is done by them in the same room."[850]

Indentured and Colonial Born Indians as Scapegoats

The authors S. Bhana and G.H. Vadeh wrote: "When the Colonial-Born Indian Association submitted a petition in April 1912 for trade licenses as a matter of "first claim," Gandhi criticized the body for seeking preferential treatment for colonial-born Indians because they were educated in English and observed "European" standards."[851] How far this claim was true? This will be seen in the following paragraphs.

In the beginning of 1910, the Natal Indian Congress though less interested in Gandhi's struggle, was active enough to pass a resolution "relating to the stoppage of indenture altogether ....."[852] Some of the Indians were of the opinion that: "*So long as the immigration of indentured laborers into Natal continues, the free Indians will never be left in peace.*"[853] Now the question arises: Why British Indians were against the "future indentured?" From their point of view: "*Our present plight is entirely due to (the whites') fear of indentured Indians. ..... The whites labour under the apprehension that a population of indentured Indians in South Africa will lead to a swelling in the numbers of the community.*"[854] Contrary to Gandhi and his followers, many Indians and whites were not against the import of labours. For the white miners and farmers, indentures were cheap labour. Indians argued that these workers definitely did not have better life in India than in S.A.

Some white politicians had inflamed the emotions of the white community by threatening the "Indian's influx." Gandhi did the same to instigate the free Indians against the indentured. He wrote: "As for free Indians, we think the immigration of indentured laborers is a great disadvantage to them. *Those free Indians who live by their labour do not get employment, or, if they do, it is on a very low wage.*"[855] After that followed his silly argument: "It must be borne in mind that even *if Indians were to give up the agitation for the prohibition of indentured labour, the Union Parliament will certainly prohibit it on its own. Indians would then look small and would lose the credit which they have a chance of earning today.*"[856]

In the beginning of 1911, Gandhi's joy knew no bound after the Government of India announced that from July 1, 1911, there would be no supply of indentured to Natal. *"This stoppage will automatically solve the Indian question in this sub-continent. After the removal of the incubus, only time and patience are necessary for a steady improvement in our position under the Union"*, wrote Gandhi.[857] Today, we know that Gandhi was absolutely mistaken. With the stopping of the indentured servants, the situation of British Indians did not change.

Even at the time of settlement, on Aug. 24, 1913, Gandhi wrote to the Secretary of Interior: "As to South Africa-born Indians, it is perfectly true that I did not raise, in the correspondence of 1912, this point. *It had entirely escaped me until a friend drew my attention to it.* But I assured the friend that no difficulty need be anticipated as the correspondence setting forth the provisional settlement of 1911 protected all existing rights of British Indians."[858]

"Natal-born Indian is useless as a worker" – Indentured "improve as animals"

Something personal: I am living in Germany for more than 25 years. During this period I came in contact with different political groups. As a teacher I have the privilege to teach children of immigrants as well as Germans. Due to different family backgrounds many immigrants' children, even by the third generation, do not manage to obtain a higher education. They are prejudiced from different quarters. They are stamped as a group, which is not willing to integrate in the society; or is not interested in education. On the same pattern Gandhi stigmatize the indentured and their children. He quoted from a report: *"'One fact was forced upon the attention of the Commission, namely, the Natal-born Indian is useless as a worker; he will play football, - sell newspapers or do low class office work but he will not undertake anything of the nature of labour."*[859] And if they were educated, they were not good enough for Gandhi, as: *"It was admitted by educated Indians that primary education made the Natal-born Indian useless in the labour market. Agriculture had nothing to hope from him."*[860]

One of the reasons for Gandhi's attack on the colonial born was that most of them did not follow him blindly. In particular, the educated members of the community did not agree to his political views. They opposed him publically. For instance at a meeting:

"... Aiyar suggested a South Africa-wide conference to gauge the strength of the action to be taken. Gandhi, according to Aiyar, was evasive as he indicated he would abide by a decision by the people if it was not in conflict with his conscience. "The African Chronicle" said in response, "*We are not aware of any responsible politician in any part of the globe making such a stupid reply as the one that Mr. Gandhi made the other day.*"

"Mr. Gandhi's superior conscience is pervading everything," said the newspaper sarcastically. .... What hurt Aiyar most was when Gandhi, in reply to Dada Osman's question as to why he had not supported Aiyar's £3 campaign, argued that Aiyar and three other Indians he named did not compare with Polak in "purity, talents, ability, and ideals." Gandhi thought of Polak as the "purest ray serene". Well, said Aiyar snidely in his columns, Gandhi, Polak, Kallenbach, and Ritch had failed to "unearth the secrecy of the immigration law." He referred to Gandhi's supporters as the local Indian "aristocracy" and his "trusted prime ministers," Kallenbach and Polak."[861]

On the private level, Gandhi wrote to H.S.L. Polak:

"*The Colonial-born Indians' attitude I can understand. It is largely due to their ignorance which in its turn owes its existence to their indifference and laziness. They have not followed the struggle, and they will not study the laws affecting Indians.* You can see the grossest ignorance betrayed in the "African Chronicle" leading article, which I undertook to read after your warning. *It is not only ignorant, but it is mischievous.*"[862]

For him, the bill suggested by him had become a matter of life and death. Cost what it may, he wanted to have it. He wrote: "However, we can only disabuse their minds of misunderstandings to the best of our ability. What I think you may safely promise, and what *I think we may have to do, is that, immediately the matter is settled and the Bill is on the Statute Book*, we will have to present our Bill of Rights throughout the Union, and work away for it, ..."[863]

Gandhi had no problem to call the natives as "animals." For him the indentured had the same status. While taking about the mistreatment of the indentured by their masters, Gandhi wrote to a friend: "*Indentured men lose terribly in moral fibre. In many cases they improve as animals*, they lose in almost every case as men."[864]

Within the German educational system, the children of the poor and immigrant families are encouraged to adopt a low level of education and profession. Gandhi had a similar suggestion for Africa-born Indians. He told them: "*The world lives on its farmers and those who are indispensable to farmers*, e.g., carpenters, shoemakers, blacksmiths, masons, bricklayers, tailors, barbers, etc. *It is a sad fact that very few Colonial-born Indians are found willing enough to learn or take up these truly noble (because useful) professions.*"[865]

Gandhi, like most of the modern conservative politicians, cannot be called a man of integrity. I personally think that if a child is born in a new country, where he is going to stay "forever", he must master the language of that country or state. It is discouraging and humiliating to tell him that he had no idea of the language, religion or history of the country of his parents. Gandhi demanded the impossible from Africa born Indians; by telling them: "*There is something missing, and that is a knowledge of real Indian thought, history, and literature. Many of them speak nothing but the English language, some few* have obtained a colloquial knowledge of their mother tongue *whilst scarcely any can read and write the great languages of India.*"[866]

Gandhi's Conflict with the Muslim Community

In a lecture Gandhi said that most of the Muslims are converted from the lower caste Hindus. He was opposed by Mahomed Seedat and other Islami Trustees. In order to appease them, Gandhi apologized and told them that the lecture was based on "The Encyclopedia Britannica", Hunter's "Indian Empire" (History of India) and other books.[867] Shortly after that two letters of protest followed. In one of them it was shown that ancestors of Bohras Muslims were Brahmin priests and Banias.[868] In response Gandhi wrote: "As I do not wish to prolong the controversy, …. I have not sought to lower Islam, nor do I hold it to be lowly. I do not think that such an impression was created on anyone's mind when I made the speech."[869] A writer under the name "A Follower of Islam" reacted more heavily and said:

> "The statement that the lower classes of Hindus had been converted to Islam is not supported by any Urdu or Gujarati books on Indian history. However, if any such thoughts are found in some wretched books of history, they must have been only the figments of Hindu imagination … Will Mr. Gandhi be pleased to give the name of the history whence he has learnt such serious things?"[870]

In the meeting of the N.I.C. in Durban, Gandhi stated that his lecture has been misinterpreted. He suggested the members that we should not waste our time in such discussion and work united for the motherland like the Japanese.[871]

In 1905, the Royal Highnesses the Duke and Duchess of Cornwall and York were on a visit. To address him only Mohammedan candidates were appointed as persons representing the Indian community. Gandhi immediately took action. A protest meeting of the English-speaking and other Indians was held. Gandhi's Christian friends: J.L. Roberts, the convener, and D.C. Andrews, seconded the resolutions. Gandhi occupied the chair. In resolutions they strongly disapproved the manners of the Mohammedans' representatives, as they were a minority in South Africa. It was demanded that at least an equal number of representatives should be from other communities. The copies of the resolutions were sent to the secretary of the Duke and Duchess of York, the Indian Reception Committee, the Mayor of Durban, and the Press of Natal.[872]

We have already seen that Anglia and Dada Osman charged Gandhi of having misled Indians. His role was characterized as being "not only worthless but highly injurious," and he was accused of leading Indians "into slavery." Anglia objection was: *"Gandhi's heavy reliance on Polak, Ritch, Kallenbach, Albert West, and other Whites."*[873] The conflict between Hindu-Muslim communities was a reflection of Indian politics. In the end of 1906, British Indians (Hindus-Muslims) sent a deputation to U.K., nearly at the same time, that is Dec., 1906, to safeguard Muslims' interest "The All-India Muslim League" was founded.[874] Another example is a letter from April 1, 1909, from Indian politician Motilal Nehru to his son

Jawaharlal Nehru (later to be called by Gandhi as "my heir in the Congress"; and India's first Prime Minister) criticizing John Morley for the split between Hindus and Muslims by promising separate representation in political power. Though he was not happy with this situation, but "out of evil, however, comes the good. *The Arya Samaj has given the best answer to Mohamedan pretensions by quietly converting the followers of Islam to Hinduism.* Reports arrive every day of their conversions. *Sometimes whole villages are converted in a single day*," wrote Motilal to his son.[875]

Double Standard of the British Empire - Indian Traders and the Issue of Finger Prints

The views of the Boer's community are well-reflected by Smuts as follows:

"Under the old law, Indians could not remain in the country unless they allowed themselves to be registered and paid a certain sum of money. Under that law, all Indians were registered. However, on account of the severe competition from the Indians, the Volksraad passed a law whereby Indians could only trade in Bazaars. *But the British Government stepped in, and said that these people were their subjects, and according to the London Convention*, all their subjects are to be treated alike. *The law thus became impracticable, and the result was that the Indians carried on trade all over the country. They carried on business without a licence, and they were thereby even better off than the white traders.* This position, however intolerable, was kept up by the British Government till the war broke out. The result may now be studied in Prinsloo Street, Pretoria, Pietersburg, Potchefstroom and other centres, *where trade is largely in the hands of the Indian storekeepers. And yet people persist in asking - Whence this depression? Why all this poverty? Indian trade is one of the causes thereof.* The Indians have tried to get the same hold here as they have done in Natal. They want to have all trade in their hands."[876]

About the finger prints Smuts stated that: "The Government has decided to have the finger-print system" because many Asiatics shopkeepers possess fraudulent certificated, which are sold in Johannesburg, Durban and Bombay."[877] However, his strongest argument was:

"*I find that these self-same people have to make their finger impressions before they leave India, ...* Any person being an ex-official or *ex-soldier in India entitled to a pension* must put his finger-prints down, otherwise he cannot draw his pension. All these things came to light when the Indians sent a deputation to England. *The Indians think that they can fool the present Government, but they will soon find out their mistake."*[878]

In order to appease the white community he said:

"I warn the Indians that the Government will insist on the strict enforcement of the law, and I trust that the newspapers will make it fairly plain that on December 31 the doors will be closed against them forever. I have no quarrel with the Indians; the object is not persecution, but a stoppage of the influx of Indians. *We have made up our mind to make this a white man's country, and, however difficult the task before us in this matter, we have put our foot down, and shall keep it there.*"[879]

However, it would be wrong to say that there was no support from the white community. In some areas, Indians bought land in lieu of their white friends.[880] In the Natal Parliament a Minister said that: "The Government should provide greater facilities for the education of Indians. He pointed out that Indians needed them and that a special responsibility devolved on the Government for the education of Natal born Indians. We should be thankful to the Honourable Gentleman for his speech."[881] Almost all of Gandhi's close workers were Europeans and without their support, he would have achieved nothing.

Appendix A

Laws against Asians until 1914[882]

Year	Law (Indenture 1859-1950) ….
1859	LAW No. 14. Law providing for the Introduction of Coolies into the Colony of Natal at Public expense, and for the regulation and governance of such Immigrants (Repealed by Law No. 2, 1870).
1859	LAW No. 15. Law enabling persons to introduce, at their own expense, Immigrants from India. (Repealed by Law No.2, 1870).
1863	LAW No.20. Law regulating payments made by the Masters or Employers of Coolie Immigrants. (Repealed by Law No.2, 1870).
1864	LAW No.17. Law extending the terms of Assignment of Coolie Immigrants from Three to Five Years. (Repealed by Law 2, 1870).
1865	LAW No. 29. Law declaring and amending Law No. 14 of 1859.
1870	LAW No.2. Law to amend and consolidate the Laws relating to the introduction of Coolie Immigrants into this Colony, and to the Regulation and Government of such Coolie Immigrants.
1885	LAW 3. Coolies, Arabs and other Asiatics Act (S.A. Republic) Transvaal: Prohibition on taking up residence except in segregated areas. Denial of all civic rights. (a) Law passed to amend Act 3 of 1885. (b) No political rights. (c) Cannot own properties. (d) Segregation in Streets, Wards and Locations.
1891	State Law of the Orange Free State. Absolute prohibition of Indians to live in the Free State. Those owning businesses had to wind them up at the time of the passing of the law.
1891	LAW 25, Natal. Regulates the life and routine work of indentured Indians.
1895	LAW 17, Natal. Imposition of the 3 Pound Tax on Indians after expiry of indenture; Indians forced to re-indenture to the Whites; failing that, either subject to imprisonment or deportation to India.
1896	The Franchise Act, Natal. Parliamentary Franchise withdrawn.

1897	The Dealers' Licences Act, No.18, Natal. Restriction on Trading Licences - Wholesale and Retail.
1897	The Immigration Restriction Act, Natal. Total Prohibition of Free Immigration into Natal.
1897	LAW 3. - Regulating the marriages of Coloured persons within the South African Republic (Transvaal); Criminal offence for an Indian to marry a White woman.
1898	LAW 15, Transvaal. Indians prohibited from operating in gold mining areas.
1899	Regulations - Separation of Trading and Residential areas in Transvaal (South African Republic).
1900	Act No. 1. Amended the Immigration Law(Natal)thereby making conditions for Indentured Indians more severe.
1902	Peace Preservation Proclamation, Transvaal.
1903	The Immorality Ordinance Law 46 (Transvaal) imposed severe penalty for "immorality" between European and Asiatic.
1903	Immigration Restriction Act.
1905	The Immigration Restriction Act (Transvaal). Indians allowed to enter the Transvaal only if they were issued a special permit.
1906	The Immigration Act (Cape Colony). Cape commenced prohibition of immigrants from India.
1906	Johannesburg Municipal Ordinance: Provided for bazaars and locations for Indians.
1906	Act No.3. Amendment to the 1903 Immigration Act (Natal) : Further restrictions on the movements of Indians.
1907	The Arms and Ammunition Act, No.10 (Transvaal) : Indians prohibited from carrying firearms.
1907	The Immigration Act, No.15 (Transvaal) : Total prohibition of Indians into the Transvaal.
1907	Asiatic Law Amendment Act : Compulsory registration of Indians; Fine of 100 Pounds or 3 months imprisonment.
1907	Education Act No. 25 (Transvaal) : Segregation in schools - compulsory education for Europeans, none for Indians.
1907	Act 27 : Vrededorp Stands Ordinance (Transvaal) : Indians who had stands

	were ejected on the pretext of unsanitary conditions.
1907	The Workmen's Compensation Act, No. 36 (Transvaal) : Denial of benefits of the Workmen's Compensation Act to Indians and restricting the term "worker" to European employees only.
1908	The Immorality Amendment Ordinance, Law 16 (Transvaal) : Long term imprisonment for immoral connections with White women.
1908	The Township Amendment Act, Law 34 (Transvaal) : Residence in town restricted to domestic servants. Trade and residence restricted to segregated areas.
1908	The Gold Law, Act 35 (Transvaal) : Absolute prohibition of Indian Traders to reside or carry on Trade in proclaimed areas.
1908	The Asiatic Registration Amendment Act, No.36 (Transvaal) : Indians required to register and to carry passes.
1909	The Public Service and Pensions Act, No. 19 (Transvaal) : No provision made for Indian Civil Servants.
1909	The South Africa Act. Asiatic affairs under direct charge of Governor-Inner-Council. No safeguard for Indian rights provided.
1910	The Public Servants Super-annuation Act, No. 1(Natal): Indian servants excluded.
1910	Education Act, No. 6 (Natal) : Compulsory education for Indians not instituted. Compulsory education for Whites only.
1910	Act No. 31 provides pensions for teachers in Government-aided Schools, Natal. Indian teachers excluded.
1913	Immigration Regulation Act : Immigration from Asia prohibited for the whole Union.
1914	Indian Relief Act Arising from the Passive Resistance of 1913, the Solomon Commission (that was subsequently appointed) made recommendations that led to the passing of the Indian Relief Act (no. 22 of 1914) which made provision for : - The abolition of the 3 pound tax; - The legalisation of marriages conducted according to Indian rites: - The relaxation of the immigration laws; and - All resisters were to be pardoned.

Notes and References

[823] The Times of India, 9-12-1899.

[824] Copley A., Gandhi against the tide, Basil Blackwell Inc., Cambridge 1989, p. 17.

[825] Indian Opinion, 17-9-1904.

[826] Indian Opinion, 1-10-1904.

[827] Gani A. to Colonial Secretary, Pretoria, March 14, 1905.

[828] Indian Opinion, 21-1-1905.

[829] Indian Opinion, 26-1-1907.

[830] Indian Opinion, 11-5-1907.

[831] Indian Opinion, 27-7-1907.

[832] Indian Opinion, 15-6-1907.

[833] Indian Opinion, 22-6-1907.

[834] Indian Opinion 6-7-1907.

[835] Indian Opinion, 13-4-1907.

[836] Indian Opinion, 4-5-1907.

[837] Indian Opinion, 27-4-1907.

[838] Indian Opinion, 27-4-1907.

[839] Indian Opinion, 27-4-1907.

[840] Indian Opinion, 26-1-1907.

[841] Dhupelia-Mesthrie U. False fathers and false sons - Immigration officials in Cape Town - Documents and verifying minor sons from

India in the first half of the twentieth century. https://www.academia.edu/9942562/False_Fathers_and_False_Sons_Immigration_Officials_in_Cape_Town_Documents_and_Verifying_Minor_sons_from_India_in_the_First_Half_of_the_Twentieth_Century, June 14, 2015.

[842] Indian Opinion, 15-1-1910.

[843] Indian Opinion, 23-2-1907.

[844] Indian Opinion, 12-10-1907.

[845] Indian Opinion, 27-5-1905.

[846] Indian Opinion, 9-2-1907.

[847] Indian Opinion, 26-1-1907.

[848] Indian Opinion, 2-2-1907.

[849] Indian Opinion, 4-1-1913.

[850] Indian Opinion, 29-7-1914.

[851] Bhana S., Vadeh G.H., The making of a social reformer – Gandhi in South Africa 1893-1914, online, http://www.mkgandhi-sarvodaya.org/social_reform/social_reform.htm, Feb. 5, 2015.

[852] Indian Opinion, 26-2-1910.

[853] Indian Opinion, 5-3-1910.

[854] Indian Opinion, 12-3-1910.

[855] Indian Opinion, 2-4-1910.

[856] Indian Opinion, 2-4-1910.

[857] Indian Opinion, 7-1-1911.

[858] Indian Opinion, 13-9-1913.

[859] Indian Opinion, 3-9-1910.

[860] Indian Opinion, 3-9-1910.

[861] http://www.mkgandhi-sarvodaya.org/social_reform/social_reform.htm, Feb. 5, 2015.

[862] Gandhi M.K. to Polak H.S.L., March 13, 1911.

[863] Gandhi M.K. to Polak H.S.L., March 13, 1911.

[864] Gandhi M.K. to Natesan G.A., May 31, 1911.

[865] Indian Opinion, 15-7-1911.

[866] Indian Opinion, 7-12-1912.

[867] Gandhi M.K. to Seedat M., May 27, 1905.

[868] C.W.M.G. 4, 1904-1905, p. 304.

[869] Indian Opinion, 3-6-1905.

[870] C.W.M.G. 4, 1904-1905, p. 316.

[871] Indian Opinion, 1-7-1905.

[872] Indian Opinion, 30-9-1905.

[873] http://www.mkgandhi-sarvodaya.org/social_reform/social_reform.htm, Feb. 5, 2015.

[874] Pandey B.N. (Ed.), The Indian nationalist movement, 1885-1947, St. Martin's Press, New York 1979, p. 17.

[875] Pandey B.N. (Ed.), The Indian nationalist movement, 1885-1947, 1979, p. 18.

[876] Indian Opinion, 12-10-1907.

[877] Indian Opinion, 12-10-1907.

[878] Indian Opinion, 12-10-1907.

[879] Indian Opinion, 12-10-1907.

[880] Indian Opinion, 8-4-1905.

[881] Indian Opinion, 6-5-1905.

[882] http://scnc.ukzn.ac.za/doc/HIST/LAWS.htm, June 14, 2015.

The Origin of M.K. Gandhi's Political Ideas

Most probably to impress the Western people, in particular the Christian missionaries, Gandhi said that he was influenced by the Holy Bible and the author Leo Tolstoy. In Oct. 1905, Gandhi had written about Tolstoy as follows:

"He spends all his time in good works and prayer. He believes that:

1. In this world men should not accumulate wealth;

2. No matter how much evil a person does to us, we should always do good to him. Such is the Commandment of God, and also His law;

3. No one should take part in fighting;

4. It is sinful to wield political power, as it leads to many of the evils in the world;

5. Man is born to do his duty to his Creator; he should therefore pay more attention to his duties than to his rights;

6. Agriculture is the true occupation of man. It is therefore contrary to divine law to establish large cities, to employ hundreds of thousands for minding machines in factories so that a few can wallow in riches by exploiting the helplessness and poverty of the many."[883]

In India Gandhi became popular due to "Salt-March or Dandi-March" and "Charkha, that is, spinning-wheel." The idea of "passive resistance and boycott of British goods" brought him to the level of immortals. Gandhi in his autobiography was not fare enough to give credit to those, whose ideas were copied by him. This part of his life is given below.

Refusal of Tax and Protest against Carrying Passes

In India, one of Gandhi's political tools was to suggest people to refuse to pay tax. The fact is that not Indians, but Zulus were the first who refused to pay the poll-tax. For the "revolt" they were blown up with cannons.[884] *Even before Gandhi, in the Cape the coloured community refused to take passes and went to gaol.* The Cape Government was unable to enforce it.[885]

Going to Prison

Gandhi's most famous method was "going to prison." Was it Gandhi's invention? According to Gandhi's autobiography: "In September 1906, there was a large gathering of Indians, ..., when the position was thoroughly faced, and, under the inspiration of deep feeling, and *on the proposal of one of our leading men*, they swore a solemn oath committing themselves to Passive Resistance."[886] Why did not Gandhi tell the name of the "leading man"? Perhaps, was he annoyed as most of his earlier followers, who were ruined, refused to follow Gandhi's dictation? The reality is that on Sept. 11, 1906, Gandhi gave a speech and called for action.[887] One of the resolutions was entitled as "The gaol resolution." Hajee Habib told the public that we are not going to get justice at the hand of the British Government. He said that if bill is passed he will never register again and he will be the first who will prefer to go to goal. He suggested the others to do so. H. Habib seems to be the person, who knew, when and how to hit the nail. He stood up and asked the audience: *"Are you all prepared to take the oath? (The Assembly stood up to a man and said, 'Yes, we will go to gaol!')."*[888] H. Habib told the public as follows:

> *"We tried this method in the days of the Boer Government also.* Some 40 of our men were once arrested for trading without licences. *I advised them to go to gaol and not to seek release on bail.* Accordingly, they all remained there without offering bail. I immediately approached the *British Agent, who approved of our action and ultimately secured justice for us.* Now that a British Government is in power, the time has come for us to go to gaol, and go we will. As he repeated the last phrase thrice, the meeting greeted his resolve with applause."[889]

He proposed that all who want to oppose the ordinance should take a solemn oath. Gandhi was rather surprised at the idea. He said: "The manner of making the resolution suggested by our friend is *as much of a novelty as of a solemnity. I did not come to the meeting with a view to getting the resolution passed in that manner, which redounds to the credit of Sheth Haji Habib as well as it (sic) lays a burden of responsibility upon him.* I tender my congratulations to him."[890]

However, he warned:

> "We all believe in one and the same God, the differences of nomenclature in Hinduism and Islam notwithstanding. *To pledge ourselves or to take an oath in the name of that*

God or with Him as witness is not something to be trifled with. If having taken such an oath we violate our pledge we are guilty before God and man. Personally I hold that a man, who deliberately and intelligently takes a pledge and then breaks it, forfeits his manhood."[891]

"The Rand Daily Mail" reported that:

"..., it must be admitted that much of *the credit for holding such a meeting goes to the Hamidia Islamic Society. ...* Both the Colonial Secretary and Mr. Chamney were invited. .... In addition, white gentlemen like Mr. Lichtenstein, a lawyer from Pretoria, Mr. Israelstram, Mr. Littmann Landsberg and Mr. Stuart Campbell's manager were present. ... The President, Mr. Abdul Gani, began his speech exactly at three o'clock. .... When he spoke of gaol-going, the audience shouted in one voice we shall go to gaol, but will not register ourselves again."[892]

How to Finance the Arrested Protesters? – Learn from British Women

To start a movement is one issue. To keep it going on, money is needed. This idea was copied by Gandhi from the case of the British women who were struggling for the right to vote. During his stay in London, and after his return from U.K., he wrote a number of articles to motivate Indians to take part in the movement, and to finance it by collecting money.[893-895] He said that the Women's Association is spending 100 pounds per week.[896] He estimated that the Indians would require 13000 pound and 13000 had to go to prison to get their rights.[897] The other point, which applied by Gandhi was to disobey the law, refuse to pay the penalty and go to goal. This he also observed in the U.K. For instance, in 1906, Gandhi wrote:

> "Last Wednesday, they (women) to the House of Commons as soon as it opened and demanded the right to vote; they caused some damage also, for which they were prosecuted and sentenced to furnish a security of £5 each. On their refusing to do so, they were sentenced to imprisonment, and they are now in gaol. Most of the women have got three months. All of them come from respectable families and some are very well educated."[898]

According to Indian culture, going to jail is identified with criminality. It is a shameful act; not only for the person, but also for his family. Most probably to convince the educated and rich, Gandhi wrote:

> "One of these is the daughter of the late Mr. Cobden who was highly respected by the people. She is serving her term in gaol. …. A third is an LL.B. On the very day these women went to gaol there was a huge meeting here in support of the resolve adopted by the brave ladies, and a sum of £650 was collected on the spot. Mr. Lawrence announced that he would pay £10 a day as long as his wife was in gaol."[899]

Martin Luther – Burn the Documents

"We are to be obliged to carry permits on our persons. *When the Pope sent a similar order to the great Luther of Germany through an envoy, he consigned it to the flames* in the presence of the envoy and said, "Go, tell the Pope that Luther is free from now on. Tell him of the fate of his bull." Since that day Luther has remained immortal. Millions may want to do what Luther did, but not everyone can succeed," wrote Gandhi.[900] Further he stated: "After reading this news-letter, many readers will want to know what we are to do now. *The answer has already been supplied by Luther. We have now earned the freedom to burn old permits, together with the new ones.* Not a single person must enter the Permit Office, for the situation is really all that hopeless."[901] Though Gandhi's description of "burning documents by Luther" was not correct, still for illiterate and Christian Indians, it was a fascinating example of protesting against the authorities. There cannot be any doubt that it attracted the attention of the Christian missionaries and Christians in South Africa. Apart from that, a good number of Indians, in particular colonial borns were converted Christians.

Spinning-Wheel and Weaving

Recently an author wrote: "A spinning wheel used by Indian independence leader Mohandas K. Gandhi to make 'homespun' *cloth as a protest against British rule*, has been sold at auction in the U.K. for $180000 – about twice as much as expected. ... Shunning British textiles in favor of homemade cloth was part of a self-reliance campaign that encompassed the larger "Quit India" independence movement championed by Gandhi."[902]

In Gandhi's Ashrams in India, followers had to do spinning. Now, the question arises, how Gandhi came to this idea? The answer is to be found in his letter from the year 1911, which he wrote to his relative Narandas Gandhi. In part it reads:

> "I read your views about weaving in your letter to ... Maganlal. They are quite right. What is required for the present is that every intelligent person should learn the craft. I see no benefit in getting the work done through hired labour."[903] However, at that time he was interesting in making money. He advised: *"The person who weaves cloth after learning that craft must secure a rich buyer*, who should make no profit from it, but should, on the contrary, be prepared to sustain a loss. If this comes about, thousands, I believe, will take to weaving."[904]

Even before that, that is, in 1870s, a particular group of the Sikh community, who protested against British rule. "They were rigid in their clothing and wore only hand-spun white attire."[905]

"Passive Resistance" – vs. "Satyagraha"

So far the term "passive resistance" is concerned; it was applied by a local newspaper. Gandhi was not quite happy with it. He wrote: "The Natal Advertiser" has taken us to task for, as it terms it, "deliberately inciting the Transvaal British Indians *to passive resistance.*" It is impossible for "The Natal Advertiser" to enter into the feelings that actuate British Indians. It is not a question of martyrdom, nor is it a question of offering resistance for the sake of it. We have no hesitation in saying that to a loyal and law-abiding community, *passive resistance, as the proposed going to gaol has been termed for want of a better word,* is a recognized method of obtaining redress; as a matter of fact, the going to gaol is a legal method of submission to law."[906]

Idea of Boycott Foreign Goods and Non-cooperation

Gandhi is often palmed for asking Indians to "boycott British textile" and support "Indian local industry." The historical fact is that in 1872 a religious-political movement, known as "Kuka movement" was started by Ram Singh, who considered political freedom a part of religion.

> "*The principles of boycott and non-co-operation*, which Mahatma Gandhi introduced in our freedom movement, *were expounded by Guru Ram Singh for the Namdharis* (a sect belonging to Sikh religion). The Guru's Non-co-operation Movement was based on a few things such as *boycott of education institutions of British and laws established by them. They were rigid in their clothing and wore only hand-spun white attire.* A large number of Kuka followers were in the police as well as army, though they did not reveal their identity. It's worth note that a special Kuka regiment was raised by the Maharaja of Kashmir was disbanded at the intervention of the British."[907]

In Bengal, the boycott of British goods began in 1905.[908] It was not limited to "textile", but all British goods. About that Gandhi wrote:

> "The strong movement that is being carried on *in Bengal to boycott British goods is of no mean significance.* Such a movement has been possible there because education is more widespread and the people in Bengal are more alert than in other parts of India. Sir Henry Cotton has remarked that Bengal holds sway from Calcutta to Peshawar. It is necessary to know the reasons for this."[909]

About three week later he informed the readers of the "Indian Opinion" as follows:

> "..., the movement is so general as to show that it results from deep feeling on the part of the people. Whatever may be the result of the present agitation against the Partition, the effect of the boycott will be productive of only good to India. *It has resulted in a wonderful stimulation of native industries* which, we trust, will grow more and more. *It is a result unlooked for*, but not the less eminently desirable. The great need of India is that national characteristics should be fostered and improved. If the resolve to use only Indian goods, so far as possible, be maintained, it will be no small help in developing the national spirit."[910]

In the 1920s, *Gandhi supposedly asked Indians to boycott the Indian administration.* The reality is that idea was due to a lawyer, Shyamji Krishnavarma, who had served Dewan in Ajmer and other States. In 1906, Gandhi wrote: "The idea underlying his service is that .... the British should quit the country, handing over power to Indians. If they do not do so, the *Indians should refuse them all help so that they become unable to carry on the administration and are forced to leave.*"[911]

The forgoing examples leave no doubt that most of the ideas connected with his name were not from him. While blowing his image (see next chapter), neither his Christian biographers, nor Gandhi himself made efforts to say few words on it.

Notes and References

[883] Indian Opinion, 2-9-1905.

[884] Indian Opinion, 7-4-1906.

[885] Indian Opinion, 20-4-1907.

[886] Gandhi M.K., Speeches and writings – M.K. Gandhi, G.A. Natesan & Co., Madras 1922, p. 181.

[887] Indian Opinion, 22-9-1906.

[888] Indian Opinion, 22-9-1906.

[889] Indian Opinion, 22-9-1906.

[890] Indian Opinion, 22-9-1906.

[891] Indian Opinion, 22-9-1906.

[892] C.W.M.G. 5, 1905-1906, pp. 343-343.

[893] Indian Opinion, 24-11-1906.

[894] Indian Opinion, 22-12-1906.

[895] Indian Opinion, 23-2-1907.

[896] Indian Opinion, 29-6-1907.

[897] Indian Opinion, 29-6-1907.

[898] Indian Opinion, 24-11-1906.

[899] Indian Opinion, 24-11-1906.

[900] Indian Opinion, 11-5-1907.

[901] Indian Opinion, 11-5-1907.

[902] http://www.npr.org/sections/thetwo-way/2013/11/05/243268093/on-the-block-gandhis-spinning-wheel-napoleons-last-will, June 17, 2015.

[903] Gandhi M.K to Gandhi N., Jan. 10, 1911.

[904] Gandhi M.K to Gandhi N., Jan. 10, 1911.

[905] http://www.gktoday.in/kuka-movement-1872/, June 17, 2015.

[906] Indian Opinion, 6-4-1907.

[907] http://www.gktoday.in/kuka-movement-1872/, June 17, 2015.

[908] Indian Opinion, 28-10-1905.

[909] Indian Opinion, 16-9-1905.

[910] Indian Opinion, 7-10-1905.

[911] Indian Opinion, 1-12-1906.

The Creation of a Legend – Christian Writers and Self Propaganda by Gandhi

In religions legends, mythos and martyrdom played/play a major role in raising the status of a person. Gandhi is often remembered to have said that *he would be a 'false mahatma' if he were to die a natural death.*[912] In Delhi after a bomb-attack he was suggested to take police security which he denied. He told to one of his followers: "And if an explosion took place, as it did last week, or somebody shot at me and I received his bullet on bare chest, without a sigh and *with Rama's name on my lips*, only then you should say that I was a true *mahatma*. (underlined in original)."[913] Unsurprisingly, he died with the last words on his lips "Hai Rama" (Oh God or Oh god Rama). Nathuram Godse, the assassinator, listened and heard only a faint "Ah!."[914] As far as I can recall, our Government schoolbooks read that Gandhi died with the last words on lips being "Hei Rama." This type of propaganda boosted and continues to boost Gandhi's image as a deep religious leader.

In "Mahatma Gandhi – Sex scandals and the missed Nobel Peace Prize"[915], I showed that for the Prize, he was nominated nearly 100 times. My aim was to find out the opinion of nominators about Gandhi; and why the Nobel Committee rejected their claim. I concluded that due to Gandhi's "Brahmacharya" experiments his associates were annoyed, thus they did not supply the necessary information to the Nobel Committee, which was willing to give a posthumous award.[916] In the same book, I discussed: Where does the positive image of the so-called "Mahatma" comes from? This part is reproduced in the second half of this chapter. It mainly deals with the time period after 1940s. The period before that is given in the following section. We shall see:

- How the Christian Baptist missionary J.J. Doke by writing "M.K. Gandhi – An Indian patriot in South Africa" created Gandhi's legend?
- Which influence had R. Rolland's Gandhi's biography in Europe?
- How Gandhi himself and his Indian friends boosted his image in India?
- What were the interests of Christian writers and Gandhi's friends in boosting his image?

Gandhi and the Christian Biographers

J.J. Doke, for the first time, met Gandhi in his office and found it poorly equipped and dusty. On the walls he saw photographs from Annie Besant, William Wilson Hunters, Richter Ranade and Jesus Christ (surprisingly nobody from India and Indian culture or religion).[917] Doke found *Gandhi's actions like the actions of Mary of Bethany, "often regarded as incomprehensible and often completely misunderstood."*[918] Gandhi told Doke that it was "The New Testament", which brought to his consciousness the accuracy and value of the liabilities of passive resistance. In the 'Sermon on the Mount' when I came to point: "But I say unto you , that ye shall not resist evil , but so somebody strikes you on your right cheek, turn to him the other" … "I was very happy and I found my opinion there confirmed. …. "The Bhagwat Gita" deepened my impression and Tolstoy's "The Kingdom of God is in you" gave him the final form."[919]

Gandhi was a practical man. So that the book "M.K. Gandhi – An Indian patriot in South Africa" has scrutiny from an influential Western politician like Lord Ampthill. He (Ampthill) was asked to write a "Foreword." On Aug. 9, 1909, Gandhi wrote to him:

> "I have now received the somewhat delayed proof of the Rev. *Mr. Doke's book, which I am very anxious to see published as early as possible. I might mention in passing that I have received a number of subscriptions from subscribers in advance.* I know you are very busy and I have hesitated to burden you further with the perusal of this proof and with the writing of the introduction, which you were good enough to promise, if the proof should meet with your approval."[920]

In order to give publicity to his biography, Gandhi took pains to circulate it widely. For instance, he wrote to his friend Polak:

> "*As many copies will have to be distributed free of charge, I thought I should pocket my own personal feelings and deal with the thing myself. I fancy that Dr. Mehta will guarantee any deficit.* I have already corresponded with him in the matter. *You may, therefore, be on the lookout for any bookseller who would care to take up the book.* The best thing will be, perhaps, for Kaliandas or Chhaganlal's cousin, or both of them, *to take the book personally to many people.*"[921]

Polak, who was at that time in India, replied: "Natesan will take 250 copies for distribution here among booksellers for sale. When Chhaganlal comes here, he will make enquiries in Bombay."[922]

The biography was published by Nasarwanji M. Cooper, editor of the "Indian Chronicle", London.[923] On Oct. 21, 1909, Gandhi asked him to send: 24 copies to Mehta, Rangoon, India; 250 copies to Messrs. Natesan & Co., Madras, India, and 250 copies to the Manager, International Printing Press, Durban, Natal, South Africa. About a week later, to Polak, he (Gandhi) sent a list of newspapers in India, to which the biography was sent. He was told that if he (Polak) thinks that a particular newspaper is left out, he can take a copy from Natesan and send. Same can be done in the case of private persons. He was informed that *"85 complimentary copies have been distributed here. Of these 81 are to newspapermen."*[924]

The U.K. newspaper seems to be the first to write a review. About it Gandhi wrote to H.S.L. Polak: "Mr. Doke's book has been reviewed in the Edinburgh "Evening News" in about 20 lines. "The Times" has just acknowledged it, giving a 4-line notice. I do not think it has been reviewed anywhere else yet."[925]

What we see from above is that Gandhi made "mass-level" propaganda and invested money to make his biography popular in political circles as well as on the local level.

"Mahatma Gandhi's ideas – Including selections from his writings – Mahatma Gandhi: His own story – Mahatma Gandhi at work – His own story continued" was written by C.F. Andrews, a Christian missionary, who spent most of his life in India. During his visit to

S.A. he met Doke. Andrews, referring to Doke, tried to represent Gandhi like Jesus. For instance, after Gandhi was arrested:

> "*Two children, greatly attached to him*, accompanied their friend on his return march to the Fort. They walked in line with him, for a long distance up the dusty road, in hope of attracting his attention, and of throwing him a word of cheer. But they failed. His face was *"steadfastly set to go to Jerusalem,"* and he saw nothing but that. I wonder what he saw in that long march. Not the immediate Jerusalem, *I imagine-the place of crucifixion.* I know of no vision more terrible than that. The Fort, with its cells and its hateful associations. Those long files of prisoners. *The white-clad, brutal native warders, swaggering along with their naked assegais.*"[926]

How far one shall believe the missionaries, the "Keepers of the truth", who were blind to Gandhi's participation in wars and his dislike for natives and African born Indians? It will be wrong to expect either rationality or objectivity from them. However, at one stage, that is, in the beginning of the 1920s, Andrews, had differences of opinion with Gandhi due to his Brahmacharya experiments and recruiting of soldiers for the British. He confessed that though he had discussed with Gandhi, yet he was unable to understand him.[927] Gandhi, the "India's freedom fighter", who with his blood and flesh was loyal to British Empire was critical of Andrews. He recalled, *Gandhi "blamed me very severely indeed for my lack of faith in British connexion* and for my publically *putting forward a demand for complete independence.* He said to me openly that *I had done a great deal of mischief by such advocacy of independence.*"[928]

Gandhi and the French Views

Gandhi's other biographer was the pacifist Romain Rolland, who got the Literature Nobel Prize in 1915. In 1923 he wrote Gandhi's biography, in which he stated:

> "I thought I had found that rampart in the revelation given to me in 1922 of the little Saint Francis of India, Gandhi. Did he bring, in the folds of his sackcloth, the word which would free us of the murders to come, the heroic non-violence which does not flee, but resists, 'Ahimsa?' I had such need to believe in it that I believed in it passionately for many years, and I poured out that faith in full buckets. I was convinced (I confess) that it *alone could bring salvation to a crime-ridden world*, its past crimes, its future crimes."[929]

Rolland, like other Christians in Europe, sought console in Hindu religion and philosophy. He wrote not only Gandhi's biography, but also that of Ramakrishna and Vivekananda. According to an author: *"He devoted his maximum attention and efforts to "advertising" Gandhi's life, method, and message.* The Gandhian movement in South Africa and India and the Gandhian thought were little known in Europe and the attitude of European intellectuals was to ignore Gandhi. RR found it incredible that Europe knew so little and so inaccurately about the impressive personality and colossal action of Gandhi."[930] And further: "As per his own assessment, RR's writings on Gandhi succeeded in spreading "Gandhism" in Europe to an "astonishing" extent and they created considerable commotion in the French, German, Russian, and other European minds. They particularly had a great impact in Protestant circles which absorbed Gandhi's words as if *"they came from the Christ himself.""*[931] Like Doke, R. Rolland saw in Gandhi *"the purest and the greatest Christian in spirit,* the purest interpreter of Christ, and the person who, above all others, resumed the direct tradition of *the spirit of the Gospel and Testament."*[932]

The Marxists like E. Roy rebutted Rolland publicly by stating that he misuses Gandhi "in order to prove his own theory that non-violence, based upon suffering, self-sacrifice, and brotherly love, is the only philosophy that can save European civilization from ultimate annihilation."[933] According to E. Roy, for Marxists, "he (Gandhi) is not and never will be - a "true revolutionary," whether of the violent or non-violent variety."[934] Like other Christians, R. Rolland: "While recognising Gandhi's belief in sacred cows and the caste system, he attempted to show that *his ultimate inspiration was Christian.*"[935] Due to Rolland's propaganda: "*The notion of Gandhi's saintly character spread throughout Anglo-Saxon Protestant Christendom, most particularly in the United States.* In Lutheran and Catholic circles it was much less widely accepted, even if Gandhi acquired followers with a Catholic background such as Jean-Joseph Lanza del Vasto, the Frenchman of Italian origin who was the main propagator of Gandhism is France."[936]

During WWII the situation had changed. When Gandhi visited France, "the dominant image of Gandhi carried by the press was of a trouble-maker, or a hypocrite, certainly not of a saint."[937] After his death "he became a figure of veneration in France, his tragic death definitely giving him the aura of a martyr."[938]

Gandhi in German literature

In 1925, E.F. Rimensberger translated J.J. Doke's book into German. The German version contains articles from the "Indian Opinion" written by Gandhi's followers Millie Graham Polak and H.S.L. Polak. It contains three chapters by G.K. Gokhale on the situation of Indians in South Africa. Polak in "Preface" wrote:

> "His enterprise was a pioneering work, a big venture - *The search for the holy soul,* who is at home in the heart of the life. As a moving knight he moved from in bright zeal and high enthusiasm. ... *He did not strive to raise a country or a race above other countries and races -* .... It was then *that Gokhale witnessed the miracle.* ... What a man (Gandhi) who knows how to make heroes from ordinary men. Gokhale was the first among Indians who understood Gandhi and the rights of Indians in South Africa. He was of the opinion that the difference is that most of us are politicians, while *he is a holy person.*"[939]

There is not a single word of criticism from Polak on Gandhi's support to British Empire in WWI. In "Foreword" Lord Amptbill wrote that in England, in official circles Gandhi is often reported as a normal agitator.[940]

Gandhi and Americans

In 1910 Doke left for U.S.A. It is not clear, which role was played by his book in the U.S.A. R. Rolland made influence on the Americans. J.H. Holmes, U.S.A., like other Christians[941], wrote: "When I think of Rolland ... I think of Tolstoy. When I think of Lenin, I think of Napoleon. *But when I think of Gandhi, I think of Jesus Christ. He lives his life; he speaks his word;* he suffers, strives and will someday nobly die, for his kingdom upon earth."[942]

A historian wrote:

> "There remained always a certain degree of ambiguity in the relationship between Gandhi and his Christian admirers. Gandhi did nothing to incite them to elevate him to sainthood, but he was shrewd enough politically to understand all the advantages he could derive from being put on such a pedestal. Actually, as Juergensmeyer rightly argues, the canonization of Gandhi had more to do with the problems of some Christian intellectuals *vis-á-vis* the modern world than with Gandhi's personality or his actions. Gandhi's saintliness was largely a proxy saintliness into which some Western Christian intellectual projected their own frustrations and expectations."[943]

According to my view, the Christian missionaries or Gandhi's Christian supporters had their own interests. Gandhi was cunning enough to manipulate the situation. For instance, until 1907, that is, the start of his so-called "satyagraha", his associates were mainly Muslims. In his speeches and writings he often used the word "Khuda" and "Ishwar", that is, God as Muslims and Hindus respectively say. After this period the Christian terms started appearing. Just to say a few examples:

- By mentioning Martin Luther who refused to follow the orders of the Pope. Gandhi gives a bit of a different or rather wrong example, that Martin Luther burnt the documents. Gandhi asked his people to refuse to take documents or burn them as Luther did.
- To Christian missionaries like Doke he said that his political ideas are due to the Bible.

Now the question is: What had missionaries gained from Gandhi? My personal opinion is:

- They use/abuse Gandhi to propagate Christianity.
- In the end of 19th and beginning of the 20th century, in particular in India, the conversion movements were quite dominant. I have quoted one such example by referring to a letter from M. Nehru to his son. History of Punjab shows that during this period, in Punjab many Sikhs converted to Christianity. One standard example is that of "Sadhu Sundar Singh."[944] His biography was written and propagated in the Christian world. Thus for missionaries there could not have been be a better example than a Hindu (Gandhi), who gave credit to Jesus and Bible, for the creation of a "peaceful" world.
- As has been referred to above, after the WWI, many intellectual Christians like R. Rolland were disillusioned by Christian Institutions. Those, who did not identified themselves with revoluationary and Marxist ideologies, had no other choice but

to see solution from other cultures. Western educated Gandhi, a mixture of East and West philosophy was the perfact example to be followed.

- C.F. Andrews with his connection on authorities and elite Indians seems to have heart for underdogs. His support to Gandhi can be seen as his will to help Indians.

- Gandhi was of the opinion that "The aim of the Christian Governments, so we read, is to raise people whom they come in contact with or whom they control. It is otherwise in South Africa."[945] Such statements leave on no doubt that for Christian States Gandhi was the right person for their aims.

Propaganda by Friends

So far as Gandhi's autobiography in Gujarati is concerned, it was published in 1922. Gandhi's friend G.A. Natesan, a politician and publisher produced: "Gandhi M.K., Speeches and writings."*Under the testimony (which contains 30 pages) we find important names*: Count Leo Tolstoy, Gilbert Murray, *Lord Hardinge, Lord Ampthill, Lord Bishop of Madras, Lord Gladstone, Sir Henry Cotton, Senator W.P. Schreiner, G.K. Gokhale, J.J. Doke, Annie Besant and Sir P.M. Mehta.*[946] All these names show that Gandhi cannot be seen as a man who wanted to get rid of the British Empire. The book is mainly based on Doke's biography and Gandhi's articles in "Indian Opinion." We have seen – How his political ideas emerged and his achievements were "marginal." But according to the book: "*Mr. Gandhi is chiefly responsible for the initiation of the policy of the passive resistance that was so successfully carried out by the Indians of South Africa during the next eight years.*"[947] Credit has been given to Gandhi for the foundation of the "Indian Opinion." For "About the middle of 1903, it had occurred to him ...it was absolutely necessary to have a newspaper, ..."[948] The fact is that Madanjit Vayaviharik (to whom, in 1899, Gandhi borrowed money to start the International Printing Press, Durban) in 1903 came to Gandhi and suggested to publish "Indian Opinion" in four languages. Gandhi agreed to write at least one article every week. Gandhi's associate Mansukhlal Nazar agreed to work as an unpaid editor.[949]

There is difference of opinion, in how Mohandas Gandhi became the "Mahatma" (the great soul). One of the versions is that Indian's Nobel Laureate R.N. Tagore, once in a talk, addressed Gandhi as "Mahatma." However, for educated members of the I.N.C. as well as for illiterates, his real name vanished. For others, it became impossible to use the right name. For instance, in a meeting, M.A. Jinnah (see Appendex A) used the word "Mr. Gandhi." As a reaction to it:

> "He was *'howled down with cries of 'shame, shame' and 'political imposter' and louder shouts of 'No. Mahatma Gandhi.' Jinnah repeated 'Mister' but the irate audience yelled 'Mahatma.'* He waited for the noise to subside, turning toward Gandhi to say, 'Standing on this platform, knowing as I do that he commands the majority in this assembly, I appeal to him to pause, to cry halt before it is too late.' But Gandhi did not respond, leaving Jinnah to step down from that platform, followed out of the crowded

Congress by ugly hisses and catcalls, this chapter of his career as India's 'Best Ambassador of Hindu-Muslim Unit' shattered by Gandhi's honorary title."[950]

Self-Promotion - Autobiography – "The story of my experiments with truth"

From day to day experience, we know that, contrasts matter. We cannot appreciate the value of light, without the existence of the darkness. This simple philosophy was applied by Gandhi in his autobiography. To show his own "positive" quality, he exposed "negative" side of his teachers, brothers and friends. He presented himself as "reformer." Here follows two examples. In his autobiography, under "A Tragedy", he wrote that his Muslim friend drank and ate meat. Gandhi was induced by him to eat the "forbidden fruit", that is meat. We know that Eva and Adam were thrown out of the "Garden of Eden" for their sin. In the autobiography, the sinner Gandhi did not suffer. He came out as a "reformer." At the time he was just a teenager. According to his autobiography: "Nevertheless I pleaded with them (parent and other well-wishers) saying, 'I know he has the weaknesses you attribute to him, but you do not know his virtues. He cannot lead me astray, as *my association with him is meant to reform him*. For I am sure that if he reforms his ways, he will be a splendid man."[951] In next paragraphs, the "reformer" turns into a patriot, who needs to eat meat, because: "*I wished to be strong* and daring and wanted my countrymen also to be such, *so that we might defeat the English and make India free. ....*"[952]

The fact is, according to his life philosophy, Gandhi was not responsible for his deeds. *He went to a brothel.* What happened: *"God in His infinite mercy protected me against myself.* I was almost struck blind and dumb in this den of vice."[953] Though he appreciated the Bible's teaching, in contrast to Jesus's teaching (if you sin in your thoughts it as if you committed the sin), Gandhi said: "But from the ordinary point of view, a man who is saved from physically committing sin is regarded as saved."[954] Surprisingly, God did not "save" or "stop" him, when he stole money from a servant's pocket or his brother's jewelry.[955] Much more exaggerated is about the "origin of non-violence." This he learnt as a child.[956] The son of a "Prime Minister" wrote: *"The poverty of my family* likewise dictated to me the same choice. This was my first journey from Rajkot to Ahmedabad and that too without a companion."[957] There are many more contradictory examples.

In "Mahatma Gandhi – ... the missed Nobel Peace Prize", it was argued that: "First of all, Gandhi was a fantastic promoter of his own ideology. He understood the power of symbols and mass media. In order to be independent from the local media, he founded his own weeklies and newspapers such as the "Indian Opinion", "Young India" and "Harijan." According to one of his followers, T.A. Raman, in 1943, "Harijan":

> "... Was printed in English at Ahmedabad .... Eleven other issues published at different places brought to total *12 editions in 9 languages.* .... *Gandhi's most important articles in the "Harijan" are reprinted the next day by all the daily newspapers of India, 37 in English and 115 in Indian*

languages. Together they cover every single newspaper reader in India, and practically all the educated adults of the country. It might also be added that while the speeches and articles of other leaders often appear in a condensed form, Gandhi's "Harijan" articles are always reported in *extenso* and prominently displayed even in the British-owned newspapers."[958]

Gandhi in Independent India

Gandhi's party, Indian National Congress boosted his image at every available opportunity. After his death his complete works were collected and published. There are "The Collected Works of Mahatma Gandhi"[959]- 98 Vol., "Gandhiji No Akshar Deha" – 97 Vol. and "Sampoorna Gandhi Vangmaya"[960] - 97 Vol. In 1977, in total there were 45 Branch offices to propagate Gandhi's ideas; in addition to a number of museums named after him, most of which financed by the Government of India and various Charitable Trusts.[961] This leaves no doubt that within India, Gandhians are powerful lobbyists and state financed propaganda is only a part of the success.

Today in Western Countries, the main driver for the positive and uncritical image of Gandhi has much to do with Richard Attenborough's movie named after the man himself. After Tenzin Gyatso (Dalai Lama) received the Nobel Peace Prize, a 50 minute long documentary about Gandhi was produced in English. From here, the foundation for two short German movies under the titles "Mahatma Gandhi - Deutsche Doku über Mahatma Gandhi"

(Mahatma Gandhi – German documentary on Mahatma Gandhi)[962] and "Mahatma Gandhi - Pilger des Friedens" (Mahatma Gandhi – The Pilgrimage of Peace) by Channel of GandhiServe Foundation[963] was laid. The film makers used original photographs and included spoken excerpts from the likes of Gandhi's grandson Arun Gandhi, Dalai Lama, Prof. X.Y., London School of Economics, Prof. X.Y., political scientist, and a journalist X.Y. It is surprising that many so-called experts, highly educated persons, say no more than an Indian school child about Gandhi and his life. The stereotype of a "Mahatma" who fought for the rights of "blacks and Indians" in South Africa and his non-violent struggle against the British has propagated well to the Western World. There are many more uncritical documentary films, which are entirely based on his autobiography – "The Making of The Mahatma - British Propaganda - BBC Documentary."[964] "Gandhi - The Road to Freedom - British Propaganda - BBC Documentary."[965] In this film – Part 4 there is talk about "critical practices of "Brahmacharya." "Gandhi - The Rise to Fame - British Propaganda - BBC Documentary."[966]

"Censorship" by the Indian State

The other cause of Gandhi's "clean" image is the "censorship" that occured in India. Following India's independence, the Congress Party took care that Gandhi's ideas were not criticised. Even internationally recognized Indian scientists like S.K. Mitra were careful when commenting on Gandhi's hand-loom and primitive agriculture methods.[967] They foresaw the solution of Indians' problems in science and technology.

In particular on a state level, Gandhi's sexuality was/is a taboo topic. For instance, Sudhir Kakar's novel "Mira and the Mahatma"[968] lead to controversy in India, as reported by the German newspaper: "Die Welt" of Oct. 22, 2004 - "Gandhi und die Schülerin – Sie hieß Madeleine Slade, eine britische Admiralstochter. War sie die Geliebte des Mahatma Gandhi? Ein neuer Roman provoziert Indien" (Gandhi and the Follower - Her name was Madeleine Slade, a British Admiral's daughter. Was she the mistress of Mahatma Gandhi? A new novel provokes India). According to my personal view, Girja Kumar has written the most critical book on Gandhi's relation with women and the misuse of his power to ensnare young women in his so-called "brahmacharya" experiments.[969] One of the reviewers stated:

> "Having brought the Father of the Nation down to his own level, Kumar gloats that Gandhiji was 'a failed hero who was too obsessed with the sexuality issue' and enjoyed controlling every aspect of the lives of these women but refused to concede that he used them for purposes of his own. …. To paraphrase Dorothy Parker, *this is not a book to be cast aside lightly; it is to be thrown away with great force.*"[970]

In 2011, after the publication of the "Great soul - Mahatma Gandhi and his struggle with India"[971], the Gujarat's state assembly unanimously voted to ban the book.[972] N. Modi in those days Chief Minister of Gujrat (presently Prime Minister of India) urged the central government to ban the publication nationwide. Sanjay Dutt from the Congress Party suggested that: *"The government should invoke a law to severely punish anyone* who tarnishes the image of the Father of the Nation." According to "The India Today" the Law Minister Veerappa Moily said, "The government has taken a serious note of the book that has made disgraceful statement on the national leader. It is demeaning for the nation."[973] The reason being is that the author hinted at a sexual relationship between Gandhi and his friend, Hermann Kallenbach.

As a reaction to propaganda and suppression of these anti-Gandhian ideas, "In India the younger generation hates Gandhiji and break his statues, burn his books and portraits, garland his statues with shoes and blackens them with tar-coal."[974]

About thirty years ago, G.D. Khosla, one of three judges, who sentenced Nathuram Godse, Gandhi's killer, wrote: "*I have, however, no doubt that had the audience of that day been constituted into a jury and entrusted with the task of deciding Godse's appeal*, they would have brought him in *a verdict of 'not guilty' by an overwhelming majority.*"[975]

One wonders, whether these so-called experts ever read Gandhi's own writings and critical books like: "Gandhi - Apostel der Unmenschlichkeit" (Gandhi – Apostle of inhumanity)[976] and "Gandhi: Behind the Mask of Divinity."[977]

In 1999 in the U.S.A., a Committee of the so-called "spiritual writers" selected Gandhi's autobiography as one of the hundred best spiritual books of the 20th century.[978] Like most of the autobiographies, as to be expected, it boosts Gandhi's own "great" achievements with the "soul power" and "truth." It presents the "war" between the "devilish" white communities vs. the "godly" Indians, who were being suppressed. The book completely ignores the grievances of the Boers, who lost 1/3rd of their population during the Anglo-Boer War. Their farms and houses were burnt by the British, who were supported by Gandhi and his friends. Equally, the Indian workers and their children, who represented majority of the Indian population in S.A., appear as "footnotes" in "The story of my experiments with truth."

His writings show that in general, Gandhi was against democracy. In Natal and the Cape Colony, under certain conditions Indians were allowed to vote and to be elected. Gandhi was least interested in voting system. His argument was: *"The weapon of franchise has been rusting, ..."*[979] In 1910, he stated:

> "It is very difficult to get rid of our fondness for Parliament. It was no doubt barbarous when people tore off the skin, burned persons alive and cut off their ears or nose; but *the tyranny of Parliament is much greater than that of Chengiz Khan, Tamerlane and others*. Hence it is that we are caught in its meshes. Modern tyranny is a trap of temptation and therefore does greater mischief. One can withstand the atrocities committed by one individual as such; but it is difficult to cope with *the tyranny perpetrated upon a people in the name of the people.*"[980]

Gandhi was not only anti-democrat, but also anti-revolutionary. In 1908, in Bengal and Punjab at the time of protests against the British Empire, he formulated the situation as follows:

> "*It would be a bad day for India when that forcible revolutionary spirit gained a substantial footing*, but he

could not help saying that Lord Elgin (Victor Bruce, Viceroy of India 1894-1899) had sown the seed. *If this had been confined to the student world, it would probably never grow in Indian soil,* but he found today that the merchant, who did not know a word of English, was steeped in the new spirit with reference to the Act and its evil."[981]

Instead of supporting Indians, he criticized their efforts. He called them mad. The journal "Bande Mataram" was forbidden to be published in India and U.K. It propagated freedom through weapons and criticized the so-called "moderate" leaders such as G.K. Gokhale. In 1909, an Indian nationalist, Madanlal Dhingra tried to assassinate Curzon Wyllie's, Viceroy of India; as the former was of the opinion that he is responsible for India's ruin. During the court-process Dhingra said that he did not see it as crime. He did it for the sake of his country. He was sentenced to death. About Dhingra's action, Gandhi wrote: *"Dhingra's statement, according to me, argues mere childishness or mental derangement."*[982] Gandhi was not willing to see the suppression by the British system, which for four months sent the editor of "The Indian Sociologist" behind the bar, because he dared to publish a "violent article", which stated "that homicide for the good of one's country was no murder."[983]

The activities of the Indian revolutionary within the country were far stronger. After an attack on Lord Hardinge, Viceroy of India, Gandhi wrote that it is due to Western influence:

"The mad youth who perpetrated the crime no doubt thought that by striking murders of distinguished men, rulers could be terrorized and an independent Indian could

be thereby secured. We should decline to share any such independence even if it were attainable, which we doubt..... *We pray, too, for Lord Hardinge's quick recovery from the effect of the wound received by him.*"[984]

In my previous book, I stated: "A lack of education, and perhaps a bit of ignorance, cause a large part of the world to believe that India won freedom from the British Empire due to Gandhi's "Ahimsa" (non-violent resistance). Such views are due to uncritical literature and the famous movie "Gandhi" by Richard Attenborough. It was heavily financed by the Government of India to use one figure as a symbol of light. This film presented Gandhi as the embodiment of India's freedom struggle while ignoring historical facts and the role played by other political groups."[985] According to historians:

"Even without Gandhi's satyagraha campaign, there was a prospect of serious unrest during the spring of 1919, although its form and extent were unclear to the government. It was simultaneously faced with Muslim apprehension about the future of the caliphate, distress in the wake of the recent influenza epidemic, prices outstripping wages, dearths and undercurrents of expectation stirred up by the news of massive upheavals in Russia and the Middle East."[986]

Indian school books ignore the role of the Bengali and Punjabi revolutionaries. The reality is that while under Gandhi's guidance, the Congress Party was "fighting" with non-violent methods; in Bengal, on "August 4th, 1929, a procession of about 100 Bengali volunteers and 25 Punjabis was taken out in Calcutta carrying placards bearing such inscriptions as 'Down with Imperialism', 'Long live revolution', and 'Death is at our door'."[987] The historian L. James explores the role played by communists and Sikh community in detail. He wrote:

> "*Communist and Sikh ultra-nationalist agitation was responsible for two significant outbreaks of unrest in 1939-40. Both were blamed for a mutiny by over 300 men of the Royal Indian Army Service Corps in Cairo in January 1940, where they refused to load stores on the lorries. Among those arrested were several Sikh reservists who had pre-war connections with the Communist journal 'Kirti Lehr', and others from a village where Ghadrite sympathies were still strong.*"[988]

In 1940, an Emergency Powers Act was introduced to control the political activities.

> "Here, *the greatest danger lay not with the major political parties, but with the smaller extremist groups which had mushroomed over the past twenty years. The loyalty of the Indian soldiers was a delicate matter,* and the Indian army was extremely touchy about allegations that its men were even susceptible to subversive propaganda, let alone willing to give it the time of day."[989]

In the 1940s, "the administrative machinery had quietly passed into Indian hands: less than a tenth of India's 2,500 judges were now British, and Indians outnumbered Britons in the ICS (Indian Civil Services)."[990] Another remarkable example to be quoted is that of S.C. Bose, who left India and went to Germany and later, Japan.

There he founded the Indian National Army, which was comprised of nearly sixty-thousand Indian troops composed primarily from a part of the former British army which previously surrendered to Japan. He acknowledged India as a free country and declared war against the British and the U.S.A. Bose's army reached Imphal; however, due to adverse weather conditions and a lack of battle worthy weapons, the I.N.A. was forced to surrender in May of 1945. In Delhi, the captured officers of the army were placed on trial while being simultaneously celebrated by the people as heroes of India's struggle for independence. This shook the loyalty of their Indian colleagues, who had fought alongside the British. It led to *a mutiny in the Royal Air Force in Dum Dum and Bombay forcing the British Empire to develop new policies to deal with those Indian soldiers, who fought against the British Empire.*[991] According to the historian S. Wolpert: *"Noncooperation brought nothing but detention and despair to Indian nationalist ranks. The Raj had proved more resilient than any of the Congress high command imagined it would be a year earlier."*[992]

Another important historical fact is that in June 1948 it was declared as the latest date for the termination of British rule in India; despite this, the British left India one year before this deadline. This occurred primarily because:

> "The Interim Government in 1946-7 at the centre revealed the utter incompatibility of the Congress and the Muslim League. *The communal riots*, which began at Calcutta on 16 August 1946, spread like a prairie fire from Calcutta to East Bengal, from East Bengal to Bihar, and from Bihar to

the Punjab. India seemed to be sliding into *an undeclared civil war with battle lines passing through almost every town and village. ... The Viceroy* seemed to have been outplayed in the face of divergent pressures which he could neither reconcile nor control; he *suggested to his superiors in London the desperate expedient of a British evacuation of India,* province by province."[993]

From the above-mentioned evidence, we see that India's independence was not a non-violent campaign. A second point to be noted is that Government had difficulty in controlling the public. The worst of the restlessness occurring after 1944 when there was revolt within the army. Such events led the British to think of a face saving solution.

The fact is that M. Gandhi was one of millions who fought for their motherland and India's freedom.

Appendex A – Muhammand Ali Jinnah

Muhammad Ali Jinnah and the All India Muslim League

The All India Muslim League, later renamed as the Muslim League, was founded in 1906. Its aim was to safeguard the rights of Muslims in a Hindu dominated country. In 1913, its target was the self-governing of India. For the following two decades, its members, in particular M.A. Jinnah, advocated for Hindu-Muslim unity in a united and independent India.[994] Jinnah rose to prominence in the Indian National Congress in the first two decades of the 20th century. In 1920, he resigned from the Congress due to disagreements with Gandhi's satyagraha method. This conflict took a worse turn in the beginning of the 1930s when Gandhi refused to accept Muslims as a minority. Elections in 1937 were an eye-opener for the Muslim League and, in 1940, the Muslim League led by Jinnah, passed the Lahore resolution, demanding a separate nation. During WWII Muslims supported the British Empire showing a straight forward way of operating and negotiating. At the same time, Congress under Gandhi was adopted under unclear strategies. After WWII, the Muslim League won a majority of the seats during a major election. When it came to the sharing of power in independent India, the Congress and Muslim League could not reach an agreement leading the participants (British, Congress and Muslim League) to create new nations – Pakistan and East Bengal as administrative units under the Muslim League. In 1955, this area was declared as East Pakistan and later in 1971 East Pakistan emerged as the People's Republic of Bangladesh.

Notes and References

[912] Kumar G., Brahmacharya Gandhi and his women associates, Vitasta Publishing Pvt. Ltd., New Delhi 2008, p. 357.

[913] Kumar G., Brahmacharya Gandhi and his women associates, 2008, p. 357.

[914] Kumar G., Brahmacharya Gandhi and his women associates, 2008, pp. 360-361.

[915] Singh R., Mahatma Gandhi – Sex scandals and the missed Nobel Peace Prize – Facts and fictions, Shaker 'Verlag', Aachen 2015.

[916] Singh R., Mahatma Gandhi – …. the missed Nobel Peace Prize, 2015.

[917] Doke J.J., Gandhi in Südafrika – Mohandas Karamchand Gandhi – Ein indischer Patriot in Südafrika, Rotapfel Verlag, Erlenbach-Zürich 1925, p. 27.

[918] Doke J.J., Gandhi in Südafrika …, 1925, p. 30.

[919] Doke J.J., Gandhi in Südafrika …, 1925, p. 120.

[920] Gandhi M.K. to Ampthill L., Aug. 9, 1909.

[921] C.W.M.G. 10, 1909-1910, p. 96.

[922] C.W.M.G. 10, 1909-1910, p. 96.

[923] C.W.M.G. 10, 1909-1910, p. 151.

[924] Gandhi M.K. to Polak H.S.L., Oct. 29, 1909.

[925] Gandhi M.K. to Polak H.S.L., Nov. 9, 1909.

[926] Andrews C.F., Mahatma Gandhi's ideas – Including selections from his writings – Mahatma Gandhi: His own story – Mahatma Gandhi at work – His own story continued, The Macmillan Company, New York 1931, pp. 376-377.

[927] Gandhi M.K., Speeches and writings – M.K. Gandhi, G.A. Natesan & Co., Madras 1922, pp. xiii-xvi.

[928] Gandhi M.K., Speeches and writings – ... , 1922, pp. xiii-xvi.

[929] Markovits C., The Un-Gandhian Gandhi – The life and afterlife of the Mahatma, Anthem Press, London 2003, pp. 17-18.

[930] www.hss.iitb.ac.in/bhole/eog/ch6.pdf, *Dec. 22, 2014.*

[931] www.hss.iitb.ac.in/bhole/eog/ch6.pdf, *Dec. 22, 2014.*

[932] www.hss.iitb.ac.in/bhole/eog/ch6.pdf, *Dec. 22, 2014.*

[933] https://www.marxists.org/archive/roy-evelyn/articles/1923/gandhi_rev_counter.htm, Dec. 22, 2014. Roy E., Mahatma Gandhi revolutionary or counter-revolutionary?, A reply to Romain Rolland and Henri Barbusseto Labour Monthly Vol. V, Sept. 1923.

[934] https://www.marxists.org/archive/roy-evelyn/articles/1923/gandhi_rev_counter.htm, Dec. 22, 2014. Roy E. Mahatma Gandhi revolutionary or counter-revolutionary?, A reply to Romain Rolland and Henri Barbusseto Labour Monthly Vol. V, Sept. 1923.

[935] Markovits C., The Un-Gandhian Gandhi – ..., 2003, pp. 18-19.

[936] Markovits C., The Un-Gandhian Gandhi – ..., 2003, p. 20.

[937] Markovits C., The Un-Gandhian Gandhi – ...., 2003, pp. 20-21.

[938] Markovits C., The Un-Gandhian Gandhi – ..., 2003, p. 26.

[939] Doke J.J., Gandhi in Südafrika – ..., 1925, pp. 9-12.

[940] Doke J.J., Gandhi in Südafrika – ..., 1925, pp. 16-21.

[941] For more detail on Gandhi's interaction with Americans, see, Reddy E.S., Mahatam Gandhi – Letters to Americans, Bharatiya Vidya Bhavan, Bombay 1998.

[942] Markovits C., The Un-Gandhian Gandhi – ..., 2003, p. 16.

[943] Markovits C., The Un-Gandhian Gandhi – ..., 2003, pp. 20-21.

[944] https://en.wikipedia.org/wiki/Sadhu_Sundar_Singh, June 14, 2015.

[945] Gandhi M.K., Speech at public meeting, Bombay, Sept. 26, 1896, in: C.W.M.G., vol. 1, 1888-1896, pp. 407-417.

[946] Gandhi M.K., Speeches and writings – ..., 1922, appendix ii, pp. 17-47.

[947] Gandhi M.K., Speeches and writings – ..., 1922, p. 15.

[948] Gandhi M.K., Speeches and writings – ..., 1922, p. 11.

[949] Gandhi R., Gandhi - The man, his people, and the empire, University of California Press, California, 2008, p. 99.

[950] Wolpert S., Gandhi's passion - The life and legacy of Mahatma Gandhi, Oxford University Press, Oxford 2001, p. 111.

[951] Gandhi M.K., An autobiography or the story of my experiments with truth, Navajivan Publishing House, Ahmedabad 1940, p. 10.

[952] Gandhi M.K., An autobiography or the story of my experiments ... , 1940, p. 11.

[953] Gandhi M.K., An autobiography or the story of my experiments ... , 1940, p. 12.

[954] Gandhi M.K., An autobiography or the story of my experiments ...., 1940, p. 12.

[955] Gandhi M.K., An autobiography or the story of my experiments ..., 1940, pp. 13-14.

[956] Gandhi M.K., An autobiography or the story of my experiments ..., 1940, p. 14.

[957] Gandhi M.K., An autobiography or the story of my experiments ..., 1940, p. 18.

[958] Raman T.A., What does Gandhi want?, Oxford University Press, London 1943, p. ix.

[959] GandhiServe Foundation - Mahatma Gandhi Research and Media Service http://www.gandhiserve.org/e/cwmg/cwmg.htm, Sept. 28, 2014.

[960] http://en.wikipedia.org/wiki/Gandhi_Heritage_Portal, Aug. 28, 2014.

[961] Mehta V., Mahatma Gandhi and his apostles, Yale University Press, New Haven 1993, p. 31.

[962] http://www.youtube.com/watch?v=F_aRBLhJjjM, Oct. 27, 2014.

[963] http://www.youtube.com/watch?v=2ZJNKiC1-ak, Oct. 27, 2014.

[964] https://www.youtube.com/watch?v=S-kytwoWkQI, Dec. 17, 2014.

[965] https://www.youtube.com/watch?v=y815_a8k4Rg, Dec. 17, 2014.

[966] https://www.youtube.com/watch?v=jyQiqRvr9nl, Dec. 17, 2014.

[967] Mitra S.K., Science and progress - The story of radio electronics, Proc. Ind. Sci. Cong. 1955, in: The shaping of Indian Science – Indian Science Congress Association, Presidential Addresses Vol. II, 1948-1981, University Press (India) Pvt. Ltd., Hyderabad 2003, pp. 720-740. For S.K. Mitra's biography see, Singh R., Nobel Prize nominator Sisir Kumar Mitra F.R.S. - His scientific work in international context, Shaker 'Verlag', Aachen 2014.

[968] Kakar S., Mira and the Mahatma, Penguin Books India, New Delhi 2004.

[969] Kumar G., Brahmacharya Gandhi and his women associates, 2008, p. 328.

[970] http://www.dnaindia.com/lifestyle/books-and-more-brahmacharya-gandhi-and-his-women-associates-1053363

[971] Lelyveld J., Great soul - Mahatma Gandhi and his struggle with India, Alfred A. Knopf, Inc., New York 2011.

[972] The Guardian, March 30, 2011.

[973] The India Today, March 30, 2011.

[974] Dhiman O.P., Betrayal of Gandhi, Kalpaz Publications, Delhi 2010, p. x.

[975] Khosla G.D., Murder of the Mahatma, Jaico Press Pvt. Ltd., Bombay 1977, p. 306.

[976] http://www.youtube.com/watch?v=VTJy4CuIQQs; Oct. 14, 2014, http://www.youtube.com/watch?v=SUpHp3yueOw; Oct. 14, 2014, http://www.youtube.com/watch?v=zXoO_1hHau0, Oct. 27, 2014.

[977] R.Singh, I have not read this book. My knowledge is based on internet documentation.

[978] http://usatoday30.usatoday.com/life/enter/books/book372.htm, May 2, 2015.

[979] Indian Opinion, 7-9-1907.

[980] Gandhi M.K. to Gandhi M., April 2, 1910.

[981] Indian Opinion, 4-1-1908.

[982] Indian Opinion, 21-8-1909.

[983] Indian Opinion, 21-8-1909.

[984] Indian Opinion, 28-12-1912.

[985] This section is taken from my previous book, Singh R., Mahatma Gandhi – Sex scandals and the missed Nobel Peace Prize, Shaker 'Verlag', Aachen 2015, pp. 7-10.

[986] James L., Raj – The making and unmaking of British India, Little, Brown and Company, London 1999, p. 470.

[987] Banerjee R., Subhas Chandra Bose and the Bengal revolutionaries, Reference Press, New Delhi 2010, p. 67.

[988] James L., Raj – The making and unmaking of British India, 1999, p. 543.

[989] James L., Raj – The making and unmaking of British India, 1999, pp. 542-543.

[990] James L., Raj – The making and unmaking of British India, 1999, p. 541.

[991] Wolpert S., A new history of India, Oxford University Press, Oxford 1997, pp. 334-341. For more detail on S.C. Bose see, Banerjee R., Subhas Chandra Bose and the Bengal revolutionaries, 2010.

[992] Wolpert S., A new history of India, 1997, pp. 334-338.

[993] Nanda B.R., Gandhi and his critics, Oxford University Press, Bombay 1985, p. 96.

[994] http://www.britannica.com/EBchecked/topic/399405/Muslim-League, Aug. 9, 2014.

Bibliography

Adam A.C.H. to Chamberlain J., July 2, 1897.

Adam A.C.H. to Governor, Natal, April 6, 1897.

Adam A.C.H. to Governor, Natal, July 2, 1897.

Adam A.K.H. et al. to Chamberlain J., May 22, 1896.

Andrews C.F., Mahatma Gandhi's ideas – Including selections from his writings – Mahatma Gandhi: His own story – Mahatma Gandhi at work – His own story continued, The Macmillan Company, New York 1931.

Banerjee P., Ray N., Gupta P., et al., Hundred years of the University of Calcutta – A history of the university issued in commemoration of the centenary celebrations, University of Calcutta, Calcutta 1957.

Banerjee R., Subhas Chandra Bose and the Bengal revolutionaries, Reference Press, New Delhi 2010.

Bawazeer I.A.K. to Chamney M., May 26, 1908.

Bhana S., Vadeh G.H., The making of a social reformer - Gandhi in South Africa, 1893 – 1914, (Online). http://www.mkgandhi-sarvodaya.org/social_reform/appendix.htm, Feb. 4, 2015.

Bhana S., Vadeh G.H., The making of a social reformer – Gandhi in South Africa 1893-1914, online, http://www.mkgandhi-sarvodaya.org/social_reform/social_reform.htm, Feb. 5, 2015.

Biswas A.K., Science in India, Firma KL Mukhopadhyay, Calcutta 1969.

Bose D.M., Scientific education and research in the Calcutta University during the last hundred years, Science and Culture 22, 405-412, 1957.

C.W.M.G. 1, 1888-1896. (Collected Works of Mahatma Gandhi Online – http://www.gandhiserve.org/e/cwmg/cwmg.htm, Copyright 2008-2012)

C.W.M.G. 2, 1897-1902.

C.W.M.G. 3, 1902-1904.

C.W.M.G. 4, 1904-1905.

C.W.M.G. 5, 1905-1906.

C.W.M.G. 6, 1906-1907.

C.W.M.G. 8, 1907-1908.

C.W.M.G. 9, 1908-1909.

C.W.M.G. 10, 1909-1910.

C.W.M.G. 11, 1910-1911.

C.W.M.G. 12, 1911-1913.

C.W.M.G. 13, 1913.

C.W.M.G. 14, 1913-1915.

Cachalia A.M. to Director of Prisons, Pretoria, Sept. 19, 1908.

Cachalia A.M. to the Governor-General, Pretoria, June 16, 1913.

Chatterjee A., Burn R., British contribution to Indian studies, Longmans, Green & Co., London 1943.

Copley A., Gandhi against the tide, Basil Blackwell Inc., Cambridge 1989.

Dhiman O.P., Betrayal of Gandhi, Kalpaz Publications, Delhi 2010.

Doke J.J., Gandhi in Südafrika – Mohandas Karamchand Gandhi – Ein indischer Patriot in Südafrika, (Translated by E.F. Rimensberg), Rotapfel Verlag, Erlenbach-Zürich 1925.

Erikson E.H., Gandhi's truth - On the origins of nonviolence, W. W. Norton & Company, New York 1971.

Fischer L., Gandhi – His life and message for the world, New American Library, New York 1954.

Fischer L., Gandhi – Prophet der Gewaltlosigkeit, Wilhelm Heyne Verlag, München 1983.

Gandhi M., Mein Leben, Suhrkamp Taschenbuch Verlag, Frankfurt 1983.

Gandhi M.K to Gandhi N., Jan. 10, 1911.

Gandhi M.K. to Ali A., Oct. 25, 1906.

Gandhi M.K. to Ali A., Aug. 30, 1909.

Gandhi M.K. to Ally H.O., Oct. 26, 1906.

Gandhi M.K. to Ampthill L., Aug. 5, 1909.

Gandhi M.K. to Ampthill L., Aug. 9, 1909.

Gandhi M.K. to Ampthill L., Aug. 10, 1909.

Gandhi M.K. to Ampthill L., Sept. 13, 1909.

Gandhi M.K. to Ampthill L., Sept.16, 1909.

Gandhi M.K. to Ampthill L., Oct. 29, 1909.

Gandhi M.K. to Bhownaggree M., Oct. 25, 1906.

Gandhi M.K. to British Agent, Pretoria, Jan. 29, 1897.

Gandhi M.K. to Campbell M., Dec. 26, 1913.

Gandhi M.K. to Campbell M., June 20, 1914.

Gandhi M.K. to Cartwright A., June 6, 1908.

Gandhi M.K. to Colonial Secretary, Maritzburg, Oct. 19, 1899.

Gandhi M.K. to Cotton H., Nov. 10, 1906.

Gandhi M.K. to Cotton H., Nov. 12, 1906.

Gandhi M.K. to Doke J.J., March 7, 1911.

Gandhi M.K. to Doke J.J., March 17, 1911.

Gandhi M.K. to Gandhi C., April 5, 1911.

Gandhi M.K. to Gandhi C., March 11, 1914.

Gandhi M.K. to Gandhi K., Nov. 9, 1908.

Gandhi M.K. to Gandhi M., April 2, 1910.

Gandhi M.K. to Gandhi M., Oct. 2, 1913.

Gandhi M.K. to Gandhi M., Nov. 11, 1913.

Gandhi M.K. to Gibson J.C., Jan. 6, 1910.

Gandhi M.K. to Gokhale G.K., Aug. 1, 1902.

Gandhi M.K. to Gokhale G.K., Nov.14, 1902.

Gandhi M.K. to Gokhale G.K., Dec. 3, 1906.

Gandhi M.K. to Gokhale G.K., Dec. 6, 1909.

Gandhi M.K. to Gokhale G.K., Aug. 4, 1912.

Gandhi M.K. to Gokhale G.K., Feb. 14, 1913.

Gandhi M.K. to Gokhale G.K., April 19, 1913.

Gandhi M.K. to Gokhale G.K., June 20, 1913.

Gandhi M.K. to Gokhale G.K., Jan. 30, 1914.

Gandhi M.K. to Gokhale G.K., Feb. 27, 1914.

Gandhi M.K. to Gokhale G.K., May 6, 1914.

Gandhi M.K. to Gokhale G.K., June 5, 1914.

Gandhi M.K. to Gorges E.M., June 30, 1914.

Gandhi M.K. to Kallenbach H., Oct. 23, 1913.

Gandhi M.K. to Kallenbach H., Oct. 27, 1913.

Gandhi M.K. to Kallenbach H., Oct. 30, 1913.

Gandhi M.K. to Kallenbach H., Oct. 30, 1913.

Gandhi M.K. to Kallenbach H., Jan. 18, 1914.

Gandhi M.K. to Kallenbach H., Feb. 27, 1914.

Gandhi M.K. to Kallenbach H., March 2, 1914.

Gandhi M.K. to Kallenbach H., June 7, 1915.

Gandhi M.K. to Kallenbach H., July 2, 1915.

Gandhi M.K. to Lane E.F.C., May 14, 1908.

Gandhi M.K. to Lane E.F.C., Aug. 20, 1908.

Gandhi M.K. to Lane E.F.C., March 4, 1911.

Gandhi M.K. to Lane E.F.C., March 29, 1911.

Gandhi M.K. to Lane E.F.C., May 31, 1912.

Gandhi M.K. to Mehta F., Aug. 9, 1895.

Gandhi M.K. to Minister of Interior, April 1, 1913.

Gandhi M.K. to Minister of Interior, June 28, 1913.

Gandhi M.K. to Minister of Interior, Telegram, Oct. 30, 1913.

Gandhi M.K. to Minister of Interior, Oct. 30, 1913.

Gandhi M.K. to Naoroji D., Sept. 18, 1897.

Gandhi M.K. to Natesan G.A., Dec. 9, 1910.

Gandhi M.K. to Natesan G.A., May 31, 1911.

Gandhi M.K. to Polak H.S.L., Nov. 9, 1906.

Gandhi M.K. to Polak H.S.L., Nov. 16, 1906.

Gandhi M.K. to Polak H.S.L., Aug. 6, 1909.

Gandhi M.K. to Polak H.S.L., Oct. 29, 1909.

Gandhi M.K. to Polak H.S.L., Nov. 9, 1909.

Gandhi M.K. to Polak H.S.L., March 7, 1911.

Gandhi M.K. to Polak H.S.L., March 13, 1911.

Gandhi M.K. to Polak H.S.L., March 20, 1911.

Gandhi M.K. to Pretoria News, March 16, 1911.

Gandhi M.K. to Qadir A., Nov. 10, 1906.

Gandhi M.K. to Registrar of Asiatics, April 11, 1913.

Gandhi M.K. to Ritch L.W., March 24, 1911.

Gandhi M.K. to Ritch L.W., April 7, 1911.

Gandhi M.K. to Ritch L.W., April 8, 1911.

Gandhi M.K. to Ritch L.W., April 21, 1911.

Gandhi M.K. to Robertson B., March 6, 1914.

Gandhi M.K. to SABIC, April 7, 1909.

Gandhi M.K. to Schlesin S., March 27, 1911.

Gandhi M.K. to Secretay to Lord Elgin, Oct. 29, 1906.

Gandhi M.K. to Seedat M., May 27, 1905.

Gandhi M.K. to Shukla D.B., Nov. 8, 1902.

Gandhi M.K. to Smith A.H., Nov. 22, 1906.

Gandhi M.K. to Smuts J.C., May 12, 1908.

Gandhi M.K. to Smuts J.C., May 21, 1908.

Gandhi M.K. to Smuts J.C., June 13, 1908.

Gandhi M.K. to the Pvt. Sec. to Lord Crewe, Aug. 11, 1909.

Gandhi M.K. to Under Sec. Colonies, Nov. 6, 1909.

Gandhi M.K., Ally H.O. to Secretary to Lord Elgin, Nov. 20, 1906.

Gandhi M.K., Ally H.O. to Secretary to Morley J., Nov. 20, 1907.

Gandhi M.K., Ally H.O., Bennett T.J., to Cotton H., Birdwood G., Griffin L., *et al.*, Nov. 15, 1906.

Gandhi M.K., An Autobiography – The story of my experiments with truth (translated from Gujarati by Mahadev Desai), Jonathan Cape Ltd., London 1972.

Gandhi M.K., An autobiography or the story of my experiments with truth, Navajivan Publishing House, Ahmedabad 1940.

Gandhi M.K., Quinn L., Naidoo T. to Colonial Sec., Transvaal, Jan. 28, 1908.

Gandhi M.K., Speeches and writings – M.K. Gandhi, G.A. Natesan & Co., Madras 1922.

Gandhi M.K., Speech at public meeting, Bombay, Sept. 26, 1896, (in: C.W.M.G. 1, 1888-1896).

Gandhi R., Gandhi - The man, his people, and the empire, University of California Press, California, 2008.

GandhiServe Foundation - Mahatma Gandhi Research and Media Service http://www.gandhiserve.org/e/cwmg/cwmg.htm, Sept. 28, 2014.

Gani A. to Private Secretary to Governor, Orange River Colony, Aug. 30, 1905.

Gani A. to Rand Plague Committee, June 24, 1904.

Gani A., Gandhi M.K. to Colonial Sec., Pretoria, Sept. 3, 1904.

Gani A. to Colonial Secretary, Pretoria, March 14, 1905.

Gani A. to Chief Sec. for Permit, Sept. 1, 1905.

Gani A. to the Registrar of Asiatics, Pretoria, March 4, 1907.

Grabner S., Schwert der Gewaltlosigkeit – Mahatma Gandhi, Leben und Werk, Pahl-Rugenstein Verlag, Köln 1984.

Hajee A.K. *et al.* to Governor, Natal, Feb. 26, 1896.

Hopwood F.G.S. to Gandhi M.K., Nov. 3, 1909.

http://en.wikipedia.org/wiki/Gandhi_Heritage_Portal, Aug. 28, 2014.

http://en.wikipedia.org/wiki/Indian_South_Africans#Orange_Free_State, May 13, 2015.

http://en.wikipedia.org/wiki/Second_Boer_War, Feb. 2, 2015.

http://scnc.ukzn.ac.za/doc/HIST/LAWS.htm, Jan. 2, 2015.

http://usatoday30.usatoday.com/life/enter/books/book372.htm, May 2, 2015.

http://www.bbc.com/news/world-africa-14094918, Feb. 2, 2015.

http://www.britannica.com/EBchecked/topic/399405/Muslim-League, Aug. 9, 2014.

http://www.dnaindia.com/lifestyle/books-and-more-brahmacharya-gandhi-and-his-women-associates-1053363

http://www.gandhi-manibhavan.org/aboutgandhi/chrono_detailed_gandhiinsafrica.htm, March 22, 2014.

http://www.gktoday.in/kuka-movement-1872/, June 17, 2015.

http://www.ismaili.net/histoire/ history08/history820.html, Aug. 17, 2014.

http://www.npr.org/sections/thetwo-way/2013/11/05/243268093/on-the-block-gandhis-spinning-wheel-napoleons-last-will, June 17, 2015.

http://www.sahistory.org.za/politics-and-society/anti-indian-legislation-1800s-1959, May 13, 2015.

http://www.sahistory.org.za/topic/history-indians-south-africa-timeline1654-2008, Jan. 14, 2015.

http://www.youtube.com/watch?v=2ZJNKiC1-ak, Oct. 27, 2014.

http://www.youtube.com/watch?v=F_aRBLhJjjM, Oct. 27, 2014.

http://www.youtube.com/watch?v=SUpHp3yueOw; Oct. 14, 2014.

http://www.youtube.com/watch?v=VTJy4CuIQQs; Oct. 27, 2014.

http://www.youtube.com/watch?v=zXoO_1hHau0, Oct. 27, 2014.

https://en.wikipedia.org/wiki/Sadhu_Sundar_Singh, June 14, 2015.

https://worldhistoriesfrombelow.files.wordpress.com/2011/08/engaging-with-immigration-laws1.pdf#page=1&zoom=auto,-107,842, Feb. 2, 2014.

https://www.academia.edu/9942562/False_Fathers_and_False_Sons_Immigration_Officials_in_Cape_Town_Documents_and_Verifying_Minor_sons_from_India_in_the_First_Half_of_the_Twentieth_Century, June 14, 2015.

https://www.lib.utexas.edu/maps/africa/safrica_provinces_95.jpg, Feb. 2, 2015.

https://www.marxists.org/archive/roy-evelyn/articles/1923/gandhi_rev_counter.htm, Dec. 22, 2014.

https://www.nelsonmandela.org/omalley/index.php/site/q/03lv01538/04lv01646/05lv01727.htm, Sept. 20, 2015.

https://www.youtube.com/watch?v=jyQiqRvr9nI, Dec. 17, 2014.

https://www.youtube.com/watch?v=S-kytwoWkQI, Dec. 17, 2014.

https://www.youtube.com/watch?v=y815_a8k4Rg, Dec. 17, 2014.

Hughes H., 'The coolies will elbow us out of the country': African reactions to Indian immigration in the colony of Natal, Labour History Review, 72, 155-168, 2007.

India, 23-11-1906.

India, 18-2-1910.

India, 18-11-1910.

Indian Opinion, 11-6-1903.

Indian Opinion, 17-9-1904.

Indian Opinion, 1-10-1904.

Indian Opinion, 12-11-1904.

Indian Opinion, 10-12-1904.

Indian Opinion, 21-1-1905.

Indian Opinion, 25-2-1905.

Indian Opinion, 8-4-1905.

Indian Opinion, 22-4-1905.

Indian Opinion, 29-4-1905.

Indian Opinion, 6-5-1905.

Indian Opinion, 27-5-1905.

Indian Opinion, 3-6-1905.

Indian Opinion, 1-7-1905.

Indian Opinion, 22-7-1905.

Indian Opinion, 2-9-1905.

Indian Opinion, 16-9-1905.

Indian Opinion, 30-9-1905.

Indian Opinion, 7-10-1905.

Indian Opinion, 28-10-1905.

Indian Opinion, 30-12-1905.

Indian Opinion, 10-3-1906.

Indian Opinion, 7-4-1906.

Indian Opinion, 14-4-1906.

Indian Opinion, 28-4-1906.

Indian Opinion, 12-5-1906.

Indian Opinion, 26-5-1906.

Indian Opinion, 2-6-1906.

Indian Opinion, 16-6-1906.

Indian Opinion, 23-6-1906.

Indian Opinion, 30-6-1906.

Indian Opinion, 21-7-1906.

Indian Opinion, 28-7-1906.

Indian Opinion, 22-9-1906.

Indian Opinion, 6-10-1906.

Indian Opinion, 20-10-1906.

Indian Opinion, 24-11-1906.

Indian Opinion, 1-12-1906.

Indian Opinion, 8-12-1906.

Indian Opinion, 15-12-1906.

Indian Opinion, 22-12-1906.

Indian Opinion, 29-12-1906.

Indian Opinion, 12-1-1907.

Indian Opinion, 26-1-1907.

Indian Opinion, 2-2-1907.

Indian Opinion, 9-2-1907.

Indian Opinion, 2-3-1907.

Indian Opinion, 9-3-1907.

Indian Opinion, 16-3-1907.

Indian Opinion, 23-3-1907.

Indian Opinion, 30-3-1907.

Indian Opinion, 6-4-1907

Indian Opinion, 13-4-1907

Indian Opinion, 20-4-1907.

Indian Opinion, 27-4-1907.

Indian Opinion, 4-5-1907.

Indian Opinion, 11-5-1907.

Indian Opinion, 18-5-1907.

Indian Opinion, 25-5-1907.

Indian Opinion, 1-6-1907.

Indian Opinion, 8-6-1907.

Indian Opinion, 15-6-1907.

Indian Opinion, 22-6-1907.

Indian Opinion, 29-6-1907.

Indian Opinion 6-7-1907.

Indian Opinion, 6-7-1907.

Indian Opinion, 20-7-1907.

Indian Opinion, 27-7-1907.

Indian Opinion, 3-8-1907.

Indian Opinion, 10-8-1907.

Indian Opinion, 17-8-1907.

Indian Opinion, 24-8-1907.

Indian Opinion, 31-8-1907.

Indian Opinion, 7-9-1907.

Indian Opinion, 14-9-1907.

Indian Opinion, 21-9-1907.

Indian Opinion, 28-9-1907.

Indian Opinion, 12-10-1907.

Indian Opinion, 19-10-1907.

Indian Opinion, 26-10-1907.

Indian Opinion, 2-11-1907.

Indian Opinion, 9-11-1907.

Indian Opinion, 16-11-1907.

Indian Opinion, 23-11-1907.

Indian Opinion, 30-11-1907.

Indian Opinion, 7-12-1907.

Indian Opinion, 14-12-1907.

Indian Opinion, 21-12-1907.

Indian Opinion, 28-12-1907.

Indian Opinion, 4-1-1908.

Indian Opinion, 11-1-1908.

Indian Opinion, 18-1-1908.

Indian Opinion, 8-2-1908.

Indian Opinion, 22-2-1908.

Indian Opinion, 29-2-1908.

Indian Opinion, 21-3-1908.

Indian Opinion, 11-4-1908.

Indian Opinion, 25-4-1908.

Indian Opinion, 2-5-1908.

Indian Opinion, 9-5-1908.

Indian Opinion, 16-5-1908.

Indian Opinion, 23-5-1908.

Indian Opinion, 30-5-1908.

Indian Opinion, 13-6-1908.

Indian Opinion, 20-6-1908.

Indian Opinion, 27-6-1908.

Indian Opinion, 4-7-1908.

Indian Opinion, 11-7-1908.

Indian Opinion, 18-7-1908.

Indian Opinion, 25-7-1908.

Indian Opinion, 8-8-1908.

Indian Opinion, 22-8-1908.

Indian Opinion, 29-8-1908.

Indian Opinion, 5-9-1908.

Indian Opinion, 12-9-1908.

Indian Opinion, 19-09-1908.

Indian Opinion, 26-9-1908.

Indian Opinion, 3-10-1908.

Indian Opinion, 10-10-1908.

Indian Opinion, 17-10-1908.

Indian Opinion, 19-12-1908.

Indian Opinion, 9-1-1909.

Indian Opinion, 23-1-1909.

Indian Opinion, 30-1-1909.

Indian Opinion, 6-2-1909.

Indian Opinion, 13-2-1909.

Indian Opinion, 27-2-1909.

Indian Opinion, 6-3-1909.

Indian Opinion, 10-4-1909.

Indian Opinion, 29-5-1909.

Indian Opinion, 5-6-1909.

Indian Opinion, 12-6-1909.

Indian Opinion, 19-06-1909.

Indian Opinion, 26-6-1909.

Indian Opinion, 31-7-1909.

Indian Opinion, 7-8-1909.

Indian Opinion, 21-8-1909.

Indian Opinion, 4-9-1909.

Indian Opinion, 2-10-1909.

Indian Opinion, 9-10-1909.

Indian Opinion, 23-10-1909.

Indian Opinion, 6-11-1909.

Indian Opinion, 13-11-1909.

Indian Opinion, 4-12-1909.

Indian Opinion, 18-12-1909.

Indian Opinion, 25-12-1909.

Indian Opinion, 15-1-1910.

Indian Opinion, 29-1-1910.

Indian Opinion, 12-2-1910.

Indian Opinion, 19-02-1910.

Indian Opinion, 26-2-1910.

Indian Opinion, 5-3-1910.

Indian Opinion, 12-3-1910.

Indian Opinion, 26-3-1910.

Indian Opinion, 2-4-1910.

Indian Opinion, 16-4-1910.

Indian Opinion, 23-4-1910.

Indian Opinion, 7-5-1910.

Indian Opinion, 28-5-1910.

Indian Opinion, 11-6-1910.

Indian Opinion, 18-6-1910.

Indian Opinion, 25-6-1910.

Indian Opinion, 2-7-1910.

Indian Opinion, 16-7-1910.

Indian Opinion, 13-8-1910.

Indian Opinion, 27-8-1910.

Indian Opinion, 3-9-1910.

Indian Opinion, 10-9-1910.

Indian Opinion, 17-9-1910.

Indian Opinion, 29-10-1910.

Indian Opinion, 5-11-1910.

Indian Opinion, 7-1-1911.

Indian Opinion, 4-3-1911.

Indian Opinion, 18-3-1911.

Indian Opinion, 8-4-1911.

Indian Opinion, 22-4-1911.

Indian Opinion, 6-5-1911.

Indian Opinion, 20-5-1911.

Indian Opinion, 27-5-1911.

Indian Opinion, 15-7-1911.

Indian Opinion, 28-10-1911.

Indian Opinion, 6-1-1912.

Indian Opinion, 3-2-1912.

Indian Opinion, 10-2-1912.

Indian Opinion, 17-2-1912.

Indian Opinion, 27-7-1912.

Indian Opinion, 10-8-1912.

Indian Opinion, 24-8-1912.

Indian Opinion, 31-8-1912.

Indian Opinion, 2-11-1912.

Indian Opinion, 9-11-1912.

Indian Opinion, 23-11-1912.

Indian Opinion, 21-12-1912.

Indian Opinion, 28-12-1912.

Indian Opinion, 4-1-1913.

Indian Opinion, 25-1-1913.

Indian Opinion, 22-3-1913.

Indian Opinion, 29-3-1913.

Indian Opinion, 12-4-1913.

Indian Opinion, 26-4-1913.

Indian Opinion, 3-5-1913.

Indian Opinion, 10-5-1913.

Indian Opinion, 17-5-1913.

Indian Opinion, 24-5-1913.

Indian Opinion, 31-5-1913.

Indian Opinion, 19-07-1913.

Indian Opinion, 13-9-1913.

Indian Opinion, 20-9-1913.

Indian Opinion, 24-9-1913.

Indian Opinion, 15-10-1913.

Indian Opinion, 22-10-1913.

Indian Opinion, 29-10-1913.

Indian Opinion, 12-11-1913.

Indian Opinion, 19-11-1913.

Indian Opinion, 24-12-1913.

Indian Opinion, 31-12-1913.

Indian Opinion, 14-1-1914.

Indian Opinion, 28-1-1914.

Indian Opinion, 4-2-1914.

Indian Opinion, 11-2-1914.

Indian Opinion, 25-2-1914.

Indian Opinion, 18-3-1914.

Indian Opinion, 3-6-1914.

Indian Opinion, 8-7-1914.

Indian Opinion, 15-7-1914.

Indian Opinion, 22-7-1914.

Indian Opinion, 29-7-1914.

Indian Opinion, 5-8-1914.

Indian Opinion, 9-9-1914.

Indian Opinion, 16-9-1914.

Indian Opinion, 30-9-1914.

Indian Opinion, 1-27-1915.

Jaffer I.A., The early Muslims in Pretoria 1881-1899, M.A. thesis, Rand Afrikaans University 1991.

James L., Raj – The making and unmaking of British India, Little, Brown and Co., London 1999.

Jeewa C.M. *et al.* to Naoroji D. *et al*, Sept. 18, 1897.

Johari O.H.A., Anglia M.C. to Colonial Secretary, Pietermaritzburg, June 2, 1906.

Johari H.A., Anglia M.C. to Principal Medical Officer, June 2, 1906.

Kakar S., Mira and the Mahatma, Penguin Books India, New Delhi 2004.

Khosla G.D., Murder of the Mahatma, Jaico Press Pvt. Ltd., Bombay 1977.

Kumar G., Brahmacharya Gandhi and his women associates, Vitasta Publishing Pvt. Ltd., New Delhi 2008.

Lane E.F.C. to Gandhi M.K., May 13, 1908.

Lelyveld J., Great soul - Mahatma Gandhi and his struggle with India, Alfred A. Knopf, Inc., New York 2011.

Mahomed T.K.H. to Colonial Sec., Pretoria, Jan. 2, 1903.

Markovits C., The Un-Gandhian Gandhi – The life and afterlife of the Mahatma, Anthem Press, London 2003.

Mehta V., Mahatma Gandhi and his apostles, Yale University Press, New Haven 1993.

Mia E.I. to Chamney M., May 26, 1908.

Mia E.I. to Colonial Sec., July 6, 1908.

Mia E.I. to Sec. of State for the Colonies, Sept. 9, 1908.

Mitra S.K., Science and progress - The story of radio electronics, Proc. Ind. Sci. Cong. 1955, (in: The shaping of Indian Science – Indian Science Congress Association, Presidential Addresses Vol. II, 1948-1981, University Press (India) Pvt. Ltd., Hyderabad 2003.

Mohamed D. to Colonial Sec. Pietermaritzburg, April 25, 1906.

Muzondidya J., Walking a tight rope - Towards a social history of the coloured community of Zimbabwe, Africa World Press Inc., Trenton 2005.

Nanda B.R., Gandhi and his critics, Oxford University Press, Bombay 1985.

Nauriya A., William Winstanley Pearson - The Natal experience, Natalia 44, 70 – 78, 2014.

Pandey B.N. (Ed.), The Indian nationalist movement, 1885-1947, St. Martin's Press, New York 1979.

Quinn L. to Chamney M., May 26, 1908.

Raj K., Knowledge, power and modern science - The Brahmins strike back (in: Science and empire – Essays in Indian context: 1700-1947, Kumar D. (Ed.)), Anamika Prakashan, Delhi 1991.

Raman T.A., What does Gandhi want?, Oxford University Press, London 1943.

Rau H., Mahatma Gandhi, Rowohlt Taschenbuch Verlag GmbH, Hamburg 1996.

Reddy E.S., Mahatam Gandhi – Letters to Americans, Bharatiya Vidya Bhavan, Bombay 1998.

Sanghavi N., The agony of arrival – Gandhi, the South Africa years, Rupa Co., New Delhi 2006.

Shah M. to Editor, The Transvaal Leader, Nov. 23, 1907.

Singh R., Mahatma Gandhi – Sex scandals and the missed Nobel Peace Prize, Shaker 'Verlag', Aachen 2015.

Singh R., Nobel Prize nominator Sisir Kumar Mitra F.R.S. - His scientific work in international context, Shaker 'Verlag', Aachen 2014.

Sunder R. to Sec. Colony, Dec. 14, 1907.

Switzer S. (Ed.), South Africa's alternative press - Voices of protest and resistance, 1880s-1960s, Cambridge University Press, Cambridge 1997.

The Diamond Fields Advertiser, 25-4-1911.

The Diamond Fields Advertiser, 26-10-1912.

The Englishman, Calcutta, 8-12-1896.

The Englishman, Calcutta, 3-8-1909.

The Guardian, March 30, 2011.

The Hindustan Times, 22-1-2011.

The India Today, 30-3-2011.

The Morning Leader, 22-10-1906.

The Natal Advertiser, 5-6-1896.

The Natal Mercury, 30-9-1893.

The Natal Mercury, 27-9-1895.

The Natal Mercury, 4-10-1895.

The Natal Mercury, 3-6-1913.

The Natal Mercury, 11-6-1913.

The Natal Mercury, 27-10-1913.

The Natal Mercury, 22-12-1913.

The Natal Mercury, 23-12-1913.

The Natal Mercury, 5-1-1914.

The Natal Mercury, 20-7-1914.

The Rand Daily Mail, 29-6-1907.

The Rand Daily Mail, 2-7-1907.

The Rand Daily Mail, 15-9-1913.

The Rand Daily Mail, 23-10-1913.

The Rand Daily Mail, 16-7-1914.

The Star, 11-5-1907.

The Star, 17-9-1908.

The Time, 8-11-1906.

The Times of India, 9-12-1899.

The Times of India, 6-1-1900.

The Times of India, 25-5-1911.

The Times of India, 25-10-1913.

The Times of India, 5-11-1913.

The Times of India, 7-11-1913.

The Transvaal Leader, 12-11-1907.

The Transvaal Leader, 31-1-1908.

The Transvaal Leader, 29-7-1908.

The Transvaal Leader, 21-8-1908.

The Transvaal Leader, 22-8-1908.

The Transvaal Leader, 24-8-1908.

The Transvaal Leader, 30-9-1913.

The Transvaal Leader, 15-7-1914.

The Tribune, 22-10-1906.

Wolpert S., A new history of India, Oxford University Press, New York 1997.

www.hss.iitb.ac.in/bhole/eog/ch6.pdf, Dec. 22, 2014.